6th International Conference on Generative Approaches to the Lexicon (GL 2013)

Generative Lexicon and Distributional Semantics

Pisa, Italy
24-25 September 2013

Editors:

Roser Saurí
Nicoletta Calzolari
Chu-Ren Huang
Alessandro Lenci
Monica Monachini
James Pustejovsky

ISBN: 978-1-62993-554-6

Printed from e-media with permission by:

Curran Associates, Inc.
57 Morehouse Lane
Red Hook, NY 12571

Some format issues inherent in the e-media version may also appear in this print version.

Printed by Curran Associates, Inc. (2014)

For permission requests, please contact the Association for Computational Linguistics at the address below.

Association for Computational Linguistics
209 N. Eighth Street
Stroudsburg, Pennsylvania 18360

Phone: 1-570-476-8006
Fax: 1-570-476-0860

acl@aclweb.org

Additional copies of this publication are available from:

Curran Associates, Inc.
57 Morehouse Lane
Red Hook, NY 12571 USA
Phone: 845-758-0400
Fax: 845-758-2634
Email: curran@proceedings.com
Web: www.proceedings.com

Table of Contents

Organizers:

Nicoletta Calzolari	Istituto di Linguistica Computazionale "Antonio Zampolli", Pisa, Italy
James Pustejovsky	Brandeis University, Waltham, MA, USA

Chairs:

Chu-Ren Huang	The Hong Kong Polytechnic University, Hong Kong
Alessandro Lenci	Università di Pisa, Pisa, Italy
Monica Monachini	Istituto di Linguistica Computazionale "Antonio Zampolli", Pisa, Italy
Roser Saurí	Barcelona Media, Catalonia, Spain

Local Organizer:

Sara Goggi	Istituto di Linguistica Computazionale "Antonio Zampolli", Pisa, Italy

Sponsors:

UNIVERSITÀ DI PISA

Endorsed by:

SIGSEM

SIGANN

SIGLEX ACL Special Interest Group

Program Committee

Marco Baroni	University of Trento
Olga Batiukova	Universidad Autonoma de Madrid
Núria Bel	Universitat Pompeu Fabra
Sabine Bergler	Concordia University
Gemma Boleda	University of Texas
Pierrette Bouillon	ETI/TIM/ISSCO, University of Geneva
Nicoletta Calzolari	ILC-CNR
Philipp Cimiano	University of Bielefeld
Ann Copestake	University of Cambridge
Laurence Danlos	Universite Paris 7
Stefan Evert	University of Erlangen
Christiane Fellbaum	Princeton University
Shu-Kai Hsieh	National Taiwan University
Chu-Ren Huang	The Hong Kong Polytechnic University
Nancy Ide	Vassar College
Hitoshi Isahara	Toyohashi University of Technology
Elisabetta Jezek	Università di Pavia
Kyoko Kanzaki	Toyohashi University of Technology
Adam Kilgarriff	Lexicography MasterClass Ltd
Alessandro Lenci	University of Pisa - Department of Linguistics
Bernardo Magnini	FBK
Louise McNally	Universitat Pompeu Fabra
Monica Monachini	ILC-CNR
Seungho Nam	Seoul National University
Fiammetta Namer	ATILF-CNRS, University of Nancy
Sebastian Padó	University of Heidelberg
Martha Palmer	University of Colorado
Massimo Poesio	University of Trento
James Pustejovsky	Brandeis University
Valeria Quochi	Instituto Di Linguistica Computazionale ”Antonio Zampolli”
German Rigau	UPV/EHU
Anna Rumshisky	University of Massachusetts
Magnus Sahlgren	Gavagai AB
Roser Saurí	Barcelona Media
Zuoyan Song	Beijing Normal University
Laure Vieu	Institut de Recherche en Informatique de Toulouse
Piek Vossen	Vrije Universiteit
Alessandra Zarcone	University of Stuttgart

Preface

The papers in this volume represent some of the most recent and exciting work being carried out both within the framework of Generative Lexicon and related approaches to the lexicon and lexical resources. With the recent emphasis in natural language processing on the development of machine learning algorithms, it has become even more important for computational linguists to work on the development of linguistically informed lexical resources, for use in the annotation of corpora and creation of gold standard data for training, as well as the collation of larger theoretical datasets for investigating linguistic phenomena in greater detail and sophistication. These works contribute to this trend as well as to the further development of the mechanisms within GL for describing and explaining semantic and lexical phenomena in language.

The GL2013 Organizers and Chairs

Dynamic Event Structure and Habitat Theory

James Pustejovsky
Computer Science Departament
Brandeis University
Waltham, Massachusetts, USA
jamesp@cs.brandeis.edu

Abstract

In this brief note, I explore the cognitive mechanisms involved in interpreting the meanings of events, as conveyed through language. Specifically, I examine the notion of *event simulation* in the construction of linguistic meaning. Simulations are a special class of minimal models, generated from linguistic input, under a number of agent-oriented cognitive constraints. An integral part of this model is a dynamic representation of processes and events, such as the *Dynamic Event Structure* presented here. I show how simulations are composed of entity and event *habitats*, which are contextualization functions, acting to embed a proposition into a minimal model.

1 Introduction

This paper presents a new interpretation of the frame-based event structures introduced in Pustejovsky and Moszkowicz (2011), in the context of Dynamic Interval Temporal Logic. The resulting model, Dynamic Event Structure (DES), has several desirable features, including its simplicity as well as its interpretation as a labeled transition system. I show how Aktionsarten distinctions are captured within this system, and point to how these can be deployed in a dynamic analysis of change predicates in language. I then explore the role that these event structures play in the construction of habitats and "event simulations" from linguistic utterances. Simulations are a special class of minimal models, generated from linguistic input, under a number of agent-oriented cognitive constraints.

2 The Semantics of Change

The topic of measuring change in linguistic theory has focused mainly on the few issues of count-mass distinctions, gradability in adjectives, and partitivity (Cresswell 1977, Klein 1991, Kennedy 2001 Link 1983, Gillon 1992, Schwarzschild 2002, Ladusaw 1982, de Hoop 1997). For our discussion, the most relevant discussion concerns telicity in predicates and gradability measures. Linguistic approaches to the analysis of gradable predicates have recently invoked a distinction between different types of scales (cf. Kennedy, 1999, 2003). For example, to explain the ability of verbs such as *eat* to shift between process and completive events, scales are invoked referencing the object extent of the theme:

(1) Incremental theme verbs:
  a. Sam ate ice cream. (atelic)
  b. Sam ate an ice cream cone. (telic)

Similarly, degree achievement behavior is available with predicates measuring some change, either existentially (2a) or quantifiably (2b).

(2) Change of state verbs:
  a. The icicle lengthened (over the course of a week). (atelic)
  b. The icicle lengthened two inches. (telic)

Most directed motion predicates exhibit this same behavior:

(3) Directed motion verbs:
  a. The plane ascended (for 20 minutes). (atelic)
  b. The plane ascended to cruising altitude. (telic)

Hence, as Levin (2009) points out, there are generalizations over scale behavior that can be noted, as summarized below.

(4) a. Property Scales: often found with change of state verbs;
b. Path Scales: most often found with directed motion verbs;
c. Extent Scales: most often found with incremental theme verbs.

While agreeing with the generalizations resulting from much of this work, we take a slightly different approach to how scales play a role in modeling the semantics of linguistic expressions. In the discussion that follows, we propose that all predication involves measuring an attribute against a scale. Further, we measure change according to this scale domain. Hence, scale theory is not peripherally involved in the semantics of selected properties, extent, and motion, but rather touches all aspects of predication in the language.

Any predication invokes reference to an attribute in our model. Often, but not always, this attribute is associated with a family of other attributes, structured according to some set of constraints. The least constrained association is a conventional sortal classification, and its associated attribute family is the set of pairwise disjoint and non-overlapping sortal descriptions (non-super types). Following Stevens (1946), we will call this classification a *nominal* scale, and it is the least restrictive scale domain over which we can predicate an individual. Binary classifications are a two-state subset of this domain.

When we impose more constraints on the values of an attribute, we arrive at more structured domains. For example, by introducing a partial ordering over values, we can have transitive closure, assuming all orderings are defined. This is called an *ordinal scale.* When fixed units of distance are imposed between the elements on the ordering, we arrive at an *interval scale.* Finally, when a zero value is introduced, we have a scalar structure called a *ratio scale.* Stevens' original classification is summarized below.

- Nominal scales: composed of sets of categories in which objects are classified;
- Ordinal scales: indicate the order of the data according to some criterion (a partial ordering over a defined domain). They tell nothing about the distance between units of the scale.
- Interval scales: have equal distances between scale units and permit statements to be made about those units as compared to other units; there is no zero. Interval scales permit a statement of "more than" or "less than" but not of "how many times more."
- Ratio scales: have equal distances between scale units as well as a zero value. Most measures encountered in daily discourse are based on a ratio scale.

Recent work has criticized approaches to the statistical analysis of data that apply Stevens' classification blindly, without acknowledging the subtlety of interpretation of the data (cf. Suppes et al., 1990, Velleman and Wilkinson, 1993, Luce, 1996). In reality, of course, there are many more categories than those given above. But our goal here is to use these types as the basis for an underlying cognitive classification for creating measurements from different attribute types. In other words, these scale types are models of cognitive strategies for structuring values for conceptual attributes associated with natural language expressions involving scalar values. We will show how adjectives and their associated verbs of change can be grouped into these scalar domains of measurement.

In the following discussion, we demonstrate how many aspects of measurement in language can be modeled dynamically. An interesting consequence of this analysis is a straightforward explanation of the distinction between non-incremental and incremental change predicates. In Pustejovsky and Jezek (2011, forthcoming), we explain how blended readings between the two arise, and how such expressions are actually to be expected, given the model.

Before we discuss how change can be structured, let us briefly discuss the domain of attributes to which individuals may be assigned values. In principle, this would refer to any attribute which may be constructed as a predicate over individuals.

Following Suppes et al (1990), we will treat measurement as a function of two variables: the *attribute* being modeled; and the *scale theory* with which it is being interpreted. One rich area of attribute classifications come from work in semantic field analysis (cf. Dixon, 1991, Lyons, 1977). In this work, attributes are categorized according to a thematic organization, centered around a human frame-of-reference, as lexically encoded in the language.

(5) a. DIMENSION: big, little, large, small, long, short

b. PHYSICAL PROPERTY: hard, soft, heavy, light

c. COLOR: red, green, blue

d. EMOTIONS: jealous, happy, kind, proud, cruel, gay

e. TEMPORAL: new, old, young

f. SPATIAL: above, up, below, near

g. VALUE: good, bad, excellent, fine, delicious

h. MANNER: sloppy, careful, fast, quick, slow

We can further distinguish between *intrinsic* (color, volume) and *extrinsic* attributes (distance, orientation) of an object. In principle, any of these attribute domains can be interpreted by means of one of the scale theories: Nominal; Ordinal; Interval; or Ratio.

But, just what is a measurement and what constitutes a scale? Below we introduce the theory as developed within measurement theory as reviewed by Krantz et al (1971) and Suppes et al (1990). Measurement, as stated above, is an assignment of a value, relative to an attribute $\mathcal{A}$ in our domain. The nature of the theory interpreting the attributes depends on what constraints we impose on how the values are assigned. Consider first Stevens' *nominal scale*. This theory has the properties that the objects in the domain $\mathcal{A}$ are distinct from one another relative to a particular attribute: that is, an object has P or does not have P; elements are not ordered relative to one another. A binary classification scheme is the simplest structure possible, as illustrated below for the attribute *animate*.

(6)

+ANIMATE	-ANIMATE
boy	plastic
tree	rock
worm	house
elephant	cup
grass	glass

Hence, no member in the scale -ANIMATE is any more or less an exemplar of that attribute. The elements of this set, $\{plastic, rock, house, cup, glass\}$, can be distinguished only if additional attributive constants are introduced, thereby creating new "scales". Obviously, this simple notion of scale reduces to the general notion of equivalence class and characteristic function.

A simple *ordinal scale* consists of a set of elements, $\mathcal{A}$, exhibiting the attribute to be measured, along with an ordering of A over this attribute, $\preccurlyeq$, where, if $a, b \in \mathcal{A}$, $a \succcurlyeq b$, then element a has at least as much of the attribute as does b: $\langle \mathcal{A}, \preccurlyeq \rangle$. An order-preserving transformation is monotonic, and hence transitivity holds; e.g., if $a \preccurlyeq b$ and $b \preccurlyeq c$, then $a \preccurlyeq c$. For lexically defined scalar positions over homogeneous sortal domains, for example, this can be used to compute transitive closure graphs, but not much else; e.g., the domain model below.

(7) a. John is short.
b. Mary is medium.
c. Bill is tall.
d. $\mathcal{M} \models j \preccurlyeq m \preccurlyeq b$

Of course, there is no clear *metric* to the ordering between two elements of the domain. An *interval scale* is a order-preserving structure that also has a composition operator, $\circ$, that maintains transitive closure within a scale of the composition of two values from that scale. This is lacking in a simple ordinal scale structure: $\langle \mathcal{A}, \preccurlyeq, \circ \rangle$. Comparisons between values on a scale are now possible because standard interval metrics are assumed to underlie the attribute values. Hence, interval scale theories are concatenation structures with commutativity and associativity properties.

3 Dynamic Event Structure

Given the above observations, the focus here is to provide a dynamic interpretation of how change is encoded within event structures. Although many event types can be adequately expressed as tree structures, Pustejovsky and Moszkowicz (2011) introduce a linear box notation, which they call an *event frame structure*, where single frames may extend linearly into frame sequences, but may also compose vertically, in parallel *tracks*. This was seen as a conceptual analogue to the structures used in Barselou's Frame Theory (Barselou, 2003).

Recall first the classic event structure distinctions of Generative Lexicon Theory (cf. Pustejovsky, 1995), shown below:

(8) a. EVENT → STATE | PROCESS | TRANSITION
   b. STATE: → e
   c. PROCESS: → $e_1 \ldots e_n$
   d. TRANSITION$_{ach}$: → STATE STATE
   e. TRANSITION$_{acc}$: → PROCESS STATE

Let us assume a GL feature structure for the meaning of a linguistic expression:

$$\begin{bmatrix} P \\ \text{ARGSTR} = \begin{bmatrix} \text{ARG1} = x \\ \ldots \end{bmatrix} \\ \text{EVENTSTR} = \begin{bmatrix} \text{EVENT1} = e1 \\ \text{EVENT2} = e2 \end{bmatrix} \\ \text{QUALIA} = \begin{bmatrix} \text{FORMAL} = P_2 \\ \text{AGENTIVE} = P_1 \end{bmatrix} \end{bmatrix}$$

Following general interpretations of qualia structure (cf. Bouillon, 1997), the qualia are naturally ordered over the temporal domain. That is, the predicates associated with each quale are interpreted as a sequence of "frames" of interpretation. This is illustrated below, where the matrix predicate, P, is decomposed into different subpredicates within these frames:

(9) $\text{V}(\text{A}_1, \text{A}_2) \Rightarrow \lambda y \lambda x \boxed{P_1(x,y)}_A \boxed{P_2(y)}_F$

In the discussion that follows, we will adopt this interpretation for qualia structure specifically, and for predicative content more generally, in order to reinterpret our model of events for language. We will assume the model of predication presented in Pustejovsky and Moszkowicz (2011). In order to adequately model change as expressed in language, the representational framework should accommodate change in the assignment of values to the relevant attributes being tracked over time.

A dynamic approach to modeling updates makes a distinction between formulae, ϕ, and programs, π. A formula is interpreted as a classical propositional expression, with assignment of a truth value in a specific state in the model. For our purposes, a state is a set of propositions with assignments to variables at a specific time index. We can think of atomic programs as input/output relations, i.e., relations from states to states, and hence interpreted over an input/output state-state pairing (cf. Naumann, 2001).
Let us now reinterpret the Vendler event classes in terms of dynamic event structures. In order to access the various states in the temporal expressions in language, we adopt the modal operators from Linear Temporal Logic (LTL), $\circ$, $\Box$, $\Diamond$, and $\mathcal{U}$ (cf. Fernando, 2004, Kröger and Merz, 2008). Consider first the definition of a state.

(10) a. Mary was sick today.
   b. My phone was expensive.
   c. Sam lives in Boston.

We assume that a *state* is defined as a single frame structure (event), containing a proposition, where the frame is temporally indexed, i.e., $e^i \rightarrow \phi$ is interpreted as ϕ holding as true at time i. The frame-based representation from Pustejovsky and Moszkowicz (2011) can be given as follows:

(11) $\boxed{\phi}_e^i$

Propositions can be evaluated over subsequent states, of course, so we need an operation of concatenation, +, which applies to two or more event frames, as illustrated below.

(12) $\boxed{\phi}_e^i + \boxed{\phi}_e^j = \boxed{\phi}_e^{[i,j]}$

Semantic interpretations for these are:

(13) a. $[\![\boxed{\phi}]\!]_{\mathbf{M},i} = 1$ iff $V_{\mathbf{M},i}(\phi) = 1$.

   b. $[\![\boxed{\phi}\boxed{\phi}]\!]_{\mathbf{M},\langle i,j \rangle} = 1$ iff $V_{\mathbf{M},}(\phi) = 1$ and $V_{\mathbf{M},j}(\phi) = 1$, where $i < j$.

While it may seem to make little difference at this point, we can interpret these two expressions in terms of trivial tree structures, as shown below.

(14)

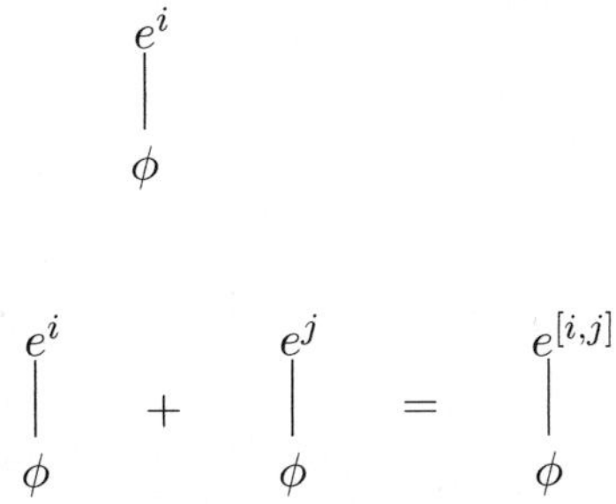

Now let's see how adjacent states can house propositions that change values. This is done with the application of a program, π, which is defined as a mapping from states to states, i.e., $[\![\pi]\!] \subseteq S \times S$ (Harel et al, 2000). Programs, like propositions, can be atomic or complex. They have the following behavior:

(15) a. They can be ordered, $\alpha;\beta$ (α is followed by β);
b. They can be iterated, a^* (apply a zero or more times);
c. They can be disjoined, $\alpha \cup \beta$ (apply either α or β);
d. They can be turned into formulas: $[\alpha]\phi$ (after every execution of α, ϕ is true);
$\langle\alpha\rangle\phi$ (there is an execution of α, such that ϕ is true);
e. Formulas can become programs: $\phi?$ (test to see if ϕ is true, and proceed if so).

Given these operations, Pustejovsky and Moszkowicz (2011) then proceed to model basic event configurations in terms of frame structures. For example, a *simple transition* can be defined in terms of two component elements: (a) a sequence of frames containing a propositional opposition over adjacent states; and (b), a representation of the program, α, which brings about the change from the first frame to the adjacent one. The state transition is shown below.

(16) $\boxed{\phi}^{i}_{e_1}\boxed{\neg\phi}^{j}_{e_2}$

A simple transition includes an atomic program, α, that changes the content of a state in the next adjacent state.

(17) $\boxed{\phi}^{i}_{e_1} \xrightarrow{\alpha} \boxed{\neg\phi}^{i+1}_{e_2}$

Because the frame representation becomes somewhat cumbersome with more complex events, we will modify the classic event structure with state-to-state labels, indicating the program being applied. We call this a dynamic event structure (DES). This is shown below.

(18)

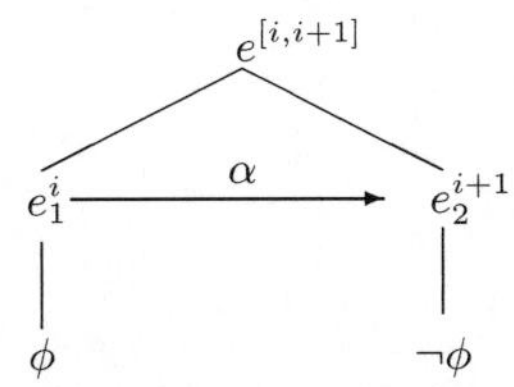

Concatenation can, of course, apply independently of the introduction of a program. Consider the sentence in (19).

(19) Mary awoke from a long sleep.

The state of being asleep has a duration, $[i, j]$, who's valuation is gated by the waking event at the "next state", $j + 1$.

(20)

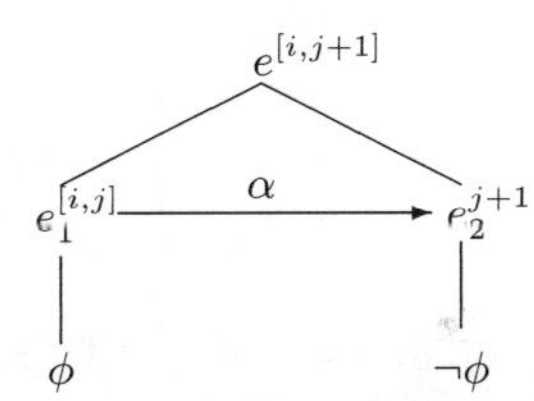

Now consider what is needed to model change to an object; that is, not just propositional change, but predicative change. Pustejovsky and Moszkowicz (2011) capture the change in an object attribute that an object with the addition of assignment functions associated with each state at a given time, in order to keep track of the values bound to variables in the expressions being interpreted. Assume an atomic program, *variable assignment*, which associates a specific value to a variable. This requires that we extend the model to pairs of assignment functions (or valuations) (u, v), in addition to temporal index pairs, (i, j). That is, every program, a, in our language, $a \in \pi$, is evaluated with respect to a pair of states, and with each state there is an assignment function. Hence, in order to evaluate a program, a pair of assignment functions is required.

(21) $x := y$ (ν-transition)
"x assumes the value given to y in the next state."
$\langle \mathcal{M}, (i, i+1), (u, u[x/u(y)])\rangle \models x := y$ iff $\langle \mathcal{M}, i, u\rangle \models s_1 \wedge \langle \mathcal{M}, i+1, u[x/u(y)]\rangle \models x = y$

We define the dynamic event structure for this transition in (22), where the attribute, $\mathcal{A}$, of an object, z, changes its value from x to y, i.e., $x \mapsto y$.

(22)

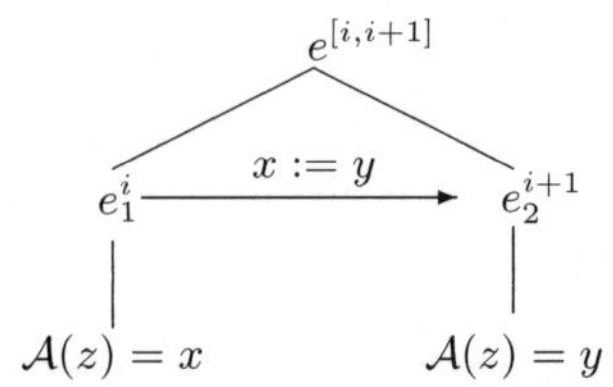

With a ν-transition defined, a *process* can be viewed as simply an iteration of basic variable assignments and re-assignments,

(23)

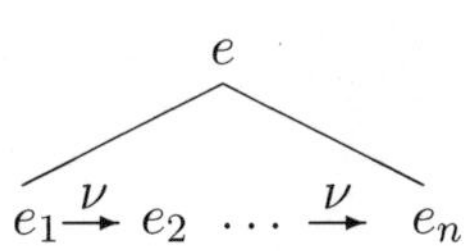

However, motion verbs (and most processes denoting change) are not simple unguarded ν-transitions, but involve a kind of directionality (directedness). Within a dynamic framework, this is accomplished with a pre-test to ensure distinctness; e.g., the object really did change to a new location.

(24) $\overset{x \neq y?}{\boxed{loc(z) = x}}_{e_1} \xrightarrow{\nu} \boxed{loc(z) = y}_{e_2}$

When this test references the ordinal values on a scale, $\mathcal{C}$, this becomes a *directed ν-transition* ($\vec{\nu}$), e.g., $x \preccurlyeq y$, $x \succcurlyeq y$.

(25) $\vec{\nu} =_{df} \overset{\mathcal{C}?}{e_i} \xrightarrow{\nu} e_{i+1}$

This is what allows us to now dynamically model "directed manner of motion verbs", such as *swim*, *crawl*, and *walk*. That is, they denote processes consisting of multiple iterations of $\vec{\nu}$-transitions, as illustrated in (26).

(26)

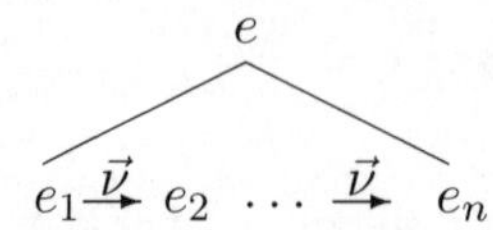

It should be clear from the present discussion that achievements are also a species of transition. They require, however, an additional test to ensure that the changed state is not altered after it is achieved. This is accomplished in terms of a pair of tests, as illustrated in (27).

(27)

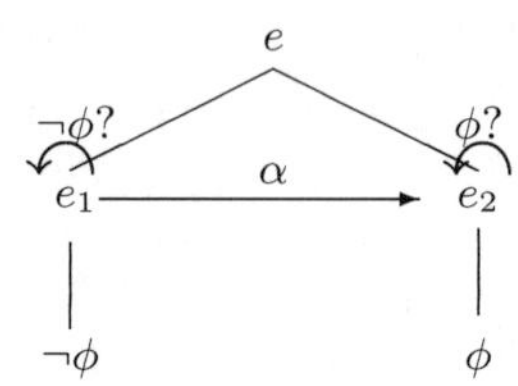

The final event class to model dynamically is that of accomplishment, such as the verbs *build*, *destroy*, and *walk to*.

(28) a. John built a table.
b. Mary walked to the store.

As discussed in Pustejovsky and Moszkowicz (2011), we can think of two parallel changes taking place in such events: there is an internal change (the Agentive activity of a building event, or the movement of the object); but there is also an external change, indicating that a predicate opposition has been satisfied (there is a table built, Mary is at the store). The DITL frame structure for such an event is given below in Figure 1.
This has an elegant treatment in first-order dynamic logic, as shown in the dynamic event structure in (29).

(29)

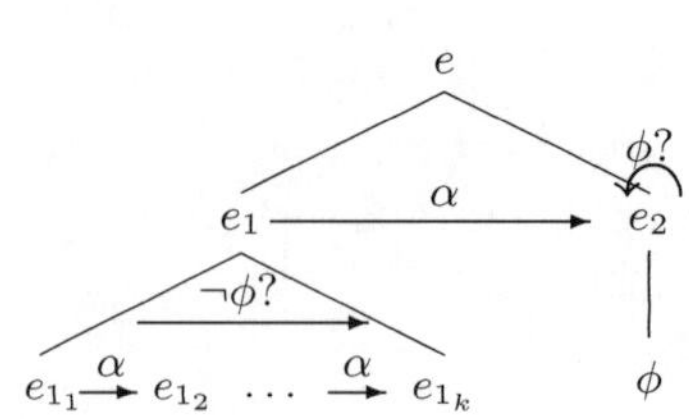

These and other change predicates receive a fuller treatment in Pustejovsky and Jezek (forthcoming), where a dynamic model of selection is developed.

$build(x,z,y)$	$build(x,z,y)^+$	$build(x,z,y), y = v$	
$\neg table(v)$		$table(v)$	(i,j)

Table 1: Accomplishment: parallel tracks of changes

4 Habitat Theory

We have focused on the development of a dynamic treatment of predication, framed within discrete event structures, as part of a larger program of research aimed at creating cognitively plausible interpretations of linguistic utterances. There is a growing community of researchers interested in "simulation semantics" (Langacker, 1987, Lakoff, 2009, Evans, 2009, Bergen, 2012), yet the philosophical foundations for this view originate in the 1980s, with Goldman (1989) and Gordon (1986), as an alternative to the "Theory-theory of mind". The intellectual connections to these various themes are explored elsewhere (Pustejovsky, forthcoming), and we concentrate here on a brief summary of how simulations are constructed from dynamic event structures.

We define an *event simulation* to be a minimal model generated in the context of a temporal trace, from linguistic input, under a number of agent-oriented cognitive constraints. These include an epistemic condition on the individual agent, imposing an evidential *point of view* (POV). The event is situated in the context through an *event localization* procedure, which is facilitated by the construction of *habitats* for the event and its participants.

We start with some general assumptions regarding entity semantics from GL, namely concerning the general structure of objects:

(30) a. Atomic Structure: Formal Quale (objects expressed as basic nominal types)
b. Subatomic Structure: Constitutive Quale (mereotopological structure of objects)
c. Event Structure: Telic and Agentive Qualia structure (origin and functions associated with an object)
d. Macro Object Structure: how objects fit together in space and activity

Now, consider how we contextualize objects through the qualia structure associated with linguistic expressions. For example, a food item has Telic value of *eat*, and an instrument for writing, of *write*, and so forth. Similarly, the artifactual object denoted by the noun *chair* carries a Telic value of "sit in", represented as: $chair : phys \otimes_T sit\_in$. As mentioned previously, this type can be seen as a shorthand for the feature structure representation below:

(31) $$\lambda x \exists y \begin{bmatrix} \textbf{chair} \\ \text{AS} = \begin{bmatrix} \text{ARG1} = x : e \end{bmatrix} \\ \text{QS} = \begin{bmatrix} \text{F} = phys(x) \\ \text{T} = \lambda z, e[sit\_in(e,z,x)] \end{bmatrix} \end{bmatrix}$$

While convention has allowed us to interpret the entire Telic expression as modal, this is inadequate for capturing the deeper meaning of functionality, and this brings in the role of the local modality.

An artifact is designed for a specific purpose, its Telic role; that much is clear. But this purpose can only be achieved under specific circumstances. Let us say that, for an artifact, x, given the appropriate context $\mathcal{C}$, performing the action π will result in the intended or desired resulting state, $\mathcal{R}$. This can be stated dynamically as follows, using the dynamic event structure from above (cf. Pustejovsky, 2012).

(32) $\mathcal{C} \rightarrow [\pi]\mathcal{R}$

This says that, if a context $\mathcal{C}$ (a set of contextual factors) is satisfied, then every time the activity of π is performed, the resulting state $\mathcal{R}$ will occur. The precondition context $\mathcal{C}$ is necessary to specify, since this enables the local modality to be satisfied.

Consider how this works with a classic example in lexical semantics, that of the domain "food". For a noun such as *sandwich*, we have a set of contexts, $\mathcal{C}$, under which, for the object denoted by x, when an individual y eats x, there is a resulting state of nourishment, which we will notate as $\mathcal{R}_{eat}$. Hence, we have the following qualia structure representation, using the dynamic event structures.

(33) $\lambda x[\text{FORMAL}(x) = phys(x) \wedge$

$\text{TELIC}(x) = \lambda y \lambda e[\mathcal{C} \rightarrow [eat(e, y, x)]\mathcal{R}_{eat}(x)]]$

This says that if the context is satisfied, then every eating of that substance will result in a "nourishing." In other words, more correctly stated, sandwiches are not "for eating", but rather "for nourishing by eating."

Now let us extend this intuition to introduce the notion of a habitat. Informally, a habitat is representation of an object situated within a partial minimal model; it is a directed enhancement of the qualia structure. Multidimensional affordances determine how habitats are deployed and how they modify or augment the context, and compositional operations include procedural (simulation) and operational (selection, specification, refinement) knowledge. As an example, consider the dynamic qualia structure for an artifact such as *table* or *chair* (shown below).

$$\lambda x \begin{bmatrix} \textbf{chair} \\ \text{AS} = \begin{bmatrix} \text{ARG1} = x : e \end{bmatrix} \\ \text{QS} = \begin{bmatrix} \text{F} = phys(x) \\ \text{T} = \lambda z \lambda e[\mathcal{C} \rightarrow [sit(e, z, x)]\mathcal{R}_{sit}(x)] \\ \text{A} = \exists w \exists e'[make(e', w, x)] \end{bmatrix} \end{bmatrix}$$

We construct the habitat for an object by contextualizing it. For example, in order to use a table, the top has to be oriented upward, the surface must be accessible, and so on. A chair must also be oriented up, the seat must be free and accessible, it must be able to support the user, etc. The habitat also includes an *embedding space* and supporting objects. An illustration of what the resulting knowledge structure for the habitat of a chair is shown below.

$$\lambda x \begin{bmatrix} \textbf{chair}_{hab} \\ \text{F} = [phys(x), on(x, y_1), in(x, y_2), orient(x, up)] \\ \text{C} = [seat(x_1), back(x_2), legs(x_3), clear(x_1)] \\ \text{T} = \lambda z \lambda e[\mathcal{C} \rightarrow [sit(e, z, x)]\mathcal{R}_{sit}(x)] \\ \text{A} = [made(e', w, x)] \end{bmatrix}$$

Event simulations are constructed from the composition of object habitats, along with particular constraints imposed by the dynamic event structure inherent in the verb itself. To best illustrate this, consider the following short discourse.

(34) a. A car entered the driveway.
b. A woman stepped out.

First minimal models are constructed from the dynamic event structure for each predicate. This proceeds informally as follows:

(35) Given an event, E: a. Compute the affordance space for each argument, a_i, to E;
b. Compute the object habitat for each a_i;
c. Compute the Event Localization on E. This is the minimal embedding for E;
d. Compute the event habitat for E.

The habitat composition resulting from these two events introduces a number of additional states, processes, and conditions, including a bridging event, statable as a precondition on the second event; namely, that the car was not moving when the woman stepped out of it. The composition creates this presupposition (defeasible as it is), and it is introduced into the event simulation as part of the model.

5 Conclusion

In this brief note, I have illustrated only some of the mechanisms involved in habitat and event simulation construction. A greater understanding of how event participants contribute towards the construction of affordance spaces for events is necessary to better articulate this process. It is clear, however, that a dynamic interpretation of the event structure and qualia structure from GL is an important aspect of modeling linguistic expressions as cognitive simulations.

Acknowledgments

I would like to thank David McDonald, Elisabetta Jezek, and Olga Batuikova, for comments and discussion of this work.

References

Bach, Emmon. 1986. The algebra of events. Linguistics and Philosophy 9:5–16.

Barker, Chris. 1998. Partitives, double genetives, and anti-uniqueness. Natural Language and Linguistic Theory 16:679–717.

Barsalou, Lawrence W. "Grounded cognition." Annu. Rev. Psychol. 59 (2008): 617-645.

Barsalou, Lawrence W. "Grounded cognition." Annu. Rev. Psychol. 59 (2008): 617-645.

Bergen, Benjamin. (2012). Louder than words: The new science of how the mind makes meaning. New York: Basic Books.

Bouillon, P. (1997). Polymorphie et semantique lexicale : le cas des adjectifs, Lille: Presses Universitaires du Spetentrion.

Carlson, Gregory. 1977. Amount relatives. Language 53:520–542.

Cresswell, M.J. 1977. The semantics of degree. In Montague grammar, ed. Barbara Partee, 261–292. New York: Academic Press.

Doetjes, Jenny. 1997. Quantifiers and selection. Doctoral Dissertation, Rijksuniversiteit Leiden.

Evans, Vyvyan. How words mean. Oxford University Press, 2009.

Fernando, Tim 2004. "A Finite-state Approach to Events in NL Semantics". *JLC* 14(1): 79-92.

Gillon, Brendan. 1992. Towards a common semantics for english count and mass nouns. Linguistics and Philosophy 15:597–639.

Goldman, A. I. (1989). Interpretation psychologized. Mind and Language 4: 161-185.

Goldman, A. I. (2006). Simulating Minds: The Philosophy, Psychology, and Neuroscience of Mindreading. New York: Oxford University Press.

Gordon, R. M. (1986). Folk psychology as simulation. Mind and Language 1: 158-171.

Gordon, R. M. (1996). Radical simulationism. In P. Carruthers and P. Smith, eds., Theories of Theories of Mind. Cambridge: Cambridge University Press.

Grosu, Alexander, and Fred Landman. 1998. Strange relatives of the third kind. Natural Language Semantics 6:125–170.

Harel, David, Jerzy Tiuryn, and Dexter Kozen. Dynamic logic. MIT press, 2000.

Hay, Jen, Christopher Kennedy, and Beth Levin. 1999. Scale structure underlies telicity in 'degree achievements'. In Proceedings of SALT IX, ed. Tanya Matthews and Devon Strolovitch, 127–144. Ithaca, NY: CLC Publications.

Heim, Irene. 1987. Where does the definiteness restriction apply? Evidence from the definiteness of variables. In The representation of (in)definiteness, ed. Eric Reuland and Alice ter Meulen, chapter2, 21–42. Cambridge, Mass.: MIT Press.

deHoop, Helen. 1997. A semantic reanalysis of the partitive constraint. Lingua 103:151–174.

Kennedy, Christopher. 2001. Polar opposition and the ontology of 'degrees'. Linguistics & Philosophy 24:33–70.

Klein, Ewan. 1991. Comparatives. chapter32, 673–691. Berlin: de Gruyter.

Krifka, Manfred. 1989. Nominal reference, temporal constitution and quantification in event semantics. In Semantics and contextual expression, ed. Renate Bartsch, Johann van Benthem, and Peter van Emde-Boas, 75–115. Stanford, CA: CSLI Publications.

Krifka, Manfred. 1998. Scope-inversion under the rise-fall contour in german. Linguistic Inquiry 29:75–112.

Kröger, Fred and Stephan Merz 2008. Temporal Logic and State Systems, Springer Verlag.

Ladusaw, WilliamA. 1982. Semantic constraints on the English partitive construction. In Proceedings of WCCFL 1.

Lakoff, George, and Mark Johnson. Philosophy in the flesh: The embodied mind and its challenge to western thought. Basic books, 1999.

Langacker, Ronald W. Foundations of Cognitive Grammar: theoretical prerequisites. Volume 1. Vol. 1. Stanford university press, 1987.

Lehrer, Adrienne. 1986. English classifier constructions. Lingua 68:109–148.

Link, Godehard. 1983. The logical analysis of plurals and mass terms: A lattice theoretical approach. In Meaning, use, and the interpretation of language, ed. R.Bäuerle, C.Schwarze, and A.von Stechow, 302–323. Berlin: de Gruyter.

Naumann, Ralf, 2001. Aspects of changes: a dynamic event semantics, Journal of Semantics 18:27-81.

Parsons, Terrence. 1970. An analysis of mass terms and amount terms. Foundations of Language 6:362–388.

Pustejovsky, J. (1995) The Generative Lexicon, MIT Press, Cambridge, MA.

Pustejovsky, J. 2001. Type Construction and the Logic of Concepts. In P. Bouillon and F. Busa (eds.), The Syntax of Word Meaning, Cambridge University Press, Cambridge.

Pustejovsky, J. 2006. Type theory and lexical decomposition. Journal of Cognitive Science 6:39-76.

Pustejovsky, J. 2011. Coercion in a general theory of argument selection, Linguistics, vol. 49, no 6. de Gruyter.

Pustejovsky, James. "The Semantics of Functional Spaces." Practical Theories and Empirical Practice: Facets of a Complex Interaction. Ed. Andrea Schalley. John Benjamins Publishing Company, 2012.

Pustejovsky, J. forthcoming. "Event Simulations as Semantic Models".

Pustejovsky, James and Elisabetta Jezek 2011. Scale-shifting and Compo- sitionality, Abstract presented at Workshop on Scalarity in Verb-Based Constructions, Heinrich-Heine-Universit?at Du?sseldorf, April 7-8, 2011.

Pustejovsky, James and Elisabetta Jezek. forthcoming. "Verbal Patterns of Change".

Pustejovsky, James, and Jessica L. Moszkowicz. "The qualitative spatial dynamics of motion in language." Spatial Cognition and Computation 11.1 (2011): 15-44.

Schwarzschild, Roger. 2002. The grammar of measurement. In Proceedings of SALT XII, ed. Brendan Jackson. Ithaca, NY: CLC Publications.

Schwarzschild, Roger, and Karina Wilkinson. 2002. Quantifiers in comparatives: A semantics of degree based on intervals. Natural Language Semantics 10:1–41.

Winter, Yoad. 2001. Measure phrase modification in a vector space semantics. In Proceedings of WCCFL 20, ed. K.Megerdoomina and L.A. Bar-el, 607–620. Somerville, MA: Cascadilla Press.

Zwarts, Joost. 2000. Vectors across Spatial domains. Paper presented at the Worksho on Axes and Vectors in Language and Space, Lincoln University, July 7, 2000. To appear in Emile van der Zee and John Slack, eds., Axes and Vectors in Language and Space. Oxford: Oxford University Press.

Zwarts, Joost. 1997. Vectors as relative positions: A compositional semantics of modified pps. Journal of Semantics 14:57–86.

Zwarts, Joost, and Yoad Winter. 1997. A semantic characterization of locative PPs. In Semantics and Linguistic Theory 7, ed. Aaron Lawson, 294–311. Ithaca, NY: CLC Publications.

Metaphor and Qualia: Embodiment or Eventuality?

Chu-Ren Huang
Hong Kong Polytechnic University
churenhuang@gmail.com

Kathleen Ahrens
Hong Kong Baptist University
ahrens@hkbu.edu.hk

Francesca Quattri
Hong Kong Polytechnic University
francesca.quattri@connect.polyu.hk

The Contemporary Theory of Metaphor heralded a whole generation of research by positing that metaphor is used because we refer to concrete and familiar object to explain abstract and potentially novel ideas. Ensuing research, picking up the two strands, can be largely classified as those focusing on embodiment (i.e. referring to familiar objects) or experiential mapping. Among those proposing mapping theories is the Conceptual Mapping Model proposed by Ahrens (2002, 2010) in which she proposes a mapping rule template that requires the description of an event. And Huang et al. (2007) adopts this approach and show that it can be mapped to ontology.

The underlining question we may ask, is whether metaphor is object-embodiment based or event-experiential driven? And if it is event-experiential driven, how can it be captured theoretically? We point out in this talk that many metaphors, especially those captured by Ahrens' mapping theory, cannot be fully explained without referring to the different event types in the qualia structure. Most shape metaphors, for instance, requires the understanding of the shaping and/or shape perception process, and can be easily captured as the agentive qualia complementing a small number of object-based metaphors which can be described by the formal qualia. For instance, a *love triangle* refers to the complex relations between three lovers because we know that a triangle is made by linking lines (as relations) among three apexes (as the three lovers). Hence, we seem to look into the formal qualae of a triangle. A vicious/virtuous circle can either spiral or be broken because we make the circle by tracing the point of the circumference. This seems to require information of the agentive qualae. And in Chinese, 规矩 gui1ju3 compass+try-square/set-square refers to rules because they are the tools to ensure that perfect circles and squares are drawn. This seems to require the telic qualae of the tools.

We propose that conceptual mapping of metaphor is experiential-eventual and makes uses of qualia structure by showing that the conceptual mapping theory of Ahrens (2002, 2010) can be better formalized and constrained with GL theory.

Selected Bibliography

Ahrens, Kathleen. 2002. When Love is not Digested: Underlying Reasons for Source to Target Domain Pairing in the Contemporary Theory of Metaphor. In Yu Chau E. Hsiao (ed.) *Proceeding of the First Cognitive Linguistics Conference*, pp 273-302. Taipei: Cheng-Chi University.

Ahrens, Kathleen. 2010. Mapping Principles for Conceptual Metaphors. In Cameron Lynne, Alice Deignan, Graham Low, Zazie Todd (Eds.), *Researching and Applying Metaphor in the Real World*. Amsterdam: John Benjamins Publishing Company. pp. 185-207.

Clausner, Timothy, and William Croft. Productivity and Schematicity in Metaphors. Cognitive Science. 21. 247-282.

Gibbs, Raymond. 2006. Metaphor Interpretation as Embodied Stimulation. Mind and Language. 21434-458.

Gong, Shu-Ping, Kathleen Ahrens and Chu-Ren Huang. 2008. Chinese Word Sketch and Mapping Principles: A Corpus-Based Study of Conceptual Metaphors Using the BUILDING Source Domain. *International Journal of Computer Processing of Oriental Languages*. 21(2): 3-17.

Huang, Chu-Ren, Siaw-Fong Chung and Kathleen Ahrens. 2007. An Ontology-based Exploration of Knowledge Systems for Metaphor. In Kishore, Rajiv, Ram Ramesh, and Raj Sharman (Eds.), *Ontologies: A Handbook of Principles, Concepts and Applications in Information Systems*. Volume 14. Berlin: Springer. pp. 489-517.

Lakoff, George, and Mark Johnson. 1980. *Metaphors We Live By*. Chicago: Chicago University Press.

Pustejovsky, James. 1998. *The Generative Lexicon*. Boston: MIT University Press.

To Coerce or Not to Coerce: A Corpus-based Exploration of Some Complement Coercion Verbs in Chinese

Chan-Chia Hsu
Graduate Institute of Linguistics,
National Taiwan University
No. 1, Sec. 4, Roosevelt Road, Taipei
chanchiah@gmail.com

Shu-Kai Hsieh
Graduate Institute of Linguistics,
National Taiwan University
No. 1, Sec. 4, Roosevelt Road, Taipei
shukai@gmail.com

Abstract

This study takes a corpus-based approach to examine twenty Chinese verbs that have been found to coerce their NP complements into an event type (cf. Lin et al. 2009), with an aim of creating a coercion profile for each verb. A cluster analysis is further conducted on the coercion profiles. The resulting clusters in our analysis show a bi-directional distribution: the verbs in Cluster 1 are found to coerce their complements more frequently, while the verbs in Cluster 2 are found to coerce more noun types. Moreover, many lexical pairs (e.g., antonyms and near-synonyms) are identified in the two clusters. Our quantitative analysis suggests that semantically related verbs can have similar coercion profiles. The empirical findings of the present study complement intuition-based studies on the complement coercion operation in Chinese (e.g., Lin and Liu 2004, Liu 2003) and shed new light on the theoretical framework of the Generative Lexicon.

1 Introduction

In our daily language, there are many mismatches in the surface form. A common example that is intriguing to semanticists is *John began a book.* Though the verb *begin* is supposed to take an event as its argument, the entity complement *a book* is also allowed for *begin.* The intended meaning can be that John began reading or writing a book. An enumerative approach may postulate another sense for *begin.* However, an economical proposal in the framework of the Generative Lexicon (Pustejovsky 1995) is the complement coercion operation, which leaves the meaning of the verb intact in different contexts by shifting the semantic type of its complement. In the above example, *a book* is shifted from an entity type to an event type.

Such an operation also works in Chinese, as Lin et al. (2009) have demonstrated using the web as a corpus. Nevertheless, the complement coercion operation in Chinese is still under-researched through a corpus-based approach. The present study thus uses corpus data to explore twenty coercion verbs in Chinese, aiming to create a coercion profile for each verb. We believe that the empirical findings of the present study will greatly enrich the explanatory power of the Generative Lexicon.

This paper is organized as follows. Section 2 reviews the coercion operations proposed in the Generative Lexicon, and Section 3 reviews some previous studies on the complement coercion operation in Chinese. Section 4 introduces the methodology of the present study. Section 5 presents the results. Section 6 discusses how the results can provide a revealing insight into lexical semantics. Section 7 provides a summary, highlights the contribution of the present study, and suggests potential directions for future studies.

2 Coercion as a Generative Mechanism in the Generative Lexicon

In the framework of the Generative Lexicon, a type coercion operation is defined as "a semantic operation that converts an argument to the type which is expected by a function, where it would otherwise result in a type error" (Pustejovsky 1995:111), and two coercion mechanisms are proposed.

First, consider the sentence in (1), which is perhaps the simplest case of coercion (Pustejovsky 1995:113):

(1) Mary drives a Honda to work.

This example is a case of **subtype coercion**: if an expression α of the type σ_1 is a subtype of σ_2, then between σ_1 and σ_2 is a possible coercion that allows the expression α to change its type from σ_1 to σ_2. In (1), *a Honda* is typed as a subtype of `car`. Further, `car` is a subtype of `vehicle`, which fulfills the selectional requirement of the governing verb *drive*.[1] A coercion chain (i.e., `Honda` → `car` → `vehicle`) is formed, and it is the subtype coercion that makes *a Honda* a legitimate argument for the verb *drive*.

Now, consider the following sentences (Pustejovsky 1995:115):

(2) a. John began a book.
 b. John began reading a book.
 c. John began to read a book.

In the above sentences, the complements of the verb *began* come in different forms. To capture their semantic relatedness and avoid treating *begin* in such a paradigm as a polysemous verb, Pustejovsky (1995) proposes a **complement coercion operation**. In the lexical representation of the verb *begin* (Pustejovsky 1995:116), the second argument of *begin* is explicitly typed as an event. Therefore, for the sentence (2a) to be semantically well-formed, the NP complement *a book* needs to be coerced into an event. This can be done by reconstructing an event reading from the qualia structure of *book*, where the values of the AGENTIVE role and the TELIC role are given as WRITE and READ, respectively. That is, *a book* in (2a) can be interpreted as an event of writing a book or an event of reading a book. Such a complement coercion is triggered by the governing verb. Moreover, without a qualia value appropriate in the context, such a complement coercion would be impossible. This proposal has two major consequences. First, an enumerative approach to the semantics of a verb can be avoided – that is, the meaning of *begin* in *begin a book*, *begin a movie*, etc. remains identical. Second, the semantic load is spread more evenly between a verb and its complement.

The complement coercion operation in the Generative Lexicon is not just a theoretical construct, but has also been empirically supported (e.g., Baggio et al. 2009, Delogu et al. 2010, Traxler et al. 2002, and Traxler et al. 2005). The hypothesis is that in processing an expression such as *began the book*, we adopt the following strategies (Traxler et al. 2005:4):

> "When encountering the noun book, comprehenders access the word's lexical entry and attempt to integrate various stored senses of this word into the evolving semantic representation of the sentence. The mismatch between the verb's selectional restrictions and the stored senses of the noun triggers a coercion process. Comprehenders use salient properties associated with the complement noun and other relevant discourse elements (including but not necessarily limited to the agent phrase) to infer a plausible action that could be performed on the noun. Comprehenders incorporate the event sense into their semantic interpretation of the VP by reconfiguring the semantic representation of the complement, converting [$_\beta$*began*[$_\alpha$*The book*]] into [$_\beta$*began*[$_\alpha$*reading the book*]]. (Conceivably, this could also require reconfiguration of an associated syntactic representation.)"

The results of various experiments (e.g., eye-tracking experiments, ERPs) have shown that the processing cost is associated with the last stage, i.e., reconstructing an event reading for the NP complement.

3 Studies on the Complement Coercion Operation in Chinese

There has been a lack of empirical studies exploring the coercion operations in Chinese. To our knowledge, the only study from the psycholinguistic perspective is Wang (2008), where the aspectual coercion operation in Chinese was investigated. Additionally, corpus-based studies are also rare. One of them is Huang and Ahrens (2003). It is suggested that some classifiers in Chinese (e.g., *tang* 'a journey' and *hui* 'a round') can coerce an individual-denoting noun to represent an event (Huang and Ahrens 2003:368). Specifically, regarding the complement coercion operation in Chinese, no psycholinguistic/neurolinguistic study has been conducted, and a corpus-based study waits until Lin et al. (2009).

[1] For the lexical representation of the verb *drive*, refer to Pustejovsky (1995:114).

The reason why the complement coercion operation in Chinese has not received adequate attention is that it is generally held that there is no true complement coercion in Chinese. This claim is based on the observation that while *John began a book* is grammatical, its literal translation into Chinese *Yuehan kaishi yi-ben shu* is unacceptable (Lin and Liu 2004, Liu 2003)—a Chinese speaker must say *Yuehan kaishi du yi-ben shu* 'John began to read a book'. Such an argument appears to be shaky (Lin et al. 2009): there are many English sentences in the literature of the complement coercion operation, but only *began a book* is translated into Chinese in Lin and Liu (2004).

To answer whether the complement coercion operation works in Chinese, Lin et al. (2009) used the web as a corpus. After collecting a set of control verbs in Chinese, they googled these verbs and randomly examined their objects. For example, one of the verb-object pairs from Google was *zhizai daxue* 'aim (at) college'. Next, the pairs were put in the template "V * O", where the asterisk enabled the search engine to get anything between the verb and its object. With the template *zhizai * daxue*, the following is one of the sentences retrieved from the web:

(3) ta zhizai shang daxue
he aim to attend college
'He aimed to attend college.'

In (3), the complement *daxue* is coerced with an event reading (i.e., attending college) for the phrase *zhizai daxue* to be semantically well-formed. Cross-linguistically, such an example shows that the complement coercion operation does work not only in English but also in Chinese. The phrase *zhizai daxue* is acceptable, and its non-coercive counterpart is also attested. Methodologically, the asterisk in the template can help to automatically identify the agentive role or the telic role of an NP complement (e.g., *shang* 'attend' for *daxue* 'college'). The method proposed in Lin et al. (2009) can be applied to further studies on the complement coercion operation in Chinese.

In summary, the study on the complement coercion operation in Chinese is still in its infancy, and corpus-based methods is worth pursuing because it can provide a language-specific insight into the complement coercion operation as a generative mechanism.

4 Method

The database for the present study was the Academia Sinica Balanced Corpus of Modern Chinese (i.e., the Sinica Corpus, for short), which can be accessed through the Chinese Word Sketch Engine.[2]

Generally, the selection of the verbs for our analysis was based on the appendix in Lin et al. (2009), where 36 complement coercion verbs in Chinese are listed.[3] First, disyllabic verbs were selected. Second, verbs with a low frequency (i.e., no more than 100 tokens in the Sinica Corpus) were not considered. Third, the present study focused on the prototypical case of the complement coercion operation in the literature, i.e., coercing an NP complement into an event type. Thus, verbs that seemingly take a proposition (i.e., *zancheng* 'approve' and *tongyi* 'agree') were not examined in the present study. Finally, 20 verbs in the appendix of Lin et al. (2009) were selected for further analysis. They are presented in the appendix of this paper.

For each of the 20 verbs, 120 sentences were randomly sampled from the Sinica Corpus. Of all the 2,400 sentences, those in which the verb was nominalized or did not take a complement were not analyzed. Here is an example:

(4) rang haizi jinliang de qu duofang tansuo yu changshi
let child as.much.as.possible DE go in.many.ways explore and try
'let children explore and try as much as possible'

In (4), the complement of the verb *changshi* is missing and hard to recover from the context. Therefore, such sentences were not analyzed in the present study. In total, 1,586 sentences were analyzed.

For each sentence analyzed in the present study, whether there was a complement coercion operation was manually checked. Consider the following example:

(5) wei jiankang er pao, zai zuotian shunli wancheng disan zhan

[2] The Chinese Word Sketch Engine is available at http://wordsketch.ling.sinica.edu.tw/. For more details about the Sinica Corpus, refer to http://db1x.sinica.edu.tw/cgi-bin/kiwi/mkiwi/mkiwi.sh.

[3] Note that the complement coercion verbs listed in the appendix of Lin et al. (2007) are not exhaustive.

for health ER run, on yesterday smoothly finish third stop

'(someone) ran for the sake of health and successfully finished the third stop yesterday'

In (5), it is the task of arriving at the third stop that is completed. This sentence was coded as showing a complement coercion operation in Chinese. The complement *disan zhan* 'the third stop' was recorded as a noun *type* that could be coerced.[4] The distance between the coercing verb and the coerced complement was coded as 1 because the complement occurs in the first word right to *wancheng*.

5 Results

Overall, of the 1,586 sentences analyzed in the present study, 264 sentences (16.64%) show a complement coercion operation. The results are presented in the appendix. The columns (D), (E), (F), and (G) are used to represent the complement coercion profiles of the verbs examined in the present study. First, the higher the value in (D) is, the more frequently the verb coerces its complement. Second, the higher the value in (E) is, the more the verb is preferred in a complement coercion operation. Generally, there is a linear relationship between the values in (D) and (E), as illustrated in Figure 1. However, it is noted that though some verbs coerce their complement often, the degree to which they are preferred in a complement coercion operation can be relatively lower. For instance, as shown in the appendix, *kangju* 'resist' (29.2%, i.e., 12 out of 41 sentences featuring *kangju*) coerces a complement marginally more often than *xuyao* 'need' (28.5%, i.e., 24 out of 84 sentences featuring *xuyao*), but the former (4.5%, i.e., 12 out of 264 sentences featuring a complement coercion operation) is slightly less preferred in a complement coercion operation than the latter (9.0%, i.e., 24 out of 264 sentences featuring a complement coercion operation). In the representation of the coercion profile of a verb, such a difference should be taken into account.

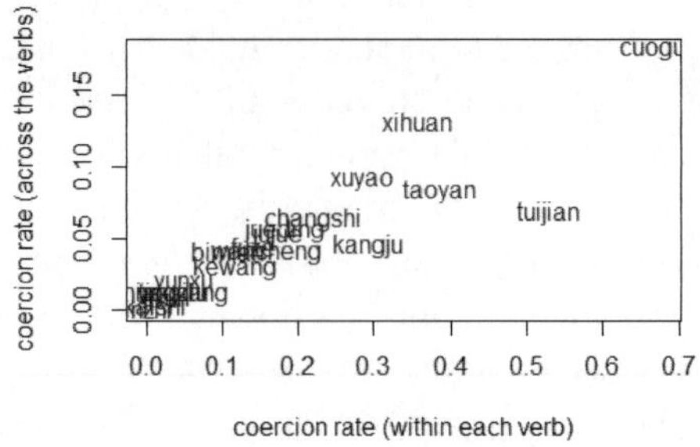

Figure 1. The coercion rates within each verb and across the verbs

Third, the higher the value in (F) is, the more noun types the verb coerces. Fourth, the higher the value in (G) is, the stronger the coercion power of the verb is — in the sense that the verb can coerce a noun that does not syntagmatically adjoin. In brief, the four columns (D), (E), (F), and (G) in the appendix are regarded as reflecting the complement coercion profile of a verb in Chinese.

The four columns (D), (E), (F), and (G) in the appendix were scaled and then used to perform a partitioning around medoids (Kaufman and Rousseeuw 1990).[5] Such a multivariate analysis is exploratory. Many variables are taken into account, and we are allowed to get a panorama of how the twenty verbs in Chinese are organized in terms of the complement coercion operation. No specific pattern is expected, but the one actually obtained with our data can be interesting and revealing to a certain degree.

In our multivariate analysis, the optimal clusters for the twenty verbs examined in the present study were estimated to be three. The results are presented in (6):

(6) Cluster 1 (8 in total): *changshi* 'try', *cuoguo* 'miss (fail to do something)', *jujue* 'refuse', *kangju* 'resist', *taoyan* 'dislike', *tuijian* 'recommend', *xihuan* 'like', *xuyao* 'need'

Cluster 2 (11 in total): *bimian* 'avoid', *fuze* 'be responsible for', *jixu* 'continue', *jueding* 'decide', *kaishi* 'begin', *kewang* 'long for', *mianqiang* 'force', *tingzhi* 'stop', *wancheng* 'finish', *yaoqiu* 'require', *yunxu* 'allow'

[4] The term *type* is used here as in ***type*** *frequency* (i.e., opposed to ***token*** *frequency*), not used to refer to a semantic type (e.g., an individual, an event, etc.).

[5] The analysis was conducted in R. The `pamk` function in the package `fpc` was used.

Cluster 3 (only 1): *jinzhi* 'forbid'

To reveal the differences between Cluster 1 and Cluster 2, the Mann-Whitney test was performed on the means of the four columns (D), (E), (F), and (G) in the appendix. Table 1 summarizes the results.

	Cluster 1	Cluster 2	*p*-value
Column (D)	0.365	0.082	0.000053 *
Column (E)	0.090	0.025	0.000106 *
Column (F)	0.799	0.992	0.000026 *
Column (G)	2.620	3.076	0.177400

Table 1. Differences between Cluster 1 and Cluster 2

The verbs in Cluster 1 coerce their complements more frequently. Moreover, they are also characterized by their greater extent to which they are preferred in a complement coercion operation. On the other hand, the verbs in Cluster 2 coerce more noun types than those in Cluster 1. Finally, the distance between a verb and its coerced complement is not found to be a statistically significant variable that distinguishes the two clusters.

Though Lin et al. (2009) found that *jinzhi* 'forbid' could coerce its complement, such a use was not attested in the Sinica Corpus. Therefore, the verb *jinzhi* itself forms a cluster.

6 Discussion

Generally, on the basis of their coercion profiles, the verbs examined in the present study can be grouped into two major clusters. In the following discussion, we will further zoom in to see how the verbs in each cluster are semantically related. Moreover, we will show that the empirical findings of the present study can shed new light on the framework of the Generative Lexicon.

Of the eight verbs in the first cluster, five denote enjoyment and volition: *xihuan* 'like', *taoyan* 'dislike', *tuijian* 'recommend', *jujue* 'refuse', and *kangju* 'resist'. They are compatible with referentially opaque nouns (cf. Pustejovsky 1995:181), i.e., nouns that are weakly constrained by their qualia roles (the AGENTIVE role and the TELIC role, in particular). For such a noun, an event reading can be reconstructed from the context. Here is an example:

(7) wo dangran xiwang guanzhong <u>xihuan</u> wo
I definitely hope audience like I
'I definitely hope that the audience like (to watch) me'

In (7), though *wo* 'I; me' is referentially opaque, an event reading (i.e., watching me) can be reconstructed from *guanzhong* 'audience'. A referentially opaque noun such as *wo* 'I; me' can have a relatively higher frequency. The semantic compatibility between a enjoyment/volition-denoting verb and a referentially opaque noun may explain why the verbs in Cluster 1 coerce a complement more frequently but coerce fewer noun types.

The verbs in the second cluster are also semantically related to some extent: four verbs denote the beginning or the ending of an event, i.e., *kaishi* 'begin', *wancheng* 'finish', *tingzhi* 'stop', and *jixu* 'continue'. Thus, they prefer referentially transparent nouns (cf. Pustejovsky 1995:181) that are given a process in the AGENTIVE role or the TELIC role, and an event reading is reconstructed from the qualia structure of a complement. Here is an example:

(8) <u>wancheng</u> le geng duo xin dianying
finish LE more many new movie
'(someone) has finished (shooting) more new movies'

The AGENTIVE role of *dianying* 'movie' can be SHOOT, which is a process that someone can start, finish, stop, or continue.

Furthermore, as can be observed in our quantitative data presented in the appendix, antonyms and near-synonyms may have similar profiles in terms of the complement coercion operation, and they can be clustered together accordingly – e.g., the antonym pair *xihuan* 'like'/*taoyan* 'dislike' and the near-synonym pair *jujue* 'refuse'/*kangju* 'resist' in Cluster 1; the anontym pairs *kaishi* 'begin'/*wancheng* 'finish' and *jixu* 'continue'/*tingzhi* 'stop' in Cluster 2. Note that though the antonyms *yunxu* 'allow' and *jinzhi* 'forbid' are in different clusters (i.e., Cluster 2 and Cluster 3, respectively), they are similar in that neither coerces a complement frequently. There are some intriguing cases, though. For example, *xuyao* 'need' and *yaoqiu* 'require' can be seen as near-synonyms in Chinese, but they are not clustered together.

In Chinese, the verb *jinzhi* 'forbid' is often used in a fairly formal style, and its context usually leaves little room for a misinterpretation. A misinterpretation can arise from the process of reconstructing an event reading, for the process is inferential. This may explain why the verb *jinzhi* is not found in our data to occur in a complement coercion operation. However, note that the semantics of *jinzhi* does not inherently keep the verb from coercing its complement. Lin et al. (2009), using the web as a corpus, have attested *jinzhi* in a complement coercion operation.

In the exploration of the complement coercion operation in Chinese, the present study makes one step more abstract in co-selectional terms. When checking whether a context features a complement coercion operation, we did not simply sort out the frequent collocations of a verb as we usually do to identify the collocational patterns of a lexical item. Rather, we needed to manually assign a semantic type (i.e., entity, event, etc.) to each complement to construct the complement coercion profile of a verb. Though many attempts have been made to investigate the abstract dimensions of a lexical profile (e.g., the semantic preference of a lexical item), few have incorporated the coercion profile of a verb into a verbal profile. The present study shows that the behavioral profile of a verb can include a more abstract dimension, i.e., how the verb interacts with the complement coercion operation. This suggests that the Generative Lexicon can provide a fresh insight into co-selectional/collocational studies.

On the other hand, the findings of the present study have shed new light on the Generative Lexicon. First, the present study is corpus-based, thus offering empirical support for theoretical operations in the Generative Lexicon. Second, the present study examines Chinese data, thus providing cross-linguistic support for the Generative Lexicon. The findings here echo Lin et al. (2009), demonstrating that the complement coercion operation is truly a useful mechanism in Chinese. Third, the present study shows that lexical relations (e.g., antonymy and near-synonymy) can be revealed through the interaction between the qualia structure and the complement coercion operation, and this suggests that the Generative Lexicon achieves its goal to capture the global organization of a lexicon (Pustejovsky 1995:61).

Finally, the theory of norms and exploitations (Hanks 2009, 2013) can be related to the Generative Lexicon (Pustejovsky 1995), though the two theories take different approaches to our language use. They are similar in two ways. First, in the two theories, semantics is given precedence over syntax. Second, the two theories attempt to account for novel usages which may seem unusual or abnormal at first sight. The type mismatch examined in the present study is an example. As have been discussed, the Generative Lexicon deals with type mismatches through the qualia structure and the complement coercion operation. In Hank's theory, two systems collaborate: the primary one governs conventional usages (i.e., norms), and the secondary one governs the exploitation of conventional usages (i.e., exploitations). The two systems cannot be sharply distinguished because a repeated exploitation may finally become a norm. Hanks suggests that the normality of an utterance depends on statistical analyses. In Chinese, the type mismatch between a verb and its complement can be seen as an exploitation: the surface form is a conventional usage in Chinese (i.e., a verb followed by a nominal complement), and it is exploited for economical reasons (i.e., the speaker does not need to explicitly specify the event). However, with the quantitative data from the Sinica Corpus, we have found that the complement coercion operation in Chinese is more dominant for some verbs (e.g., *cuoguo* 'fail to do something') than for others (e.g., *jixu* 'continue'). In other words, the complement coercion operation in Chinese can be seen as a norm for some verbs yet as an exploitation for others. This is exactly the insight that such a data-based model as the theory of norms and exploitations can provide for a generative model. While the Generative Lexicon can provide mechanisms to account for how a complement can be coerced, the theory of norms and exploitations can focus on how compatible an individual word is with the complement coercion operation. In short, the former is a model of rules and restrictions, while the latter is a model of preferences and probabilities. The two models can thus complement each other.

7 Concluding Remarks

Our corpus-based study explores the complement coercion operation in Chinese. The present study examined twenty verbs, creating a coercion profile for each verb. A multivariate analysis was conducted on the coercion profiles to cluster the twenty verbs. There are two major clusters: the verbs in Cluster 1 coerce a complement more frequently, while the verbs in Cluster 2 coerce more noun types. The differences can be attributed to the semantics of the verbs. Moreover, many lexical pairs (e.g., antonyms and near-synonyms) are identified in the two clusters. Our quantitative analysis suggests that semantically related verbs can have similar coercion profiles.

As suggested in our review, empirical studies on the complement coercion operation in Chinese are still rare. Our study is corpus-based, complementing intuition-based studies in Chinese (e.g., Lin and Liu 2004, Liu 2003). Additionally, the distributional patterns identified in the present study show that a data-based approach can complement a generative model that places more emphasis on rules and restrictions. The present study can be extended with more verbs analyzed and perhaps more variables taken into account.

Further studies can adopt other empirical approaches to explore the complement coercion operation in Chinese. For example, psycholinguistic/neurolinguistic studies can be conducted to see how Chinese speakers process the complement coercion operation, and acquisition studies are also needed. The framework of the Generative Lexicon can thus benefit from the integration of various empirical approaches.

References

Chiung-Yi Liu. 2003. *Dynamic Generative Lexicon*. M.A. thesis, National Tsing Hua University.

Chu-Ren Huang and Kathleen Ahrens. 2003. Individuals, kinds and events: Classifier coercion of nouns. *Language Sciences* 25:353-373.

Francesca Delogu, Francesco Vespignani, and Anthony J. Sanford. 2010. Effects of intensionality on sentence and discourse processing: Evidence from eye-movements. *Journal of Memory and Language* 62:352-379.

Giosuè Baggio, Travis Choma, Michiel van Lambalgen, and Peter Hagoort. 2009. Coercion and compositionality. *Journal of Cognitive Neuroscience* 22:2131-2140.

James Pustejovsky. 1995. *The Generative Lexicon*. MIT Press, Cambridge, Massachusetts.

Leonard Kaufman and Peter J. Rousseeuw. 1990. *Finding Groups in Data: An Introduction to Cluster Analysis*. Wiley, New York.

Matthew J. Traxler, Brian McElree, Rihana S. Williams, and Martin J. Pickering. 2002. Context effects in coercion: Evidence from eye movements. *Journal of Memory and Language* 53:1-25.

Matthew J. Traxler, Martin J. Pickering, and Brian McElreec. 2002. Coercion in sentence processing: Evidence from eye-movements and self-paced reading. *Journal of Memory and Language* 47:530-547.

Patrick Hanks. 2009. The linguistic double helix: Norms and exploitations. *After Half a Century of Slavonic Natural Language Processing*, Dana Hlaváčková, Aleš Horák, Klára Osolsobě, and Pavel Rychlý (eds.), pp. 63-80. Masaryk University, Brno, Czech Republic.

Patrick Hanks. 2013. *Lexical Analysis: Norms and Exploitations*. MIT Press, Cambridge, Massachusetts.

Shu-Yen Lin, Shu-Kai Hsieh, and Yann-Jong Huang. 2009. Exploring Chinese type coercion: A web-as-corpus study. The 5th International Conference on Generative Approaches to the Lexicon.

T.-H. Jonah Lin and C.-Y. Cecilia Liu. 2004. Coercion, event structure, and syntax. *Nanzan Linguistics* 2:9-31.

Zhijun Wang. 2008. Context coercion in sentence processing: Evidence from Chinese. *Proceedings of the 20th North American Conference on Chinese Linguistics*, Marjorie K. M. Chan and Hana Kang (eds.), pp. 959-974.

Appendix. The coercion profiles of the Chinese verbs examined in the present study

Verb	(A) # of the sentences analyzed	(B) # with a complement coercion operation	(C) # of the coerced noun types	(D) = (B)/(A)	(E) = (B)/264	(F) = (C)/(B)	(G) The average distance
bimian **'avoid'**	101	11	11	0.10891	0.04167	1.00000	3.81818
changshi **'try'**	77	17	14	0.22078	0.06439	0.82353	3.52941
cuoguo **'miss'**	71	48	37	0.67606	0.18182	0.77083	3.41667
fuze **'be responsible for'**	84	12	11	0.14286	0.04545	0.91667	3.75000
jinzhi **'forbid'**	86	0	0	0.00000	0.00000	0.00000	0.00000
jixu **'continue'**	116	2	2	0.01724	0.00758	1.00000	4.50000
jueding **'decide'**	82	15	15	0.18293	0.05682	1.00000	2.60000
jujue **'refuse'**	80	14	11	0.17500	0.05303	0.78571	2.00000
kaishi **'begin'**	78	1	1	0.01282	0.00379	1.00000	3.00000
kangju **'resist'**	41	12	11	0.29268	0.04545	0.91667	1.83333
kewang **'long for'**	68	8	8	0.11765	0.03030	1.00000	2.87500
mianqiang **'force'**	87	3	3	0.03448	0.01136	1.00000	1.00000
taoyan **'dislike'**	57	22	16	0.38596	0.08333	0.72727	2.22727
tingzhi **'stop'**	86	3	3	0.03488	0.01136	1.00000	2.00000
tuijian **'recommend'**	34	18	14	0.52941	0.06818	0.77778	2.94444
wancheng **'finish'**	69	11	11	0.15942	0.04167	1.00000	3.09091
xihuan **'like'**	98	35	28	0.35714	0.13258	0.80000	2.25714
xuyao **'need'**	84	24	19	0.28571	0.09091	0.79167	2.75000
yaoqiu **'require'**	85	3	3	0.03529	0.01136	1.00000	3.00000
yunxu **'allow'**	101	5	5	0.04950	0.01894	1.00000	4.20000

Towards the automatic classification of complex-type nominals

Lauren Romeo[1], Sara Mendes[1,2], Núria Bel[1]
[1]Universitat Pompeu Fabra, Roc Boronat, 138, Barcelona (Spain)
[2]Centro de Linguística da Universidade de Lisboa, Av. Prof. Gama Pinto, 2, Lisboa (Portugal)
{lauren.romeo, sara.mendes, nuria.bel}@upf.edu

Abstract

The work presented here depicts experiments toward the automatic classification of complex-type nominals using distributional information. We conducted two experiments: classifying complex-type nominals as members of multiple individual lexical classes, and building a dedicated classifier for complex-type nominals, distinguishing them from simple types. We discuss the promising results obtained, with a focus on asymmetries observed and on lines to be explored in the future.

1 Introduction

In this article we evaluate the possibility to automatically identify dot-type nominals using distributional information extracted from corpus data. This work has a two-fold motivation. First, to contribute to a more accurate modeling of the lexicon, by providing a method towards a cost-effective inclusion of dot-type information in Language Resources (LRs), which will thus mirror a complex, systematic and productive linguistic phenomenon. Second, to make this type of semantic information available in LRs to provide useful and often crucial information to Natural Language Processing (NLP) applications.

Differing from simple-type nouns, complex types are composed of more than one constituent sense that can be recovered both individually and simultaneously in context, as illustrated below.

(1) a. The church discussed its role in society at the gathering. (ORGANIZATION)
b. The choir rehearses on Saturdays at the church. (LOCATION)
c. There is a collection organized (ORGANIZATION) by the church on Mulberry Street (LOCATION) this Sunday.

In this example the noun *church*, in (1a) denotes an ORGANIZATION, in (1b) a LOCATION and in (1c) the context requires the same single occurrence of the noun to denote both an ORGANIZATION and a LOCATION. The complexity of dot-object selectional behavior in context, as illustrated in (1), makes it difficult to apply to complex types the standard notion of word sense, as used in automatic text processing tasks. Traditional word sense disambiguation (WSD) systems, for instance, might be able to correctly identify the senses in both (1a) and (1b), however in (1c) a decision for a single sense would have to be made, despite the fact that both senses are simultaneously activated by the context.

Having rich information available on complex types not only can reduce the search space in disambiguation tasks, and thus the number of decisions needed, but can also provide grounds to opt for the non-disambiguation of instances when relevant, for example in co-predication contexts like (1c). Moreover, knowledge of the entire sense potential of a given word is sometimes required for specific tasks (see for instance Rumshisky et al. (2007) and Lenci et al. (2010)).

Thus, information on the sense composition of complex types can be crucial in NLP, as it allows for the reduction of the amount of lexical semantic processing (Buitelaar, 2000) in tasks such as Information Retrieval, semantic role annotation, high-quality Machine Translation and Summarization, as well as Question Answering.

In this paper we evaluate the possibility to employ information from actual language use as encoded in corpus data to acquire information on the sense composition of complex types. In line with approaches that explore corpus-based definitions of fine-grained distinctions that emerge as abstractions over the combinatorial patterns of lexical items (Ježek and Lenci, 2007), we use a classification approach based strictly on distributional evidence available in a corpus to automatically identify complex types.

As most approaches in lexical semantic classification do not distinguish among related senses of the same word, considering it either as part of a class or not (Hindle, 1990; Bullinaria, 2008; Bel et al., 2012), our goal is to outline a strategy which automatically accounts for those nouns that belong to multiple classes, specifically to pinpoint complex-type nouns using distributional evidence. In this context we discuss an experiment involving two complex types in English: LOCATION•ORGANIZATION (LOC•ORG) and EVENT•INFORMATION (EVT•INF). Our hypothesis is that complex-type nouns demonstrate characteristic and indicative lexico-syntactic traits of more than one class, which allow us to use lexico-syntactic patterns over corpus data to automatically identify nouns for which there is distributional evidence of their membership to more than one class.

In the following, we review the motivation and theoretical background of this work (Section 2); discuss data preparation (Section 3); present two classification experiments, discuss the results obtained (Section 4), and conclude with promising directions for future research (Section 5).

2 Motivation and theoretical background

2.1 Complex types

Dot objects, or nouns with complex types, are composed by more than one constituent type, each representative of a distinct sense, between which holds a regular and predictable relation. As thoroughly discussed in the literature (Pustejovsky, 1995; 2005), there is strong linguistic motivation for considering the existence of such objects. First, the knowledge we have of concepts associated with *books* and *doors*, for instance, is not characterizable as a conjunction of simple types. Second, the notion of complex types captures a type of inherent logical polysemy, occurring in regular, predictable patterns, i.e. systematically recurrent, namely cross-linguistically.

Building on arguments that show traditional sense-enumerating lexicons are not only uneconomical, but also present instances of systematic phenomena as arbitrary and idiosyncratic features of single words, which do not account for the productive nature of their potential underlying regularities (Pethrö, 2000), and thus render unfeasible the task of listing all possible meanings of a word (Kilgariff, 1992), the Generative Lexicon Theory (GL) (Pustejovsky, 1995) explores and formalizes the shifts of meaning of these objects in context. This represents an important step towards implementing systems that can assign meaning to words dynamically depending on the context in which they occur (Cooper, 2005).

Here we assume Pustejovsky's (1995) definition of dot types as a Cartesian product of types with a particularly restricted interpretation. This means that the product $\tau_1 \times \tau_2$, of types τ_1 and τ_2, each denoting sets, alone does not adequately determine the semantics of the dot object. The relation *R*, which structures the component types, must also be seen as part of the definition of the semantics of the lexical conceptual paradigm of the complex type. Thus, for the dot object $\tau_1 \bullet \tau_2$ to be well-formed, there must be a relation R that structures the elements τ_1 and τ_2, a concept that is formalized in GL (Pustejovsky, 1995: 149) as:

$$\begin{bmatrix} \alpha \\ ARGSTR = \begin{bmatrix} ARG1 = \mathbf{x}: \tau_1 \\ ARG2 = \mathbf{y}: \tau_2 \end{bmatrix} \\ QUALIA = \begin{bmatrix} \tau_1\tau_2\_\mathbf{lcp} \\ FORMAL = R(x,y) \end{bmatrix} \end{bmatrix} \quad (2)$$

This formalization accounts for one of the properties that makes complex types unique and distinguishes them, for instance, from cases of homonymy[1]: the possibility for their distinctive senses to be active at the same time (Pustejovsky, 1995: 223), illustrated in (1c). The levels of representation and generative mechanisms in GL predict a noun like *church*, represented below, occurs not only in contexts typical of class x: ORG (see (1a)) and of class y: LOC (see (1b)), but also in contexts which activate the relation $R_1(x,y)$, i.e. contexts where both ORG and LOC senses are simultaneously activated (see (1c)).

$$\begin{bmatrix} \mathbf{church} \\ ARGSTR = \begin{bmatrix} ARG1 = \mathbf{x: organization} \\ ARG2 = \mathbf{y: location} \end{bmatrix} \\ QUALIA = \begin{bmatrix} \mathbf{org \bullet loc\_lcp} \\ FORMAL = R_1(x,y) \end{bmatrix} \end{bmatrix} \quad (3)$$

These properties distinguish dot objects from simple types, unified types or standard generalization on types (cf. Pustejovsky, 1995: 141 and ff.). Moreover, the possibility to have word

[1] Utt and Padó (2011) consider the importance of this distinction, proposing an automatic polysemy classifier. Boleda et al. (2012) also put forth an approach for predicting regular sense alternations in corpus data. However, both methods are based on external rich language resources, which besides only being available for a very restricted set of languages, do not necessarily mirror language use, as noted in the latter work.

senses that semantically compose these words either individually or simultaneously activated, depending on the selectional environment, presents a challenge to NLP systems that deal with identifying word senses in context. In fact, these follow a one-word, one-sense approach, designed to identify a single sense in each decision. Thus, as argued in Section 1, including information on the semantics of dot objects in LRs can contribute to an overall improvement in performance of NLP systems.

2.2 Exploring the Distributional Hypothesis to identify complex-type nouns

Considering the above characterization of dot types, we assume them to be members of more than one lexical class, more precisely members of each class corresponding to the senses they are composed of. As members of more than one class, complex types are expected to occur in indicatory contexts of more than one individual class. With this in mind, we evaluate the possibility to automatically identify complex types using a cue-based classification methodology.

Based on the Distributional Hypothesis (Harris, 1954), cue-based lexical semantic classification (Merlo and Stevenson, 2001) builds on the assumption that lexical semantic classes are emergent properties of a number of words that recurrently co-occur in a number of particular contexts. Thereby, as proposed by Bybee and Hopper (2001) and Bybee (2010), we understand lexical semantic classes as generalizations that come about when there is a systematic co-distribution for a number of words in a number of contexts. Different contexts where a number of words tend to occur thus become linguistic *cues* of a particular semantic property that a set of words has in common. Using these cues to gather indicatory distributional information provides evidence that discriminates members of a class from other lexical items.

We hypothesize that the classification of a noun as a member of the different individual classes that correspond to the senses that compose a complex type indicate its potential to belong to a given dot type. Parting from the cue-based nominal lexical semantic classification work reported in Bel et al. (2012), we apply this methodology to complex-type nominals. This allows us to analyze the distributional behavior of nouns belonging to more than one class and to which extent binary classifiers can accurately deal with such items.

As members of more than one class, we expect complex-type nouns to disperse their occurrences between indicatory contexts of different classes. Thereby, one of our goals consists in evaluating to which extent this can be problematic to binary classifiers. Specifically, we will verify whether the available distributional information indicatory of each individual class is strong enough for an automatic cue-based classification for this type of noun to work.

3 Data preparation

The sense composition of complex types discussed in previous sections forms the basis of our hypothesis in which we claim that these nominals should exhibit linguistic behavior characteristic of each simple-type class that makes up their sense composition. To verify this hypothesis and thus provide empirical evidence of multiple class membership for complex-type nouns, we implemented the cue-based lexical semantic classification experiment described below.

3.1 Classes considered

In line with the argument presented above, we focus on two complex types representative of the general characteristics of dot objects (Pustejovsky, 1995; 2005; Rumshisky et al., 2007; Melloni and Ježek, 2009; Copestake and Herbelot, 2012):

ORGANIZATION·LOCATION $(\lambda x \bullet y\ \exists R\ [\alpha\ (\textsc{org}(x) \bullet \textsc{loc}(y) \wedge R(x,y)])$: "the *church* prays during mass" vs. "the *church* is a large building"

EVENT·INFORMATION $(\lambda x \bullet y\ \exists R\ [\alpha\ (\textsc{evt}(x) \bullet \textsc{inf}(y) \wedge R(x,y)])$: "the *interview* lasted for two hours" vs. "the *interview* was interesting"

3.2 Description of the gold standard

In their nominal classification experiments, Bel et al. (2012) used gold standards created by extracting nouns from WordNet (Miller et al., 1990) which contained a sense corresponding to each of the lexical classes they studied. As our aim in this work is to automatically identify which nouns are complex-type nominals, we needed gold standards composed of nouns with the potential to be systematically interpreted in more than one sense to evaluate the results obtained in our experiments. As this information is usually not included in LRs, and specifically in Wordnet (see Boleda et al., 2012), we resorted to human annotation to create the gold standards.

Three experts, either native or highly proficient English speakers, annotated each noun from the original Bel et al. (2012) lists for their potential to contain another known sense. The annotators were given the automatically extracted list of nouns from each class and were asked to annotate whether those nouns could have a specific sense, different from the one encoded in the original gold standard.

Being simply provided with the original gold standard lists and a general definition of a target sense, annotators were asked to mark with *yes* or *no* whether they thought each individual noun in the list could be interpreted as a member of the target class, besides potentially having any other sense. With this annotated information, we used a voting scheme to build the gold standard, including in it the nouns considered to be members of more than one class by at least two annotators.

3.2.1 Asymmetry of sense components

Previous work has reported asymmetries regarding the prominence of senses that compose complex types (see, for example, Rumshisky et al. (2007) and Ježek and Melloni (2011)), as one sense is more generally used or constitutes a preferred interpretation[2]. Confirming this observation, evidence from psycholinguistic studies (Frisson and Pickering, 2001) demonstrated that although more than one sense interpretation is available for a given word, the vast majority of speakers tend to consistently choose one interpretation over the other.

Several authors established relations between this type of asymmetry and complex types, particularly with regard to the nature of the relations holding between their sense components. An important part of the work developed on this matter has focused on classes whose sense components are ontologically related, in particular on the PROCESS•RESULT complex-type.

Ježek and Melloni (2011) characterize the properties of the polysemy involved in this case arguing it arises from the fact that a RESULT object type is temporally and causally dependant on a PROCESS type as an event is the pre-condition for the (coming into) existence of the object (RESULT). Thus, PROCESS readings can be considered more prominent as they are also reflected when the RESULT sense is active while the reverse does not hold true. The EVT•INF complex type, can be considered a sub-case of the former. Formalized in (4), the aforementioned unique properties of this dot type are represented in the AGENTIVE role.

$$\begin{bmatrix} \textbf{illustration} & \\ \mathit{ARGSTR}= \begin{bmatrix} \mathit{ARG1} = \mathbf{x:event} \\ \mathit{ARG2} = \mathbf{y:information} \end{bmatrix} \\ \mathit{QUALIA}= \begin{bmatrix} \tau_1 \bullet \tau_2\text{\_lcp} \\ \mathit{FORMAL} = R(x,y) \\ \mathit{AGENTIVE} = x(z,y) \end{bmatrix} \end{bmatrix} \quad (4)$$

Just as is the case for PROCESS•RESULT nominals, we expect the prominence of senses for this complex type to be asymmetric. The data obtained in our annotation task are consistent with this expectation (see Table 1), as 90 of the 149 INFORMATION nouns in Bel et al.'s (2012) gold standard are considered to also have an EVENT sense, whereas only 9 of the 273 EVENT nouns are annotated as also having an INFORMATION sense. Moreover, these human annotation results constitute a source of quantitative information providing evidence that support the existence of asymmetries of prominence of the different sense components of complex types.

	# of complex types per class	ratio of complex types per class
ORG as LOC	38	0.28
LOC as ORG	46	0.37
INFO as EVT	90	0.60
EVT as INFO	9	0.03

Table 1. Distribution of dot types per lexical class

Regarding the LOC•ORG complex type, there is neither an ontological relation between its meaning components nor such a clear asymmetry in the prominence of its sense components. Yet, differences observed can be attributed to relations generally holding between objects in the world. For instance, an ORGANIZATION, as a more abstract concept, is typically associated to a physical reality, namely the LOCATION which hosts this abstract object and makes it "perceivable". Reversely, LOCATION, as a physical point in space, is often independent of any other reality. Thus, in the lexicon, we observe words primarily denoting an ORGANIZATION that also refer to the LOCATION that hosts it, whereas the reverse is observed only in considerably stricter conditions, as illustrated by *congress* and *schoolyard* in (5).

(5) a. The *congress* (ORG) decided to vote the new rule into power after the recess.
b. The new rule was voted to power in the *congress* (ORG or LOC).
c. #The *schoolyard* decided to vote the new law into power after the recess.
d. The new rule was voted to power in the *schoolyard* (LOC).

[2] As often discussed in the literature (e.g. Bybee, 2010), these two aspects are not independent from each other: frequency of use tends to impact preferred interpretations. This is nonetheless a debate outside the scope of this work.

Asymmetry in the prominence of complex-type sense components is thus related to the nature of the systematic relation holding between them, which is different for each complex-type paradigm. Moreover, the ratio of nouns in each individual class annotated as having more than one potential sense, makes apparent the representativity of this phenomenon for each class (see Table 1). This provides crucial insight when analyzing our results, particularly to evaluate whether the asymmetries reported in this section have an overall impact in the automatic identification of complex types.

4 Experiments

In our experiments, we considered English nouns from the LOCATION, ORGANIZATION, INFORMATION, and EVENT classes. We used a part of the UkWaC corpus (Baroni et al., 2009) consisting of 60 million PoS-tagged tokens. To gather distributional evidence, we employed lexico-syntactic patterns indicatory of each individual class including prepositions, selectional preferences, grammatical functions and morphological information (see Bel et al. (2012) for a detailed description of patterns used). Each pattern was translated into a regular expression used over the corpus to identify occurrences of nouns in marked contexts. The relative frequency of occurrence of each noun in each cue was stored in an n-dimensional vector, where n is the total number of cues used for each class. To classify, we used a Logistic Model Trees (LMT) (Landwehr et al., 2005) Decision Tree classifier in the WEKA (Witten and Frank, 2005) implementation.

As detailed in Section 3.2, our gold standards are derived from the lists used by Bel et al. (2012) to reflect the phenomenon of multiple class membership of complex types. As there is a larger ratio of simple types in language, which is mirrored in our gold standards (see Table 2), a baseline based on the majority class would not allow us to assess the quality of the results depicted here. Thereby, to evaluate our results, we compare them against the performance of state-of-the-art classifiers for simple types, reported in Bel et al. (2012).

4.1 Complex types as members of individual simple-type classes

As mentioned earlier, the basic hypothesis for our experiments is that complex-type nominals, as members of more than one lexical class (see Section 2 for more details), demonstrate characteristic lexico-syntactic traits of multiple classes, and thus occur in indicatory contexts of the different classes that correspond to their sense components. However, as members of more than one class, the distributional behavior of complex-type nouns is expected to be more disperse, as occurrences are divided between indicative contexts of different classes. Given this, the experiment reported in this section aims to provide evidence as to whether this distributional information, though disperse, is strong enough to allow for an automatic identification of the different sense components of complex types in a classification task.

To accomplish this, we used the binary classifiers described in Bel et al. (2012), which were developed to automatically classify nouns into previously known lexical semantic classes, not taking into consideration polysemy. Based on word occurrences in specific contexts in a corpus, these classifiers simply consider a given noun either as a member of a class or not.

In the experiment reported in this section, we used a binary classifier for each sense component (organization, location, event and informational object) of the complex types considered. We started by verifying the binary classifiers capacity to identify complex-type nouns as members of the class corresponding to their most prominent sense, indicated in bold in Table 2.

	complex types correctly classified as members of the class (%)	ratio of classified complex types per members of the class
ORG•LOC as ORG	58.69	0.22
ORG•**LOC** as LOC	89.47	0.25
EVT•**INFO** as INFO	71.11	0.43
EVT•INFO as EVT	77.78	0.03

Table 2. Complex types correctly identified as members of the class corresponding to their prominent sense

The results reported in Table 2 make apparent that dot-type nominals provide enough distributional evidence indicatory of their most prominent sense so that their automatic classification as members of the class it corresponds to is possible. The results obtained are actually in line with the performance of the same classifiers with simple-type nominals reported by Bel et al. (2012), where a 66.21% and a 73.05% accuracy are obtained respectively for the LOCATION and the EVENT nouns classifiers.

With this in mind, we proceeded to verify whether this is also observed when considering less prominent sense components by performing a cross-classification of the nouns in our study using the binary classifiers mentioned above, essentially emulating the human annotation task described in Section 3.2. More precisely, we used trained binary classifiers for each class to classify the human-annotated lists of nouns, i.e. each classifier trained for simple-type classification of nouns of semantic type τ_1 was provided with a list of nouns with τ_2 as their prominent sense.

To illustrate this, a noun like *church*, defined as a LOCATION (τ_1) in Bel et al.'s (2012) gold standards, was checked for its occurrence in lexico-syntactic patterns indicatory of ORGANIZATION (τ_2) nouns, i.e. whether it shows distributional evidence indicatory of another class. Our claim is that having τ_1 nouns that occur in contexts indicatory of τ_2 allowing them to be classified as members of τ_2 provides evidence toward our hypothesis: given the sense composition of complex types, they should be considered members of more than one lexical semantic class, a fact that automatic classifiers should account for.

Table 3 presents the results of precision and recall of the cross-classification of complex-type nouns as members of the class corresponding to non-prominent sense components, in bold.

	Precision	Recall	Ratio
ORG•**LOC** as LOC	77.78	15.21	0.06
ORG•LOC as ORG	57.14	21.05	0.06
EVT•INFO as EVT	64.44	32.22	0.19
EVT•**INFO** as INFO	6.67	66.67	0.03

Table 3. Results of cross-classification (in %)

With our cross-classification, we replicate the annotation task automatically (see Section 3.2). The results in Table 3 allow us to make three main observations. First, the performance of cross-classification is in line with that of the classifiers used when dealing with simple-type nominals and when classifying complex types as members of the class corresponding to its most prominent sense component[3]. This indicates that complex types do occur in contexts typical of the different classes corresponding to their sense components, i.e. they belong to more than one class and behave as such.

The second aspect made apparent from the results in Table 3 is the overall low recall. These results are consistent with the work of Rumshisky et al. (2007) and the discussion in Section 3.2.1, specifically the asymmetries in terms of prominence of the different meaning components of complex types. This is reflected in the frequency of occurrences in contexts indicatory of a given class, which represents the information provided to our classifiers.

[3] The low precision reported for EVT•**INFO** as INFO is not independent of the reduced amount of nouns (9) of this type in the gold standard (see Table 1).

The noun *church*, for instance, occurred in contexts typical of LOCATION nouns with a relative frequency of 0.015 and of 0.030 in contexts typical of ORGANIZATION nouns. This is also the case of the noun *jurisdiction,* which occurred with a relative frequency of 0.039 in contexts typical of ORGANIZATION nouns and just 0.014 in contexts typical of LOCATION nouns. This provides evidence that more distributional information is available toward one sense over another, which is bound to affect classification results, particularly when the asymmetry is large.

Thus, the representation of senses in distributional data has an impact on our classification results, being responsible, in particular, for insufficient distributional evidence towards class membership for an important part of nouns in our list, which explains the low recall observed.

Thirdly, although the absolute numbers are lower due to the aforementioned recall, the ratio of complex types per class shows similar tendencies to the human annotation results. In fact, the ratios of complex types for the ORGANIZATION and LOCATION classes are balanced, along the lines of the human annotation results (see Table 1), whereas a big asymmetry is observed for the INFORMATION and EVENT classes, again mirroring the human annotation results (see Section 3.2.1).

Given our objective to verify whether complex-type nominals provide distributional evidence concurrent with more than one semantic class, our cross-classification experiment shows that the distributional information available generally indicates that complex types demonstrate a distributional behavior typical of members of more than one class, though the information available is not enough to correctly classify a part of the nouns studied, as indicated by the low recall observed in Table 3.

However, in this experiment we only consider a part of the distributional data for each complex type at a time. Having demonstrated that complex types show distributional behavior typical of members of more than one class and being clear that more information has to be considered for classifiers to achieve a better performance, we propose to include indicatory contexts of each of the classes composing the complex type in the same classifier, this way accounting for its full sense potential in the classification task.

4.2 Distinguishing complex types from simple-type nouns

The experiments described in Section 4.1 show that complex-type distributional evidence is indicatory of class membership to more than one class, but also that individually this information is often not sufficient for automatic systems to perform accurately and robustly. Thus, we put forth a new experiment to classify complex types built upon these observations. Our cross-classification experiments considered distributional information available for each word in contexts indicative of each class corresponding to one of its senses individually. In this section we depict an experiment where we combine contextual cues indicatory of each individual class that corresponds to the different sense components of a complex type to train a classifier.

The goal of this experiment is to automatically distinguish complex types from simple types by training a dedicated classifier. This approach combines the distributional information characteristic of each individual sense component of the complex type in a single classifier, providing it with more information at a time, which we expect to raise both precision and recall. Along this line, we collected distributional evidence of nouns by simultaneously using the cues for each class corresponding to the different sense components of the complex types considered in this work. We provided this information to the classifier as well as the human annotated gold standard for training. As in the previous experiment, we used LMTs (Landwehr et al., 2005), this time in a 10 fold cross-validation setting. Table 4 presents the results of the classification of ORG•LOC and EVT•INF complex types.

	Accuracy	Precision	Recall	F-Measure
ORG•LOC	67.68%	0.62	0.67	0.62
EVT•INFO	78.75%	0.72	0.78	0.72

Table 4. Results of complex-type classifiers

The results above demonstrate that by combining cues indicatory of different individual semantic classes and thus providing distributional evidence of the entire sense potential of a complex-type to the classifier we are able to automatically classify complex types, distinguishing them from simple-type nominals. As in the previous experiment, in order to be distinguished from simple-type nominals, complex types must demonstrate sufficient distributional evidence in contexts indicatory of classes corresponding to their different sense components.

By combining the distributional information indicatory of two classes and providing it simultaneously to the classifier, we improve the results previously obtained and attain accuracy in line with state-of-the-art simple-type classifiers (see Bel et al.'s (2012) results regarding nominal lexical semantic classification in English). Moreover, this approach overcomes the main issue in the results depicted in Section 4.1, which was low recall.

A final observation on the results attained regards the difference of more than 10% of accuracy between the classifiers for both complex types considered. Previously discussed work by Ježek and Melloni (2011) (see Section 3.2.1) help us identify possible causes for these contrasts, such as an ontological dependence between component types of dot types like EVT•INF, whose occurrences have both sense components of the dot object generally simultaneously present. However, the same is not true for complex types such as ORG•LOC nouns, which results in a more disperse distributional behavior between indicatory contexts of each sense component of the dot object, constituting a challenge for classifiers, which naturally impacts performance.

5 Final Remarks

The classifiers developed in this work consider contexts indicatory of each nominal class that corresponds to a sense component of a complex-type. As shown, our classifiers are able to automatically identify nouns that display characteristic properties of different simple types, namely LOCATION and ORGANIZATION, and EVENT and INFORMATION. By achieving this, we demonstrate the validity of our hypothesis that dot-object nouns simultaneously display distributional characteristics of the different classes that correspond to their sense components.

Although, we obtain results in line with state-of-the-art performance of simple-type classifiers by combining contextual information for the different sense components of complex types, we still do not capture those contexts where only dot-type nouns can occur (i.e. contexts that are unique to these nouns and clearly separate them from simple types and homonyms). Given the specific properties of EVT•INF nouns, the weight of this type of contexts can be hinted by the different performance of the classifiers developed, as discussed in the previous section.

In future work we will evaluate to which extent using the contexts specific to complex types, i.e. contexts which "convoke" different sense components simultaneously (see, for instance, Šimon and Huang (2009), Pustejovsky (2007) and Cruse (2000)), can result in a still more reliable classifier, with the potential to contribute to cost-effectively create more accurate LRs for NLP.

Acknowledgments

This work was funded with the support of the SUR of the DEC of the Generalitat de Catalunya and the European Social Fund, by SKATER TIN2012-38584-C06-05 and by Fundação para a Ciência e a Tecnologia (FCT) post-doctoral fellowship SFRH/BPD/79900/2011.

References

M. Baroni, S. Bernardini, A. Ferraresi & E. Zanchetta. 2009. The WaCky Wide Web: A Collection of Very Large Linguistically Processed Web-Crawled Corpora. *Language Resources and Evaluation*, 43(3): 209-226.

N. Bel, L. Romeo & M. Padró. 2012. Automatic Lexical Semantic Classification of Nouns. In *Proceedings of the 8th International Conference on Language Resources and Evaluation (LREC 2012)*, Istanbul, Turkey: 1448-1455.

G. Boleda, S. Padó & J. Utt. 2012. Regular Polysemy: A Distributional Model. In *Proceedings of the 1st Joint Conference on Lexical and Computational Semantics (*SEM),* Montreal, Canada: 151-160.

P. Buitelaar. 2000. Reducing lexical semantic complexity with systematic polysemous classes and underspecification. In *Proceedings of NAACL-ANLP 2000 Workshop: Syntactic and Semantic Complexity in NLP Systems*: 14-29.

J. A. Bullinaria. 2008. Semantic Categorization Using Simple Word Co-occurrence Statistics. In M. Baroni, S. Evert & A. Lenci (eds.), *Proceedings of the ESSLLI Workshop on Distributional Lexical Semantics*, Hamburg, Germany: 1-8.

J. Bybee. 2010. *Language, usage and cognition*. Cambridge University Press, Cambridge.

J. Bybee & P. Hopper. 2001. *Frequency and the emergence of language structure*. John Benjamins, Amsterdam.

R. Cooper. 2005. Do delicious lunches take a long time?, *GSLT internal conference*.

A. Copestake & A. Herbelot. 2012. *Lexicalised compositionality*. Unpublished draft.

A. Cruse. 2000. Aspects of the micro-structure of word meanings. In Y. Ravin & C. Leacock (eds.), *Polysemy: Theoretical and Computational Approaches*. Oxford University Press.

S. Frisson & M. J. Pickering. 2009. Semantic Underspecification in Language Production. *Language and Linguistics Compass*, 3(1). Blackwell Publishing, Ltd.

Z. Harris. 1954. Distributional structure. *Word*, 10(23): 146-162.

D. Hindle. 1990. Noun classification from predicate-argument structures. In *Proceedings of the 28th Annual Meeting of the Association for Computational Linguistics*: 268-275.

E. Ježek & A. Lenci. 2007. When GL meets the corpus. A data driven investigation of semantic types and coercion phenomena. In P. Bouillon, L. Danlos & K. Kanzaky (eds.), *Proceedings of the 4th International Workshop on Generative Approaches to the Lexicon*, Paris, France.

E. Ježek & C. Melloni. 2011. Nominals, polysemy and co-predication. *Journal of cognitive science*, 12.

A. Kilgariff. 1992. *Polysemy*. PhD Thesis, University of Sussex, UK.

N. Landwehr, M. Hall & E. Frank. 2005. Logistic Model Trees. *Machine Learning*, 95(1-2): 161-205.

A. Lenci, M. Johnson & G. Lapesa. 2010, Building an Italian FrameNet through semi-automatic corpus analysis. In *Proceedings of the 7th International Conference on Language Resources and Evaluation (LREC 2010)*: 12-19.

C. Melloni & E. Ježek. 2009. Inherent Polysemy of Action Nominals, presented at *Journées Sémantique et Modélisation (JSM 2009)*, Paris, France.

P. Merlo & S. Stevenson. 2001. Automatic verb classification based on statistical distribution of argument structure. *Computational Linguistics*, 27(3): 373-408.

G. A. Miller, R. Beckwith, C. Fellbaum, D. Gross & K. J. Miller. 1990. Introduction to WordNet: An on-line lexical database. *International Journal of Lexicography*, 3(4): 235-244.

J. Utt & S. Padó. 2011. Ontology-based distinction between polysemy and homonymy. *Proceedings of the Ninth International Conference on Computational Semantics (IWCS'11)*, Stroudsburg, PA: 265-274.

G. Pethö. 2001. What is polysemy? A survey of current research and results. In E. T. Ne´meth & K. Bibok (eds.), *Pragmatics and Flexibility of Word Meaning*. Elsevier, Amsterdam: 175-224.

J. Pustejovsky. 1995. *Generative Lexicon*. The MIT Press, Cambridge.

J. Pustejovsky. 2005. *A survey of dot objects*. Unpublished manuscript, Brandeis University, Waltham.

J. Pustejovsky. 2007. Type Theory and Lexical Decomposition. In P. Bouillon & C. Lee (eds.), *Trends in Generative Lexicon Theory*. Kluwer Publishers.

A. Rumshisky, V. Grinberg & J. Pustejovsky. 2007. Detecting Selectional Behavior of Complex Types in Text. In *Proceedings of the 4th International Workshop on GenerativeApproaches to the Lexicon*, Paris, France.

P. Šimon & C. Huang. 2010. Cross-sortal Predication and Polysemy. In *Proceedings of the 24th Pacific Asia Conference on Language, Information and Computation (PACLIC 2010)*: 853-861.

I. H. Witten & E. Frank. 2005. *Data Mining: Practical machine learning tools and techniques*. 2nd Edition, Morgan Kaufmann, San Francisco.

Qualia Relations in Metaphorical Noun-Noun Compounds

Zuoyan Song
School of Chinese Language and Literature,
Beijing Normal University, Beijing, China,100875
meszy@163.com

Qingqing Zhao
School of Chinese Language and Literature,
Beijing Normal University, Beijing, China,100875
874540721@qq.com

Abstract

This paper aims to find out the qualia roles involved in metaphorical noun-noun compounds in Mandarin Chinese. Metaphor concerns the resemblance between things. From the perspective of qualia structure proposed by Generative Lexicon, the resemblance in metaphorical compounds can be interpreted in the way that a compound and its metaphorical component share the same quale role. A preliminary investigation shows that no matter which constituent (the modifying noun or the head noun) takes on a metaphorical meaning, only three qualia roles are found in metaphorical compounds, which are FORMAL, CONSTITUTIVE and TELIC, ordered from the most to the least frequent. AGENTIVE role is excluded. Among the values of FORMAL role, shape is the most frequent. CONSTITUTIVE role mainly relates to body part terms. TELIC role is mainly concerned with artifactual type nouns. Also, this study reveals some fine-grained distinctions between nouns of different types.

1 Introduction

It is clear that there are many types of nominal compounds, but as it is well known that the majority are composed of two nouns, i.e. noun-noun compounds. Compounds of this type present the result of productive compounding processes (Packard 2002:85; Li and Thompson 1981). In noun-noun compounds, the most common construction is modifier-head with the head on the right. The relatedness between the meaning of a compound and those of its components is always a hot topic and there are numerous studies are available, among which, the most innovative are works within the Generative Lexicon (GL) perspective.

In GL, Qualia structure contains four basic qualia roles (Pustejovsky 1995:85-86):

- Constitutive role: The relation between an object and its constituents or proper parts.
  e.g. material, weight, parts and component elements.
- Formal role: That which distinguishes the object within a large domain.
  e.g. shape, color, orientation, magnitude, dimensionality and position.
- Telic role: purpose and function of the object.
  i.e. purpose that an agent has in performing the object and built-in function or aim which specifies certain activities.
- Agentive role: factors involved in the origin or "bringing about" of an object.
  e.g. creator, artifact, natural kind and causal chain.

The qualia are taken as representing an essential component of word meaning, capturing how language speakers understand objects and relations in the world and providing the minimal explanation for the linguistic behavior of lexical items.

Under the theoretical framework of qualia structure, Johnston and Busa (1999) analyze the nominal compounds in English and Italian and propose Qualia Modification observing the relational structure between modifiers and heads in compounds. They focus on three types of qualia modification: TELIC, AGENTIVE and CONSTITUTIVE. Bassac and Bouillon (2013) offer a detailed analysis of the telic relationship in nominal compounds both in French and in Turkish. Recently, the approach of qualia modification has been adopted in several research works to analyze Chinese compound nouns. Lee et al. (2010) demonstrate the qualia modification in noun-noun compounds found in Chinese as well as a couple of other languages like German, Spanish, Japanese and Italian. Wang and Huang (2011) specifically investigate the modifier-head type in compound event nouns. Song and Qiu (2013) examine the qualia relations in the nominal compounds containing verbal elements (NCCVs) and identify some productive compounding patterns. Unlike previous studies, which focus on the qualia relation between the two elements in a compound, this study also pays attention to the qualia relation between a compound and its components.

Following the generative perspective in works mentioned above, this paper aims to investigate the qualia roles involved in a special class of the noun-noun compounds in Mandarin Chinese, which contain metaphorical nouns. Huang (2008) first introduces qualia roles into the analysis of metaphorical noun-noun compounds and gives some examples. Based on more data, we will make a deeper analysis from both quantitative and qualitative perspective.

The rest of this paper is organized as follows. Section 2 introduces the data and method. Section 3 and section 4 demonstrate the qualia roles involved in noun-noun compounds containing metaphorical modifiers and heads respectively. Section 5 summarizes the paper.

2 Data and Method

Different from qualia modification which focus on the modifiers, this work expects to reveal what qualia information a metaphorical component can contribute to the compound no matter it is a modifying noun or a head noun. Metaphor is an imaginative way of describing something by referring to something else which is the same in a particular way. It emphasizes the resemblance between things. From the perspective of qualia structure proposed by Generative Lexicon, the resemblance in metaphorical compounds can be interpreted in the way that a compound and its metaphorical component share the same quale role. For example, compound *shisun* (石笋 stone-bamboo shoot) 'stalagmite' is not a bamboo shoot but a stone in the shape of bamboo shoot. *Sun* specifies the formal role of *shisun*. In other words, *shisun* and *sun* share the same formal role. More precisely, they share the same value of the formal role, namely shape.

According to Packard (2002:220), Metaphorical Lexicalization refers to words whose components lose their original meaning and take on a related, figurative or metaphorical interpretation, while the grammatical relationships within the compound continue to obtain. There are two types of metaphorical Lexicalization can be distinguished: that which occurs at the component level (component metaphorical lexicalization) and that which occurs at the level of the gestalt word (word metaphorical lexicalization). In component metaphorical lexicalization, one or both of the individual word components take on a metaphorical meaning, while the overall meaning of the compound continues to be a compositional sum of the meanings of its metaphorical parts. Our study will focus on component metaphorical compounds which are composed of two nouns and have modifier-head structure. These metaphorical compounds can be further divided into two types. Conceptual metaphor acts upon the modifying noun in one type and the head noun in the other type.

Of course, metaphor and metonymy can act simultaneously upon the meaning of a noun-noun compound, as suggested by Goossens (1995), who created the term *metaphtonymy* to refer to this phenomenon. He identified two types of metaphtonymies: metaphor from metonymy and metonymy within metaphor. Exactly speaking, the compounds examined in this paper are all metaphtonymic compounds. That is to say, metonymy is also at work in these compounds. Compounds Containing Metaphorical modifier involve CATEGORY FOR PROPERTY metonymy. "Metaphor from metonymy" is at work in these compounds. *Mojing* (墨镜 ink-glasses) 'sunglasses' is such an example, where *mo* (ink) refers metonymically to the color of ink , and the compound as a whole is a metaphor (it refers metaphorically to something black). On the other hand, Compounds Containing Metaphorical head involve SPECIFIC FOR GENERIC metonymy. "Metonymy within metaphor" is at work in these compounds. For example, in the compound (石狮 stone-lion) 'stone lion', *shi* (狮) refers metonymically to something lion-shaped (SPECIFIC FOR GENERIC metonymy), and there is also a metaphor at work, by which a lion is linked to an artifact.

The interaction of metaphor and metonymy are complicated, we will not go into details since this is not the focus of this paper. More discussion can be seen in Warren (1992), Geeraerts (2002), Benczes (2006), among others.

Generally, the compounds for our analysis come from *Modern Chinese Dictionary (version 6)*, which are disyllabic, and each noun in a compound is either a natural type or an artifactual type and refers to a physical object[1]. First, a total of 666 metaphorical compounds are selected, out of which, 480 (72%) contain metaphorical modifiers and 186 (28%) contain metaphorical heads. Then, the qualia role in every compound is annotated. Finally, statistical analysis was performed.

In the following two sections, these two types will be examined one by one.

3 Compounds Containing Metaphorical Modifiers

In the compounds of this type, the modifying noun is used metaphorically. It does not refer to an object but some properties of the object, i.e. a quale role of the modifier. More precisely, modifying noun specifies some characteristic of head noun.

Such compounds bear a metaphorical relationship between the modifying noun and the compound: the entity denoted by the compound (or N_2) is metaphorically understood through the entity denoted by N_1. N_1 is a metaphorical description of N_2.This metaphorical relationship can be based upon a number of features, relations or functions. In other words, the modifying noun and the compound share the same quale role or the same value(s) of a quale role. Our examination shows that there are three qualia roles can be seen in compounds of this type, among which FORMAL is the most common, followed by CONSTITUTIVE and TELIC. Their distribution information is summarized in Table 1.

FORM	CONS	TELIC
165(89%)	11(6%)	10(5%)

Table 1: Distribution of qualia roles in compounds containing metaphorical modifiers

3.1 FORMAL Qualia Modification

In these compounds, metaphorical nouns modify the formal role of the head noun by exploiting their own formal role. As shown in table 2, the values of the formal role vary wildly from noun to noun, including shape, color, size and so on. The most common formal values are shape (63%) and color (15%). For example, *luanshi* (卵石), which literally means 'egg stone', refers to egg-shaped stone. *Luanshi* 'boulder' is similar to *luan* 'egg' in shape. *xuecheng* (血橙) 'blood orange' denotes a kind of orange which is as red as blood. Some metaphorical modifying nouns can activate more than one values of the FORMAL role as seen in compound *yican* (蚁蚕) 'cockscomb', in which *yi* indicates the size, color as well as the shape of silkworms.

luan-shi	egg -stone	'boulder'	shape
ta-lou	tower-building	'tower building'	shape
qiu-guo	ball-fruit	'cone'	shape
xing-yan	almond-eyes	'almond- eyes'	shape
lang-gou	wolf-dog	'wolf-dog'	shape
chuan-xie	boat-shoe	'boat-shaped shoes'	shape
yi-can	ant-silkworm	'newly-hatched silkworm'	size,shape, color
mo-jing	ink-glasses	'sunglasses'	color
xue-cheng	blood-orange	'blood orange'	color
hua-xian	flower-thread	'colored thread'	color
niu-wa	bull-frog	'bullfrog'	sound
feng-niao	bee-bird	'hummingbird'	sound and feeding method
mi-zao	honey-jujube	'jujube'	taste

Table 2: The formal values in metaphorical modifier

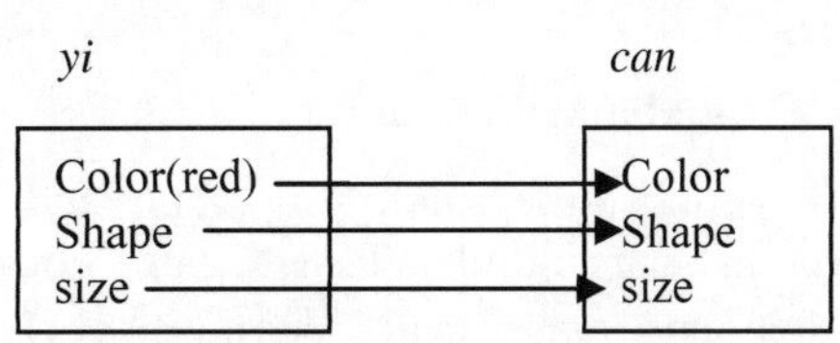

Figure 1: Mapping between the formal roles of *yi* and *can*

The metaphor-base modifiers such as *luan* and *xue* are used as adjectives. But they are quite different in qualia modification. Adjectives such as *elliptical* and *red* directly modify some aspects of the head noun. Metaphor-base modifiers, on the other hand, make reference to the FORMAL role of the head noun through their

[1] Compounds containing deverbal nouns (e.g.*meipi*) and trisyllabic compounds (e.g.*jiqiren*) are not in the scope of statistics. To illustrate our point, some of these compounds are analyzed in this paper.

own FORMAL role. In other words, to get the qualia role of the head noun, we have to get the qualia role of the modifying noun. For instance, the formal role of the modifier *yi* is mapped onto the head *can* as illustrated in Figure 1.

3.2 CONSTITUTIVE Qualia Modification

The CONSTITUTIVE quale explains the relation between an object and its constituents, or proper parts. In the compound *erfang* (耳房,ear-room) 'side room', *er* specify the relation between *erfang* and *zhengfang* (正房, principle-room) 'principal room'. Side rooms are on the sides of the principle room, just as the ears are on the sides of the head. This information is encoded in the CONSTITUTIVE role of *er*. Different from FORMAL qualia modification in 2.1, which indicates the similarity between objects in attributes, CONSTITUTIVE modification shows the parallelism between two pairs of objects in relationship as shown in (1)

(1) on_ the _sides_ of<*er* 'ear', *tou* 'head'>
on_the_sides_of<*erfang* 'side room', *zhengfang* 'principle room'>

Therefore, there is a location-located relationship between the two constituents of the compound: the modifier specifies the location of the head noun. Object metaphorically stands for its position in a relation. More examples include *jiaozhu* (脚注) 'footnote', *jiaodeng* (脚灯) 'footlight', *weizhu* (尾注 tail-note) 'endnote' and *meipi* (眉批 eyebrow-comment) 'head note'. The modifying nouns in these compounds are all body-part terms. It is not hard to understand since the relation *Is_a_part_of* is proposed as a defining element for this type of nouns (Lenci et al. 2000).

3.3 TELIC Qualia Modification

In these compounds, the modifying noun and compound noun share similar TELIC role. For instance, compound *fangche* (房车, house-car) 'recreational Vehicle' refers to a car which is similar to a house in function. *fang* modifies the purpose of *che*, which is to live in. While in non-metaphorical compounds, TELIC qualia modification exhibits a ***used_for*** relation, in metaphorical compounds it presents a ***used_as*** relation. For example, *caidao* (菜刀 vegetable-knife) 'cleaver' is used for cutting vegetables, whereas *fangche* is used as a house. In fact, *fangche* is a house as well as a car, which is used both for living and transportation, although it essentially belongs to Vehicles.

Pustejovsky(1995:142-148) proposes that a lexical item is able to inherit information according to the qualia structure it carries from multiple parents. For example, *dictionary* can inherit different roles from different types as shown in (2).

(2) Dictionary **is_formal** book
Dictionary **is_telic** reference
Dictionary **is_agent** compiled-material

In terms of multiple inheritance, the inheritance relations in *fangche* can be illustrated by figure 2. *fangche* inherits telic role from both *fang* and *che*.

(3) *fangche* **is_formal** *che*
fangche **is_telic** *che*
fangche **is_telic** *fang*

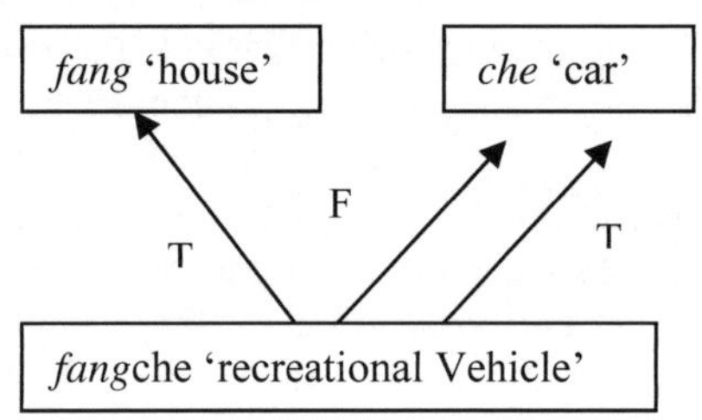

Figure 2: Multiple inheritance in *fangche*

Note that both *fang* and *che* are typical artifactual types which relate with concepts making reference to TELIC (purpose or function), or AGENTIVE (origin) (Pustejovsky 2001, 2006).

Another typical example is *zhahe* (闸盒 floodgate-box) 'fuse box', which can cut the lights off just as a floodgate can dam up water.

4 Compounds Containing Metaphorical head

FORM	CONS	TELIC
336(**70%**)	87(18%)	54(12%)

Table 3: Distribution of qualia roles in compounds containing metaphorical head

This section will focus on compounds where it is the second, headed noun that is understood metaphorically. There are also three qualia roles involving in compounds of this type, which are FORMAL, CONSTITUTIVE and TELIC, ordered from the most to the least frequent. Table 3 shows the frequencies of the qualia roles.

Unlike other noun-noun compounds, which usually involve only one qualia relation, compounds of this type can present two qualia roles, because the head nouns also indicate qualia information. In addition to referring to an object, the metaphorical head noun stands for some property, relation or function of an object as the metaphorical modifier does. In the case of *shishi*, *shi* 'stone' and *shi* 'lion' show CONSTITUTIVE role and FORMAL role of the compound respectively (see 4.1).

4.1 FORMAL Roles

Different from the metaphorical modifying nouns, which can indicate various values of formal role, the majority of the metaphorical head nouns (81%) are extended towards the reading 'shape or image of an object'. The object that is denoted by the head noun is understood to be an image of that object, i.e. not an instance of the object itself. For instance, *shishi* (石狮 stone-lion) 'stone lion' is not a real lion but a thing resembling a lion in appearance and made of stone. The head noun *Shi* is interpreted as the shape of an object.

Generally speaking, this pattern of metaphorical compounds seems to be morphologically productive. Nouns like *hua* (花) 'flower', *qiu* (球) 'ball', *yan* (眼) 'eye', *si* (丝) 'silk', *ta* (塔) 'tower', *zhu* (柱) 'post' and *xing* (星) 'star' often occur at the head position and form a group of compounds. What is common in these nouns is that shape is one of the prominent features of the objects denoted by them regardless of natural type or artifactual type nouns. Some compounds containing *hua* and *qiu* are shown in (4) and (5).

(4)-花 *hua*'flower':
雪花 *xue-hua* (snow-flower) 'snowflake'
水花 *shui-hua* (water-flower) 'water spray'
火花 *huo-hua* (fire-flower) 'spark'
浪花 *lang-hua* (wave-flower) 'spindrift /spray/waves'
纸花 *zhi-hua* (paper-flower) 'paper flower'
绢花 *juan-hua*3 (silk-flower) 'silk flower'

(5)-球 *qiu*'ball':
火球 *huo-qiu* (fire-ball) 'fire ball'
雪球 *xue-qiu* (snow-ball) 'snowball'
血球 *xue-qiu* (blood-ball) 'blood cell'
棉球 *mian-qiu* (cotton-ball) 'cotton ball'
煤球 *mei-qiu* (coal-ball) 'eggette'.

Note that *hua* (花) 'flower' tends to be metaphorically extended towards color reading when it serve as modifying noun as compound *huaxian* '*coloured* thread' shows (see table 1). When serving as head noun, however, it is much more likely to be interpreted as the shape of a flower.

Of course, besides shape, metaphorical head nouns can reveal other values of the formal role. For instance, *songtao* (松涛 pine-billow) 'the soughing of the wind in the pines' is resembling billows in sound.

The interpretation of such compounds as *shishi* and *xuehua* typically involves a shift from object to image, and seems to be triggered by the combination of lexical entries. Consider, for example, the compound *shishi* 'stone lion'. Some property that is normally understood in the interpretation of lion is excluded when it is modified by stone, i.e. a stone lion cannot be a natural kind. This interpretation effect is called Metonymic Type Coercion (MTC) in Kluck (2007). According to our preliminary investigation, TELIC and CONSTITUTIVE qualia modification nouns are most likely to lead to MTC.

4.1.1 TELIC qualia Modification

The compound *jiqiren*[2] (机器人machine-man) 'robot' denotes a kind of machine in the shape of a man. *ren* is a natural type which has no specific TELIC role. When combining with *jiqi*, it gets a TELIC role and AGENTIVE role since *jiqi* is a typical artifactual type. The noun *ren* has to be interpreted as a type that does not conflict with the TELIC role, i.e. an image. Therefore, the compound is an artifactual type, too. This is also an example of multiple inheritance (see figure 2). Similarly, *wanjuche* (玩具车 playing-utensil-car) 'toy car' is not a car but a toy in the shape of a car. In compound *jiqiren*, a TELIC role is imposed on the natural type noun *ren.* In the case of *wanjuche*, however, the normal TELIC role of *che* ('transportation') is, at least in part, replaced by the TELIC role of *wanju* (' playing') .

It is worth noting that *wanjuche* and *fangche* are quite different in that a toy car is a toy in the shape of a car but a recreational Vehicle is a car that has some functions of a house. It is easy to tell the difference from figure 2 and figure 4.

[2] We found no similar examples in bisyllabic compounds.

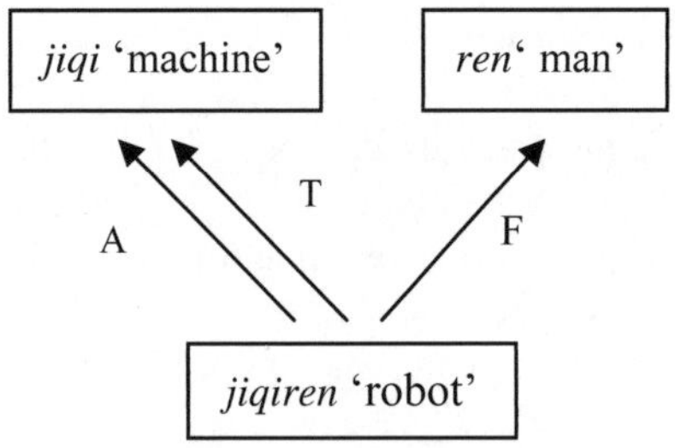

Figure 3: Multiple inheritance in *jiqiren*

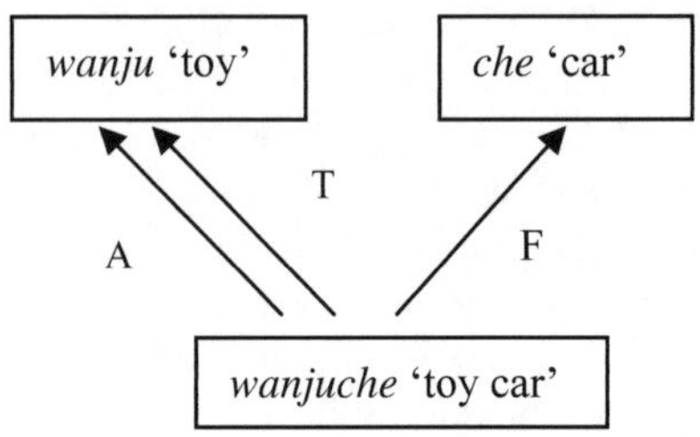

Figure 4: Multiple inheritance in *wanjuche*

4.1.2 CONSTITUTIVE Qualia Modification

In the compound *shishi* 'stone lion', the modifying noun *shi* 'stone' is used to specify a subpart of or the material of the denotation of the head noun, which is usually not contained in a lion. So, the head noun *shi* 'lion' is reanalyzed to an image of a lion. More similar examples are given in (6) and (7).

(6)石羊 *shiyan* (stone-sheep) 'stone sheep'
泥人 *niren* (clay-man) 'clay figurine'
纸花 *zhihua* (paper-flower)'paper-flower'
纸鹤 *zhihe* (paper-crane) 'paper-crane'
(7)石笋 *shisun* (stone-bamboo shoot) 'stalagmite'
雪花 *xue-hua* (snow-flower) 'snowflake'

While stone and clay are natural substances which can be used as material, paper is artifactual material. All the compounds in (6) are artifactual types, which are interpreted structurally as 'objects that are shaped like N_2 and made of N_1'. For example, *niren* is shaped like a man and made of clay. On the other hand, the compounds in (7) are all natural types, which are interpreted structurally as 'objects that are shaped like N_2 and composed of N_1'. For example, *xuehua* is shaped like a flower and composed of *shui*.

4.2 CONSTITUTIVE Role

Some body part nouns like *jiao* (脚) 'foot', *tou* (头) 'head' and *ding* (顶) 'the peak of a head' can occur in the head position and metaphorically extended towards the reading 'the position of the body part'. For Instance, *yejiao*(页脚 page-foot) 'footer' is at the bottom of a page, just as a foot is at the bottom of a man. The relation between *mei*(眉'eyebrow') and *ren*(人'person') is also similar to the relation between *yemei*(页眉 'header') and *ye* (页'page') as shown in (8) and (9).

(8)At _the_bottom_of <*jiao* 'foot', *ren* 'person'>
At_the_bottom_of<*yejiao* 'footer', *ye* 'page'>

(9)At_the_top_of <*mei* 'eyebrow', *ren* 'person'>
At_ the_ top_ of <*yemei* 'head', *ye* 'page'>

Generally speaking, body parts terms can serve as both modifier and head nouns with a location meaning as seen in *meipi* (眉批) and *yemei*（页眉）. However, there are some exceptions. As a head noun, *er* assumes a metaphorical meaning 'something shaped like an ear' as seen in *yin'er* (银耳 silver-ear) 'tremella' and *mu'er* (木耳 wood-ear) 'agaric'. The CONSTITUTIVE role that is activated in modifier position while the FORMAL role (shape) is activated in the head position. In other words, both CONSTITUTIVE and FORMAL roles of *er* are salient. On the other hand, *xin* 'heart' can stand for a central location only in the head position as *jiaoxin* (脚心 foot-heart) 'the underside of the arch of the foot' and *dixin* (地心 earth-heart) 'the earth's core' shows.

4.3 TELIC Role

In some compounds, the head nouns can show the TELIC role of the compound. For example, *naoqiao* (脑桥 brain-bridge) 'pons' denotes a part of the brain acting as a bridge, which is used for connecting different sides. Similar compounds include *chiqiao* (齿桥 tooth-bridge) 'retainer', *shangu* (扇骨 fan-bone) 'the ribs of a fan', *zhijin* (纸巾 paper-towel) 'facial tissue', *zhiqian* (纸钱 'paper money') and *bimao* (笔帽 pen-cap) 'cap of a pen'

It is noted that the metaphorical head nouns in these compounds are either artifactual types or body part nouns. Moreover, their FORMAL roles are often activated as well. That is, the comparison is based on function and possibly shape. Consider the compound *zhijin*. It is not only used as a towel, but also looks like a towel. Likewise, *shangu* looks like a rib and *bimao* looks like a cap.

5 Conclusion and Discussion

In previous sections, we examine the qualia roles involved in metaphorical noun-noun compounds. Compared to non-metaphorical noun-noun compounds, these compounds demonstrate two major characteristics.

First, no matter which constituent (the modifying noun or the head noun) takes on a metaphorical meaning, only three qualia roles are found in these compounds, which are FORMAL, CONSTITUTIVE and TELIC, ordered from the most to the least frequent. AGENTIVE role is excluded.

(10)FORMAL>CONSTITUTIVE>TELIC

From these observations, we can infer that metaphor emphasizes the resemblance between things in physical properties (e.g. shape, color, sound), location relation and function rather than origin. Among the values of FORMAL role, shape is the most frequent. It is reasonable since it is an attribute that can be perceived most directly through the senses. Shape is the primary way we recognize what an object is. CONSTITUTIVE role mainly relates to body part terms. TELIC role is mainly concerned with artifactual type nouns and body part terms.

Second, in compounds containing metaphorical head, the qualia roles of the compound not only can be activated by the modifier but also by the head noun, because the head noun as well as the modifying noun can indicate qualia information.

Also, this study reveals some fine-grained distinctions between nouns of different types. First of all, different nouns highlight different qualia roles or different values of a quale role. On this view, TELIC role are salient for artifactual nouns such as *house*, *car* and *bridge*. CONSTITUTIVE role (especially part/whole relation and location relationship) is prominent in body part terms like *head, foot* and *heart*. Shape and color are typical features of a flower in that we often creates a comparison between an object and a flower based on shape or color, as the examples of *huaxian* and *zhihua* show.

Secondly, artifactual type nouns are quite different from natural type ones. Metaphorical artifactual type nouns, especially those in head position, often exhibit both FORMAL role and TELIC role as seen in compounds *zhijin* and *shangu*.

It is particularly interesting that although both *zhuancha* (砖茶 brick-tea) 'brick tea' and *chazhuan* (茶砖) refer to the same object and *zhuan* takes on a metaphorical meaning in both compounds, they have different meaning. While *zhuancha* means 'tea that is shaped like a brick', *chazhuan* means 'a brick-like object made of tea'. *zhuan* plays different role in these two nouns. In modifier position, it only describes an object, but in head position, it also refers to an object.

In this paper, we only discuss metaphorical noun-noun compounds. For further study, we will extend the generative lexicon perspective to metaphorical noun-noun phrases.

Acknowledgments

This work is partially supported by the National Social Science Foundation of China (No. 10CYY032), the Open Project Program of Shandong Key Laboratory of Language Resource Development and Application and Major Project of National Social Science Foundation (No. 12&ZD227).We are grateful to the two anonymous reviewers for highly constructive input.

References

Bassac, Christian and Pierrette Bouillon. 2013. The Telic Relationship in compounds. In: Pustejovsky et al.(eds),*Advances in Generative Lexicon Theory Text*, Speech and Language Technology Volume 46:109-126.

Benczes,Réka.2006.Creative Compounding in English. Amsterdam/Philadelphia: John benjamins.

Geeraerts, Dirk.2002. The Interaction of Metaphor and Metonymy in Composite Expressions. In: René Dirven and Ralf Pörings (eds.), *Metaphor and Metonymy in Contrast*, pp435-65. Berlin: Mouton de Gruyter.

Goossens, Louis. 1990. Metaphtonymy: The Interaction of Metaphor and Metonymy in Expressions for Linguistic Action. *Cognitive Linguistics*, 1.3: 323–340.

Huang, Jie.2008. A Cognitive Perspective to Semantic Interpretation of Metaphtonymic Noun-Noun Compounds in Chinese and English. Foreign Language Education, 29.4:25-29.

Johnston, Michael and Federica Busa. 1999. Qualia Structure and the Compositional Interpretation of

Compounds. In: E. Viegas (ed). *Breadth and Depth of Semantics Lexicons*, pp. 67-187. Dordrecht, Kluwer.

Kluck,Marlies.2007. Optimizing interpretation from a Generative Lexicon: a case study of Metonymic Type Coercion in modified nouns. 4th International Workshop on Generative Approaches to the Lexicon (GL 2007), Paris : France (2007)

Lee, Chih-yao, Chia-hao Chang, Wei-chieh Hsu and Shu-kai Hsieh. 2010. Qualia Modification in Noun-Noun Compounds: A Cross-Language Survey. In: *Proceedings of the 22nd Conference on Computational Linguistics and Speech Processing (ROCLING-2010)*, pp.379-390.

Lenci, Alessandro, Busa F., Ruimy N, et al. 2000. *SIMPLE Work Package 2 – Linguistic Specifications*, Deliverable D2.1. ILC-CNR, Pisa, Italy.

Li, Charles N. and Thompson, S. A. 1981. *Mandarin Chinese: A Functional Reference Grammar.* Berkeley: University of California Press.1981.

Packard, J.L. 2000.*The Morphology of Chinese*. New York: Cambridge University Press.

Pustejovsky, James. 1995.*Generative Lexicon.* MIT Press, Cambridge.

Pustejovsky, James.2001.Type Construction and the Logic of Concepts, In: Bouillon, P., Busa, F. (eds.) *The Syntax of Word Meanings*, pp.91-123. Cambridge University Press, Cambridge.

Pustejovsky, James. 2006.Type Theory and Lexical Decomposition. *Journal of Cognitive Science* 6:39–76.

Song, Zuoyan and Likun Qiu. 2013. Qualia Relations in Chinese Nominal Compounds Containing Verbal Elements. *International Journal of Knowledge and Language Processing.* 4(1):1-15.

Wang, Shan and Chu-Ren Huang. 2010. Adjectival Modification to Nouns in Mandarin Chinese: Case Studies on "cháng+ noun" and "adjective+ túshūguan". In: *Proceedings of Pacific Asia Conference on Language, Information and Computation.* Tohoku University, Sendai, Japan.

Wang, Shan and Chu-Ren Huang. 2011. Compound Event Nouns of the 'Modifier-head' Type in Mandarin Chinese. In: Proceedings of the 54th PacificAsia Conference on Language, Information,and Computation. Nanyang Technological University, Taiwan.

Warren, Beatrice. 1992. *Sense Developments. A contrastive study of the development of slang senses and novel standard senses in English* [Stockholm Studies in English 80].Stockholm: Almqvist and Wiksell International.

From Glosses to Qualia: Qualia Extraction from Senso Comune

Tommaso Caselli
Trento Rise / Via Sommarive 18
IT-38122 Povo
t.caselli@trentorise.eu

Irene Russo
ILC-CNR / Via G. Moruzzi, 1
IT-56124 Pisa
irene.russo@ilc.cnr.it

Abstract

This paper describes a case study on methods for automatically extracting qualia relations from dictionary glosses in Italian, namely the Senso Comune De Mauro Dictionary (SCDM). The qualia extraction has been addressed by means of a pattern-based approach and lexical match with an Italian generative lexicon based language resource, PAROLE-SIMPLE-CLIPS (PSC). The evaluation of the extraction approaches has been performed with respect to a manually built Gold Standard containig 174 different qualia. The results obtained are encouraging (P = 0.84, R = 0.08 for the pattern extraction approach and P=0.73 and R=0.16 for the merging of pattern extraction and lexical match) and suggest that the information contained in the SCDM glosses is complementary with that in PSC.

1 Introduction

This paper describes a case study on methods for automatically extracting qualia relations (Pustejovsky, 1995) information from lexicographic dictionary glosses in Italian, namely the Senso Comune De Mauro (SCDM henceforth) Dictionary[1] for a specific semantic class, i.e. the ARTIFACT class in the Senso Comune ontology.
Qualia structure is a distinctive feature of the Generative Lexicon (GL) theory (Pustejovsky, 1995). It is a simple and powerful structure which contribute to the representation of the meaning of the nouns. The Qualia Structure consists of four roles:

- Formal role: the conceptual super category from which the object inherits its properties;
- Agentive role: the origin of the object, its coming into being into the world;
- Telic role: the purpose, or typical function of an object;
- Constitutive role: the internal constituents (parts, material, weight etc.) of an object.

The actual realization of each role is also dependent on the associated semantic type (or ontological class(es)) of the entity analyzed. For instance, an entity denoting a Natural Object (e.g. *tree*, *flower*, *fruit*, etc.) will never have information for the Agentive role. On the contrary, this information is relevant for Artifacts (*wheel*, *pen*, *table*, etc.).
The qualia extraction task has been mainly addressed in NLP by means of pattern-based approaches on corpora and from dictionaries. Pattern-based approaches for extracting semantic relations are well known in literature (Calzolari (1991); Montemagni and Vanderwende (1992); Hearst (1992); Bouillon et al. (2002); Cimiano and Wenderoth (2005); Pantel and Pennacchiotti (2006), among others) and have proved highly reliable, namely in terms of precision, for extracting the different types of qualia. One the advantages of our work is that the extracted qualia are associated with both a word sense and an ontological class (see Section 3 for details on the SCDM Dictionary). Furthermore, the SCDM dictionary glosses are richer and more descriptive than the WordNet glosses. The data collected can be exploited in different ways, namely:

- to reduce the complexity of the lexicographic entries, thus facilitating dictionary entry merging and sense alignment with other lexica like, for instance, WordNet (even in languages other than Italian);

[1] www.sensocomune.it

- to enrich already existing lexica such as PAROLE-SIMPLE-CLIPS (PSC henceforth) (Ruimy et al., 2003);
- to improve the performance of Natural Language Processing tools for complex tasks involving encyclopedic knowledge such as Question Answering and Textual Entailment, among others.

The remainder of this paper is structured as follows: Section 2 will briefly describe related works on the automatic extraction of qualia information. In Section 3 we will highlight the characteristics of the two lexica, namely the SCDM Dictionary and the PSC lexicon. A detailed description of the methodology used to identify the linguistic patterns coding the qualia information and their evaluation with respect to a manually built gold standard is reported in Section 4. In addition to this, we have also carried out experiments i.) to exploit the qualia information in the PSC lexicon to identify additional qualia which were not extracted by means of the patterns; and ii.) to evaluate the coverage of the extracted qualia with respect to the entries in the PSC lexicon in order to enrich it. Finally, Section 5 reports on conclusions and highlights on-going and future research directions.

2 Related Works

In recent years there has been a continuous interest in the NLP community on discovering novel instances of semantic relations. Most of this earlier work was based on surface pattern matching (Hearst (1998); Cimiano and Wenderoth (2005); Yamada and Baldwin (2004) among others). Other works start from matches extracted with this method and then use supervised training data to learn semantic constraints to improve precision (Girju et al. (2003); Katrenko and Adriaans (2010)). Much of previous works concentrated on extracting hypernyms (Snow et al. (2005); Sang and Hofmann (2009). Other works have applied pattern classification approaches to extract larger set of relations. The results obtained proved that extracting a pattern distribution between occurrences and performing supervised classification based on this distribution is a viable and promising solution for extending the range of semantic relations beyond hyperonymy (Ó Séaghdha and Copstake (2007); Herdağdelen and Baroni (2009)). With respect to previous research and similarly to what was done in the ACQUILEX Project, we tackle the task of extracting qualia relation from dictionary glosses. However, the SCDM glosses are augmented with ontological information whereby each sense is associated with a top level ontology class. This allows us to have at disposal qualia associated with specific senses and ontological classes.

3 The Senso Comune Lexicon and PAROLE-SIMPLE-CLIPS

The SCDM lexicon is part of a larger research initiative, *Senso Comune* (Vetere et al. (2011) Oltramari et al. (2013)). Senso Comune aims at building an open knowledge base for the Italian language, designed as a crowd-sourced initiative that stands on the solid ground of an ontological formalization and well-established lexical resources. The lexicon entries have been obtained from the De Mauro GRADIT (DMG) dictionary and consists in the 2,071 most frequent Italian words. In SCDM, word senses are encoded following lexicographic principles and are associated with lexicographic examples of usage. Senso Comune comprises three modules: i.) a top level module for basic ontological concepts; ii.) a lexical module for linguistic and lexicographic structures; and iii.) a frame module for modeling the predicative structure of verbs and nouns. The top level ontology is inspired by DOLCE (Descriptive Ontology for Linguistic and Cognitive Engineering) (Masolo et al., 2002), which has been developed in order to address core cognitive and linguistic features of common sense knowledge. 4,586 word senses from De Mauro Dictionary, corresponding to 1,111 fundamental noun lemmas and covering about 80% of the occurrences in texts (Oltramari et al., 2013), have been manually classified according to the ontological concepts.
PSC (Ruimy et al., 2003) is an Italian syntactic-semantic lexicon based on the GL theory. Lexical units are structured in terms of a semantic type system and are characterized by means of a rich set of semantic features and relations. The type system consists of 157 language- and domain-independent semantic types designed for the multilingual lexical encoding of concrete and abstract entities, events and properties. The type system of the resource reflects the GL assumption that lexical items are multidimensional entities. Multidimensionality is encoded by means of

the Extended Qualia Structure, a revisited version of the GL representational tool which extended each of the qualia roles with subtypes (e.g "*Concerns*" is a subtype of the Constitutive qualia). The PSC lexicon has been connected with ItalWordNet (Ruimy et al., 2008), an Italian version of WordNet based on the EuroWordNet principles, and contains 31619 nominal lemmas, for a total of 38092 senses, 38153 associated semantic type (ontological category) and 65539 qualia.
Although the structure of the two lexica is different, there are some common aspects (e.g. the ontological classes associated with word senses) which suggest both the possibility of merging them and respectively enriching their entries with the encoded information. Finally, the GL theory is based on the inclusion of basic encyclopedic information about nouns to model compositionality, and lexicographic glosses offer this kind of knowledge.

4 Experiments

In order to identify reliable patterns expressing qualia relations on the basis of the glosses in the SCDM lexicon, we developed a specific dataset. We first restricted the exploration of the SCDM entry to nouns which have been assigned the ontological class ARTIFACT in the Senso Comune ontology. We then extracted 35 lemmas with a total of 97 different senses as a development set. We manually explored both glosses and lexicographic examples and identified a set of 48 different syntagmatic patterns expressing the four qualia roles in a unique way. In particular, we identified 23 patterns for the telic role, 13 for the constitutive role, 5 for the formal role and 7 for the agentive role. In Table 1 we report some pattern examples and their associated qualia. In the templates N, V and ADJ refer to the target noun, verb and adjective expressing the qualia, respectively and "det" refers to the presence of articles (partitive, definite and indefinite ones). The item expressing the qualia is in bold in the pattern template and in the example.
The possibility of restricting the qualia extraction to word senses with explicit ontological classification is an advantage of using the SCDM lexicon, as this allows to disambiguate inherently ambiguous patterns. For instance, the pattern "*prodotto da (det) N*" [produced by (det) N] can express both the Constitutive quale, if it applies to the class of Natural Object such as fruit names, or the Agentive quale, if it applies to the class of Artifact such as man-made objects.
In order to evaluate the quality of the qualia extracted by the identified set of patterns in terms of coverage and to identify limitations of this methodology, such as the presence of qualia which cannot be collected by means of pattern templates and additional missing patterns, we developed a manually annotated gold standard. We selected 46 nominal entries in the SCDM lexicon with at least one sense associated with the ontological type ARTIFACT. This has provided us with a set of 50 different senses and a total of 173 different qualia, namely 79 for the constitutive role; 3 for the agentive role; 46 for the telic role; and 45 for the formal role. None of the entries in the Gold Standard is part of the development set described above. We automatically analyzed part-of-speech and lemmas in the glosses by means of the TextPro tool suite (Pianta et al., 2008), applied the pattern extraction script and then evaluated with respect to the Gold Standard. The results are reported in Table 2; all measures have been computed in terms of Precision (P), Recall (R) and F-measure (F1). We evaluated the reliability of the patterns both globally (Overall Evaluation) and for each qualia.

Evaluation Type	**P**	**R**	**F1**
Overall Evaluation	**0.84**	**0.08**	**0.14**
Agentive	1	0.5	0.66
Formal	1	0.01	0.02
Telic	0.92	0.16	0.27
Constitutive	0.73	0.07	0.12

Table 2: Evaluation of the patterns with respect to the Gold Standard.

The results obtained are quite satisfactory. Precision is extremely high but this has a cost in terms of recall, both for the overall evaluation and for each single qualia. A detailed error analysis (namely false positives and false negatives) has shown: i.) that some (additional) patterns were missing, thus preventing the extraction of qualia fillers which have been manually identified, namely for the constitutive qualia. This also explains the very low level of recall for the constitutive quale; and ii.) that some qualia are expressed in the glosses by using general expressions or as arguments of specific verbs which cannot be codified into general pattern structures at the moment. The recall (and f-measure) for the formal

Template Pattern	Example	Qualia
usare per (fare—mettere) **V** [used to (make—put) V]	usato per **cacciare** [used for hunting]	telic
costituito da (det adj—det) **N** [made of N]	costituito da **metallo** [made of metal]	constitutive
di colore **ADJ** [of ADJ color]	di colore **grigio** [of grey colour]	constitutive
prodotto da [det] **N** [produced by N]	prodotto dalla **lavorazione**	agentive
un tipo di **N** [a kind of N]	un tipo di **strumento** [a kind of instrument]	formal

Table 1: Qualia and patterns extracted from the development noun set.

qualia is the lowest. This is due to the fact that the SCDM dictionary very rarely uses explicit definitional patterns for indicating the supertype (e.g. "*è un N*" [(it) is a N]) but tends to directly use the hypernym item (e.g. as the first noun in the gloss). However, not all glosses exploit hypernyms for the sense descriptions, they sometimes contain synonyms. We thus reduced the identification of formal qualia only to instances expressed in well formed patterns during the pattern template development phase. Although the quantity of correct qualia is not large (we extracted 32 qualia relations from our data), their reliability and quality is extremely high. In the following section, we will describe i.) the methodology we adopted in order to extend the extraction of the qualia from the SCDM glosses by exploiting the information encoded in the PSC lexicon; and ii.) an evaluation of the coverage of the extracted qualia with respect to those in the PSC lexicon to enrich it with them.

4.1 Extending Qualia Matches with PSC

In order to extend the qualia extracted from the SCDM lexicon, we decided to exploit the information encoded in the PSC lexicon. Although the two lexica have different structures, they have common aspects, as described in Section 3. The ontological models, which inform the semantic typing of the word senses and contribute to keep distinct the linguistic and the conceptual levels of representation, can be exploited in order to start merging the two resources. The working hypothesis is that the ontologies of the two lexica can be merged together by means of equivalence relations and subsumption. This will allow us to have sets of ontologically compatible entries which can be further aligned for word senses (word sense alignment; WSA) by means of different methods, such as lexical match on the glosses (Niemann and Gurevych (2011); Meyer and Gurevych (2011)), exploitation of qualia information and graph-based approaches (Matuschek and Gurevych (2013); Navigli and Ponzetto (2012)).

At this stage of development, we partially tackled the task of aligning the ontological models of the two lexica by restricting our analysis of the PSC semantic types to those which are compatible with or equivalent to the SCDM semantic type ARTIFACT, namely *Instrument* and *Artifact*. Notice that we excluded the PSC types *Artifactual_food* and *Artifactual_drink* which in SCDM are assigned to the type SUBSTANCE.

We then extracted all qualia information for the 46 lemmas in the Gold Standard which have a corresponding lemma entry and ontological class *Artifact* or *Instrument* in the PSC lexicon. In this way we obtained 333 couples lemma - qualia. We then applied a baseline method for extracting additional qualia from the glosses based on token match. For each matched lemma in the PSC lexicon we grouped all its associated qualia and looked for an exact match in the gloss tokens of the corresponding lemmas in the SCDM lexicon. To avoid repetitions and to get also a preliminary evaluation both of the coverage of the PSC qualia and of the richness of the SCDM glosses in terms of qualia, we excluded from the SCDM glosses all qualia which had been extracted by means of the patterns. We then merged together the data obtained from the PSC lexicon with those obtained from the pattern extraction and evaluated this new data set against the manually built Gold Standard (DirectMatch_Extracted). Additionally, we also evaluated the data obtained from the direct match only against the Gold (DirectMatch_only) so to get a preliminary estimate of the coverage of the PSC qualia. The figures obtained are reported in Table 3.

By comparing the results of the DirectMatch_Extracted with those obtained from the pat-

Evaluation Type	P	R	F1
DirectMatch_Extracted	**0.73**	**0.16**	**0.26**
DirectMatch_only	0.60	0.06	0.12

Table 3: Evaluation of extraction by direct match of the PSC qualia in the SCDM glosses.

tern extraction method only (see Table 2), we can notice that the decrease in precision (0.84 *vs.* 0.73) is balanced by an increase in recall (0.08 *vs.* 0.16). Furthermore, by observing the figures of the results of DirectMatch_only, the lower level of precision (i.e. high number of false positives; 0.60 *vs.*0.84) suggest that the qualia information in PSC, for the great part, contains information which is additional and complementary with respect to the qualia which can be extracted from and are actually contained in the SCDM glosses, namely for the constitutive and formal roles.
To identify further support to this observation, we conducted three further evaluation assessments. We computed precision and recall between: i.) the manual gold standard and the PSC qualia (Gold-PSC), with the PSC data as the key and the manual gold standard as the response; ii.) the results of the pattern extraction and the PSC data (Extracted-PSC), with the PSC data as the key and the pattern extracted data as the response; iii.) the false positives items from the Extracted-PSC evaluation and the manual gold standard (FP_PSC-Extracted), with the manual gold as the key and the false positives as the response. We report in Table 4 the results obtained.

Evaluation Type	P	R
Gold-PSC	0.16	0.04
Extracted-PSC	0.12	0.006
FP_PSC-Extracted	0.85	0.07

Table 4: PSC qualia, manual Gold qualia and extracted qualia coverage.

It is interesting to notice that both for the Gold-PSC and the Extracted-PSC data the recall and precision values are extremely low. On the other hand, the results for the PF_PSC-Extracted are in line, both for precision and recall, with those obtained for the pattern extraction against the Gold. On the basis of these figures we claim that: i.) the pattern-based extraction method has some issues in coverage but it provides highly reliable data; ii.) the data in PSC are complementary to those which can be extracted from the SCDM glosses and that, in the perspective of merging the two resources, we can obtain a richer lexicon with a better coverage of qualia information. However, the process of integration of the SCDM extracted qualia into the PSC is not straightforward as qualia in PSC are assigned with a semantic type and a specific semantic unit (i.e. a sense). So far, we have provided a partial enrichment of the PSC entries with ontological type *Instrument* and *Artifact* for the type of relation (telic, agentive, formal or constitutive) and lemma(s) of the relation filler(s). For instance, the PSC entry for "*arco*" [bow], type *Instrument*, has the following qualia information: formal "*strumento*" [instrument]; agentive "*fabbricare*" [to make]; telic *tirare*" [to throw]. We have integrated the entry with the following additional qualia obtained from the gloss: telic "*caccia*" [hunt]; constitutive "*asta*" [rod], "*flessibile*" [flexible]. With respect to these latter aspects, we are currently experimenting with similarity measures between words and planning a crowd-sourcing task for word sense disambiguation (WSD) through the Senso Comune platform.

5 Conclusions and Future Work

This paper has reported an on-going research on the extraction of semantic information from dictionary glosses and merging of lexica at the semantic level. We have experimented a pattern-based method for qualia extraction from ontologically annotated dictionary entries (SCDM glosses) which has allowed us, on the one hand, to add high quality semantic information to the Senso Comune repository and, on the other hand, has provided a set of data for the automatic enrichment of an existing lexicon containing qualia information, namely PSC. At the current stage of development we are facing an issue related to the recall, i.e. a quantity issue rather than a quality issue. The solution can be only in part addressed by adding missing patterns, as most qualia concerning the constitutive and the formal roles are not always expressed in the SCDM glosses by means of collocation patterns. As a way to boost the extraction of additional qualia we have explored the possibility of using the information in the PSC lexicon. As a preliminary strategy we have adopted the "direct match" solution, i.e. lexical match of the token in the SCDM gloss. The results obtained are quite surprising as most of the qualia manually identified in the process of creation of the gold standard are not contained in the PSC entries. This signals that the two lexica contains complementary information and both of them could benefit from their merging. In order to accomplish this, as a preliminary task the two ontological models representing the conceptual backbone of the two lexica must be manually aligned. To improve the recall we are planning: i.) to run a new pattern extraction experiment by exploiting full parsing of the glosses and dependency relations, though parsing errors may not contribute to improve recall (Sang and Hofmann, 2009) and ii.) to exploit similarity measures between the qualia data obtained by the patterns and the lexical items in the the gloss which have not been extracted.

The availability of qualia information associated with word senses can be further exploited for achieving word sense alignment (WSA) among different lexica. As a matter of fact, words sharing the same sense, or meaning, must have a common subset of qualia roles. To prove the validity of our hypothesis, we are currently trying to achieve WSA between MutiWordNet synsets (Pianta et al., 2002) and Senso Comune entries by exploiting qualia extraction from the glosses, hypernyms relations and meronyms.

Finally, an analysis of the manually annotated data has highlighted that, at least for the SCDM lexicon, the constitutive and the telic roles have a primary function in describing the meaning of a nominal instance of type ARTIFACT, more than the formal and the agentive roles. This suggests an interesting working hypothesis for the identification of what could be called "core qualia" in order to express and identify the core lexical semantics characteristics of the entities belonging to different ontological classes. On the basis of the results we have obtained from the manual exploration, it seems that as far as the ARTIFACT type is concerned the core qualia are the constitutive and the telic roles.

References

P. Bouillon, V. Claveau, C. Fabre C, and P. Sébillot. 2002. Acquisition of qualia elements from corpora - evaluation of a symbolic learning method. In *Proceedings of the Third International Conference on Language Resources and Evaluation (LREC-2002)*, Las Palmas, Spain.

N. Calzolari. 1991. Acquiring and representing semantic information in a lexical knowledge base. In J. Pustejovsky and S. Bergler, editors, *Lexical Semantics and Knowledge Representation. First SIGLEX ACL Workshop. Lecture Notes in Computer Science*, pages 235–244. Springer Verlag.

P. Cimiano and J. Wenderoth. 2005. Automatically learning qualia structures from the web. In *Proceedings of the ACL-SIGLEX Workshop on Deep Lexical Acquisition*, pages 28–37, Ann Arbor, Michigan, June. Association for Computational Linguistics.

R. Girju, A. Badulescu, and D. Moldovan. 2003. Learning semantic constraints for the automatic discovery of part-whole relations. In *Proceedings of the 2003 Conference of the North American Chapter of the Association for Computational Linguistics on Human Language Technology - Volume 1*, NAACL '03, pages 1–8, Stroudsburg, PA, USA. Association for Computational Linguistics.

R. Girju, D. Moldovan, M. Tatu, and D. Antohe. 2005. On the semantics of noun compounds. *Comput. Speech Lang.*, 19(4):479–496, October.

M. A. Hearst. 1992. Automatic acquisition of hyponyms from large text corpora. In *Proceedings of the 14th conference on Computational linguistics - Volume 2*, COLING '92, pages 539–545, Stroudsburg, PA, USA. Association for Computational Linguistics.

M. Hearst. 1998. Automated discovery of wordnet relations. In Christiane Fellbaum, editor, *WordNet: An Electronic Lexical Database*. MIT Press, Amsterdam.

A. Herdağdelen and M. Baroni. 2009. BagPack: A general framework to represent semantic relations. In *Proceedings of the Workshop on Geometrical Models of Natural Language Semantics*, pages 33–40, Athens, Greece, March. Association for Computational Linguistics.

S. Katrenko and P. Adriaans. 2008. Semantic types of some generic relation arguments: Detection and evaluation. In *Proceedings of ACL-08: HLT, Short Papers*, pages 185–188, Columbus, Ohio, June. Association for Computational Linguistics.

S. Katrenko and P. Adriaans. 2010. Finding constraints for semantic relations via clustering. In *Proceedings of CLIN-2010*.

C. Masolo, A. Gangemi, N. Guarino, A. Oltramari, and L. Schneider. 2002. Wonderweb deliverable D17: the wonderweb library of foundational ontologies. Technical report.

M Matuschek and I. Gurevych. 2013. Dijkstra-wsa: A graph-based approach to word sense alignment. *Transactions of the Association for Computational Linguistics (TACL)*, 2:to appear.

C. Meyer and I. Gurevych. 2011. What psycholinguists know about chemistry: Aligning wiktionary and wordnet for increased domain coverage. In *Proceedings of 5th International Joint Conference on Natural Language Processing*, pages 883–892, Chiang Mai, Thailand, November. Asian Federation of Natural Language Processing.

S. Montemagni and L. Vanderwende. 1992. Structural patterns vs. string patterns for extracting semantic information from dictionaries. In *Proceedings of the International Conference on Computational Linguistics - COLING-92*, pages 546–552, Nantes, France.

R Navigli and S. Ponzetto. 2012. BabelNet: The automatic construction, evaluation and application of a wide-coverage multilingual semantic network. *Artificial Intelligence*, 193:217–250.

E. Niemann and I. Gurevych. 2011. The peoples web meets linguistic knowledge: Automatic sense alignment of wikipedia and wordnet. In *Proceedings of the 9th International Conference on Computational Semantics*, pages 205–214, Singapore, January.

D. Ó Séaghdha and A. Copstake. 2007. Cooccurrence contetxs for noun compound interpretation. In *ACL Workshop on A Broader Perspective on Multiword Expressions*. Association for Computational Linguistics.

D. Ó Séaghdha. 2007. Annotating and learning compound noun semantics. In *Proceedings of the 48th Annual Meeting of the Association for Computational Linguistics*. Association for Computational Linguistics.

A. Oltramari, G. Vetere, I. Chiari, E. Jezek, F.M. Zanzotto, M.Nissim, and A. Gangemi. 2013. Senso Comune: A collaborative knowledge resource for italian. In I. Gurevych and J. Kim, editors, *The Peoples Web Meets NLP, Theory and Applications of Natural Language Processing*, pages 45–67. Springer-Verlag, Berlin Heidelberg.

P. Pantel and M. Pennacchiotti. 2006. Espresso: Leveraging generic patterns for automatically harvesting semantic relations. In *Proceedings of 21st International Conference on Computational Linguistics and 44th Annual Meeting of the Association for Computational Linguistics*. The Association for Computer Linguistics, July.

E. Pianta, L. Bentivogli, and C. Girardi. 2002. Multiwordnet: developing an aligned multilingual database. In *First International Conference on Global WordNet*, Mysore, India.

E Pianta, C. Girardi, and R. Zonoli. 2008. Textpro tool suite. In *Proceedings of the Sixth International Conference on Language Resources and Evaluation (LREC-08)*, volume CD-ROM, Marrakech, Morocco. European Language Resources Association (ELRA).

J. Pustejovsky. 1995. *The Generative Lexicon*. MIT Press.

A. Roventini, N. Ruimy, R. Marinelli, U. Marisa, and M. Michele. 2007. Mapping concrete entities from parole-simple-clips to italwordnet: Methodology and results. In *Proceedings of the 45th Annual Meeting of the Association for Computational Linguistics Companion Volume Proceedings of the Demo and Poster Sessions*, Prague, Czech Republic, June.

N. Ruimy, M. Monachini, E. Gola, N. Calzolari, M.C. Del Fiorentino, M. Ulivieri, and S. Rossi. 2003. A computational semantic lexicon of italian: *SIMPLE. Linguistica Computazionale XVIII-XIX, Pisa*, pages 821–64.

N. Ruimy, A. Roventini, R. Marinelli, and M. Ulivieri. 2008. Linking and integrating two electronic lexicon. In *Proceedings of the First International Conference on Global Interoperability for Language Resources - ICGL 2008*, pages 197 – 204, Hong Kong, January.

E. T. K. Sang and K. Hofmann. 2009. Lexical patterns or dependency patterns: which is better for hypernym extraction? In *Proceedings of the Thirteenth Conference on Computational Natural Language Learning*, CoNLL '09, pages 174–182, Stroudsburg, PA, USA. Association for Computational Linguistics.

R. Snow, D. Jurafsky, and A. Y. Ng. 2005. Learning syntactic patterns for automatic hypernym discovery. In *NIPS 17*.

G. Vetere, A. Oltramari, I. Chiari, E. Jezek, L. Vieu, and F.M. Zanzotto. 2011. Senso Comune, an open knowledge base for italian. *JTraitement Automatique des Langues*, 53(3):217–243.

I. Yamada and T. Baldwin. 2004. Automatic discovery of telic and agentive roles from corpus data. In *Proceedings of the 18th Pacific Asia Conference on Language*, pages 115–141, Tokyo, Japan.

Expanding VerbNet with Sketch Engine

Claire Bonial, Orin Hargraves & Martha Palmer
Department of Linguistics,
University of Colorado at Boulder
Hellems 290, 295 UCB
Boulder, CO 80309-0295
{Claire.Bonial, Orin.Hargraves, Martha.Palmer}@colorado.edu

Abstract

This research describes efforts to expand the lexical resource VerbNet with additional class members and completely new verb classes. Several approaches to this in the past have involved automatic methods for expansion, but this research focuses on the addition of frequent, yet particularly challenging verbs that require manual additions after a survey of each verb's syntactic behaviors and semantic features. Sketch Engine has been an invaluable tool in this process, allowing for a comprehensive, yet detailed view of the behavior of a given verb, along with efficient comparisons to the behaviors of other verbs that might be included in VerbNet already. The incorporation of light verbs into VerbNet has presented particular challenges to this process, these are described along with a proposed resource to supplement VerbNet with information on light verbs.

1 Introduction

VerbNet (VN) (Kipper et al., 2008) is a classification of English verbs, expanded from Levin's (1993) classification. VN serves as a valuable lexical resource, facilitating a variety of Natural Language Processing (NLP) tasks such as semantic role labeling (Swier and Stevenson, 2004), inferencing (Zaenen et al., 2008), and automatic verb classification (Joanis et al., 2008). VN currently contains entries for about 6300 verbs, with continuous efforts to expand VN's coverage. VN is one resource included in SemLink (Palmer, 2009; Loper et al., 2007), which is both a mapping resource, unifying a variety of complementary lexical resources, and an annotated corpus. Through its unification of resources, SemLink provides an efficient way in which to compare resources and understand their strengths in weaknesses, including deficiencies in coverage. In an investigation of the coverage of VN for verbs found in the SemLink corpus, which consists of 112,917 instances of the Wall Street Journal, approximately 20 verbs were discovered with relatively high frequencies that were not accounted for in VN. These instances make up 14,878, or 78%, of the 19,070 SemLink instances missing VerbNet classes. These verbs include, for example, *account, be, benefit, cite, do, finance, let, market, tend, trigger,* and *violate*. Thus, while past efforts to expand VN have used automatic methods (Korhonen and Briscoe, 2004) primarily grouping verbs by syntactic patterns, these efforts take these highly frequent verbs as a starting point, as their addition to VN would greatly expand its coverage and completeness. The drawback of this approach is that many of these verbs were not already included in VN precisely because they are quite unique in their syntax and semantics, thus making them difficult candidates for incorporation into VN's class structure, which is described in more detail in the sections to follow.

Sketch Engine's (Kilgarriff et al., 2004) Word Sketch and Thesaurus functions were found to be extremely helpful in the process of considering these verbs for addition, because these resources give a detailed snapshot of syntactic and collocational tendencies. Particularly difficult cases for addition are those where common, polysemous verbs are used in their 'light' sense while combining with another predicating element; for example, *Jessica* ***made an offer*** *to buy the house.* These cases are especially problematic for VN to account for because the structure of the lexicon assumes that the verb is the primary predicating element. The steps and challenges of these additions are discussed in turn. The overall successes of this expansion demonstrate the value of utilizing both the complementary lexical resources included in SemLink, as well as Sketch Engine.

2 Background

VN and Sketch Engine are two lexical resources that provide a wealth of information on the syntactic behaviors of certain lexical items. In the case of VN, these behaviors are expressed primarily through syntactic frames and alternations common to verb class members, listed in each class. The syntactic information of VN draws heavily from Levin's (1993) work, which documented the syntactic behavior of verbs as reflected in a survey of primarily literary sources. In the case of Sketch Engine, syntactic and collocational information is drawn algorithmically from very large corpora. Thus, the two resources are quite complementary because VN makes theoretically-grounded useful generalizations about the behaviors of classes of verbs, while Sketch Engine provides empirically-based statistical information about the behavior of verbs. SemLink is also instrumental in this process because the annotated corpus can reveal which verbs should be prioritized for addition to VN. Each of these resources is discussed in more detail in the next sections.

2.1 VerbNet Background

Class membership in VN is based on a verb's compatibility with certain syntactic frames and alternations. For example, all of the verbs in the Spray class, which includes the verb *load*, have the ability to alternate the Theme or Destination as a noun phrase (NP) object or as a prepositional phrase (PP): *Jessica loaded the boxes into the wagon*, or *Jessica loaded the wagon with boxes*. VN's structure is somewhat hierarchical, comprised of superordinate and subordinate levels within each verb class. In the top level of each class, syntactic frames that are compatible with all verbs in the class are listed. In the lower levels, or 'sub-classes,' additional syntactic frames may be listed that are restricted to a limited number of members. In each class and sub-class, an effort is made to list all syntactic frames in which the verbs of that class can be grammatically realized. Each syntactic frame is detailed with the expected syntactic phrase type of each argument, thematic roles of arguments, and a semantic representation; for example:

Frame NP V NP PP.destination
Example Jessica loaded boxes into the wagon.
Syntax Agent V Theme Destination
Semantics Motion(during(E), Theme)
Not(Prep-*into*(start(E), Theme, Destination))
Prep-*into*(end(E), Theme, Destination)
Cause(Agent, E)

The class numbers in VN also reflect larger groups of what can be thought of as meta-classes. Thus, for example, all classes beginning with the number 9 (9.1-9.10) are verbs of placement. Although this classification is primarily based on shared syntactic behaviors, there is clear semantic cohesion to each of the classes. As Levin hypothesizes, this is a result of the fact that verb behavior is determined by verb meaning.

The syntactic information of VN is intended to be comprehensive in the sense that it includes all grammatical realizations of core, or frequent arguments, including some that can be optional. As a result, it can be quite difficult to add class members and classes to VN. To add a member, the verb must firstly be compatible with the primary diathesis alternation characterizing that class, and it must be compatible with all other syntactic frames listed in its class (or subclass). To add a class, two or more verbs that share a diathesis alternation and other syntactic behaviors must be discovered. In many cases, finding existing classes that are compatible with a candidate for addition is not possible, and determining what verbs warrant a new class is also a difficult question. Sketch Engine is in many ways an ideal supplement to this process because its Word Sketch function provides detailed information on the syntactic behaviors of a verb, and the Thesaurus tool can offer verbs that are used very similarly that may be candidates for new classes.

2.2 Sketch Engine Background

Sketch Engine is a corpus query and processing system for the automatic extraction of lexical information (Kilgarriff et al., 2004). Used in conjunction with a large corpus, it can generate data that efficiently summarizes the behavior of any word representing a major part of speech (noun, verb, adjective, adverb). Sketch Engine was developed for the use of lexicographers compiling dictionaries but has found widespread use in NLP because of its sophisticated and varied corpus query tools.

The two Sketch Engine tools most pertinent to our inquiry are the Word Sketch and the Thesaurus function. A Word Sketch is an HTML-formatted listing of a keyword's functional distribution and collocation in a corpus. This information includes syntactic information, such as which parts of speech and lexical items frequently act as complements of verbs. This is very useful for considering VN class membership, as membership is based on compatibility with certain syntactic frames. The Thesaurus function in Sketch Engine provides a list of words with the same part of speech for a given word that are assigned a score above a certain threshold. The score is based on the number of triples that two words share across a corpus. The higher the score, the more similar the behavior of the two words, and thus the more likely they are to be synonyms for computational purposes. This function is also useful when considering VN membership, because similar words will often share classes.

2.3 SemLink Background

SemLink (Palmer, 2009; Loper et al., 2007) is both a mapping resource and an annotated corpus. It provides mappings between complementary lexical resources: PropBank (Palmer et al., 2005), VN, FrameNet (Fillmore et al., 2002), and the recently added OntoNotes sense groupings (Pradhan et al., 2007). Each of these lexical resources varies in the level and nature of semantic detail represented, since each was created independently with somewhat differing goals. Nonetheless, all of these resources can be used to associate semantic information with the propositions of natural language. SemLink serves as a platform to unify these resources and therefore combine the fine-granularity and rich semantics of FrameNet, the syntactically-based generalizations of VN, and the relatively coarse-grained semantics of PropBank, which has been shown to be effective training data for supervised Machine Learning techniques. The recent addition of the OntoNotes sense groupings, which can be thought of as a more semantically general, or coarse-grained, view of WordNet (Fellbaum, 1998), provides even broader coverage for the resource.

The SemLink annotated corpus consists of approximately 112,000 instances of the Wall Street Journal, wherein ideally each verb is annotated with its VN class, PropBank 'roleset,' (i.e. coarse-grained sense), FrameNet frame, and OntoNotes sense number. Each argument of the verb is labelled with its VN theta role, PropBank argument number and FrameNet frame element label. The current version of SemLink includes about 78,000 instances with complete annotation; yet there are about 19,000 instances with PropBank annotations but no VN annotations because the verb is simply not present in VN. PropBank is the most comprehensive resource because, unlike FrameNet and VN, the primary goal in developing PropBank was not lexical resource creation, but the development of an annotated corpus to be used as training data for supervised machine learning systems. PropBank, like FrameNet, also includes relations other than verb relations, with annotations for noun, adjective, and complex light verb construction predicates (see http://verbs.colorado.edu/propbank/EPB-Annotation-Guidelines.pdf for full annotation guidelines, see Hwang et al., 2010-a for a description of the annotation of light verbs). As mentioned previously, verbs that are present in PropBank, and therefore SemLink, but not present in VN are prime candidates for addition.

3 Challenges of Adding VerbNet Members

The motivation for the expansion of VN is to make it a more robust tool for use in NLP by increasing its coverage. Pursuant to that, we work from a list of verbs that are relatively frequent in SemLink. In some cases, intuitive or lexicographic examination of a verb is sufficient for locating its destination in VN. When a verb has the same syntactic behavior as its super-type, for example, and the super-type is already in VN, it's possible that a new verb can simply be added to the same class its super-type is in. The relatively infrequent verb *abominate* is a synonym/subtype of *hate* and instantiates syntactic patterns similar to those of *hate*. It can be added to VN in the Admire class, where *hate* is already present.

A more complicated scenario arises when a verb shares some but not all syntactic or semantic properties of a synonym or super-type verb already in VN. In these cases, it is helpful to consult the Thesaurus function of Sketch Engine to see what verbs share the greatest number of patterns with a candidate for addition to VN. If any of these verbs is already in VN, its class can be examined for suitability with regard to the new verb. As a case in point: the transitive verb *authenticate* is not currently in VN. A thesaurus query in Sketch Engine shows *authenticate* to be syntactically and semantically similar to (in descending order) *substantiate, verify, validate, falsify,* and *corroborate*. Of these verbs, two are in the VN Indicate class (*verify* and *corroborate*), and in fact, *authenticate* fits well in the Indicate class as well.

Sketch Engine is less successful at predicting the appropriate target class of a candidate for addition to VN in three general cases:

1. when there is a sparsity of data for the candidate verb in the corpus
2. when the candidate verb's behavior does not closely match any class existing in VN
3. when the candidate verb has strong semantic ties or syntactic ties with verbs in more than one VN class but doesn't exactly fit in any of them.

In the first case there is little to be gained from examining Sketch Engine data. In cases of data sparsity, Sketch Engine may show words that are not even the same part of speech as the queried word. A query on the verb *dissimulate*, for example, returns only the adjective *glum* in Sketch Engine, with an extremely low similarity score. In the latter two cases above, examination of Sketch Engine data is still useful because it may point out possible weaknesses in VN: it may indicate a need to subdivide or reanalyze a current class, or to create a new class.

3.1 Case Studies: Successful Additions

The highly frequent verb *discuss* has recently been added to VN, in the Chit_Chat class. Information from the Thesaurus function in Sketch Engine was instrumental in helping us to arrive at the correct placement for *discuss*, which involved a minor reanalysis of the Chit_Chat class.

Most of the verbs sharing significant patterns with *discuss* as reported in Sketch Engine are already located in either of two broad classes in VN. There is *explain, mention, suggest,* and *note* (all located in the Chit_Chat class), and *consider, describe, accept,* and *believe* (all located in the larger group of classes beginning with 29, including the Characterize, Consider and Conjecture classes). Examination of the subclasses in these two broad classes did not turn up an exact match for *discuss* that allowed for instantiation of all frames, but we found that the formerly undivided Chit_Chat class could easily be split into two sibling classes that would enable us to find a perfect fit for *discuss* (which is now in 37.6-2, a subclass of Chit_Chat). It also resulted in a more rational organization for the class overall, with verbs in each of the two sibling classes fully functional in all the frames listed.

Here it is interesting to note that Levin's work, largely theoretical, insight-based, and undertaken before the availability of examining verb behavior in large corpora, is largely supported by empirical data, based entirely on the behavior of words computed statistically. Verbs that Levin had classified as near neighbors and that occupy adjacent classes in VN are demonstrably similar in their behavior as shown by the distributional analysis delivered by Sketch Engine.

3.2 Case Studies: Difficult Additions

A case where Sketch Engine fails to deliver information that facilitates the placement of a verb in VN can be illustrated with the rather complex and frequent verb *cite*. In PropBank, *cite* is represented by two senses or numbered 'rolesets': the far more frequent cite.01, which covers uses such as 'cite an example/source/case/reason' and 'Weed control is cited as the single most important challenge in organic farming,' and the less frequent cite.02, which has only the single pattern 'cite (a person) for (a violation).'

The statistical analysis delivered by Sketch Engine for *cite* draws far more from cite.01 than from cite.02 and offers verbs with high similarity scores that in VN are located mainly in classes beginning with the number 37, which are verbs of reporting: *mention, note, acknowledge, discuss, claim, explain,* and *state*. Despite these many similarities, there is not a class or subclass of 37.* that accounts well for the behavior of *cite*, mainly because it has more selectional restrictions than many verbs in those classes. *Cite*, for example, is not typically followed by a relative clause, which is characteristic of reporting verbs.

The 17th verb in terms of similarity scores provided by the Sketch Engine thesaurus for *cite* is *criticize*. This verb is in VN's Judgment class, and this seems to be a recognition of the less frequent use of *cite*, that is, cite.02 from PropBank, 'cite the witness for contempt.' The statistical algorithm for generating word similarities is surely the explanation for this much lower similarity score, because of the relative infrequency of this meaning of *cite*. Nonetheless, *cite* has been added to the

Judgment class, after reorganization and the addition of a subclass that allowed for the class to not only accommodate this verb, but also more precisely the capture the behaviors of all verbs in the class.

4 Adding Classes

When Sketch Engine shows no easily interpretable pattern for the placement of a verb in VN, and the verb is frequent, with many reportable patterns, it provides an occasion to examine whether VN is deficient in having no established class that captures the syntax and semantics of such a verb. A case we recently examined is the verb *benefit*.

4.1 Benefit Class

Benefit is reported in Sketch Engine to share significant patterns with several verbs: *gain, encourage, enable, help, attract,* and *suffer*, for example. We used the Word Sketch function in Sketch Engine for an analysis of the patterns exemplified by *benefit*, and it indicates that *benefit* has an important diathesis alternation that is not possible for any of these verbs. We can say, for example,

4. The program benefits minorities.
5. Minorities benefit from the program.
6. Minorities benefit.

and get approximately the same meaning. Like ergative English verbs, there is a strong overlap between the most frequent subjects and objects of the verb *benefit*. In one corpus we examined, for example, the five nouns *people, community, patient, child,* and *student* were the most frequent as both the subjects and the objects of *benefit*. None of *benefit's* pattern-similar verbs show this, and as a result, none of the verbs noted above that were already in VN could accept *benefit* as a new member in their class. On the basis of this analysis, we created a new class for *benefit* (Benefit-72.1), which instantiates the patterns noted above. The verb *profit* has also been added to this class since it can also instantiate these patterns.

5 Adding Light Verbs to VerbNet

Comparisons of VN and PropBank reveal another important difference in coverage: PropBank provides annotations recognizing the unique semantics of English light verb constructions (LVCs). LVCs include expressions like *do an investigation, give a groan, have a drink, make an offer,* and *take a bath*. These constructions therefore consist of a highly polysemous, semantically 'light' verb (Jespersen, 1942) as well as a noun predicate, denoting an event or state, found either in a noun phrase or prepositional phrase complement (e.g. *take into consideration*). In Goldberg's terms (2006: 109), the verbs found in these constructions have relatively low 'cue validity,' indicating that they are not a good predictor of overall sentence meaning. Rather, it is the noun that carries most of the event semantics. The verb does, however, modulate the event semantics in different manners and extents, depending on the LVC. For example, we can clearly see the contribution of the verb when comparing two LVCs with the same eventive noun: *give a bath* versus *take a bath*. Namely, the *give* LVC licenses an additional argument.

It should be noted that both the delimitation and labeling of the constructions outlined here remain nebulous and in debate. What is termed 'LVC' here has also fallen under the labels 'support verb construction,' and 'complex predicate' among others. Furthermore, since Jespersen's (1942, Volume VI:117) application of the term 'light verb' to English V + NP constructions, the term has been extended to constructions with Japanese *suru* 'do' (Grimshaw and Mester, 1988), Romance causatives (Rosen, 1989), Hindi N + V constructions (Mohanan, 1994), Urdu V + V constructions (Butt, 1994), as well as a Chinese variant on control/raising constructions involving *ba* and *de* (Huang, 1992).

It is extremely important for NLP resources to recognize the distinct semantics of LVCs. To support automatic semantic role labeling and inferencing, it is necessary to know, for example, that *Sarah took a bath* does not mean that Sarah grasped a bathtub and went dragging it around somewhere. Instead, this should be recognized as a bathing event. While VN has good coverage of most of the common English light verbs (*do, give, have, make, take*), it does not currently recognize the potential for these verbs to be used within LVCs, and would therefore inevitably misrepresent the semantics of such constructions.

Unfortunately, LVCs can be extremely difficult to detect. LVCs arguably exist on a continuum from purely compositional language that can be interpreted compositionally (e.g. *She made a dress*) to fixed idiomatic expressions with meanings that go far beyond that of the individual lexical items (e.g. *She kicked the bucket*) (Nunberg, Sag and Wasow, 1994). LVCs share some properties of each of these extremes of language because their interpretation is somewhat idiomatic in that the listener must be able to recognize firstly that the verb shouldn't be interpreted in its normal, literal ('heavy') sense, and secondly that the overall meaning stems primarily from the noun. However, they are not completely idiomatic because the noun can usually be interpreted literally, and they certainly cannot be classed with fixed idiomatic expressions because there is quite a bit of syntactic flexibility and, to some extent, substitutability of terms, reflecting LVC's semi-productivity (Nickel, 1978).

LVCs are semi-productive in the sense that novel LVCs are theoretically possible in the pattern of *light verb + eventive/stative noun*, but there are constraints on this productivity. This results in what appear to be semantically similar families of LVCs (e.g. *make a statement, make a speech, make a declaration*), yet other arguably similar LVC combinations are not acceptable to most speakers (e.g. *?make a yell, *make advice*). Additionally, LVCs tend to be syntactically indistinguishable from compositional, heavy usages of the same verb, and in some cases their semantics can be interpreted as either heavy or light: *She made a backup*, which can be thought of as either *She created a backup* (reflecting the heavy sense) or *She backed up...* (reflecting the light sense). For these reasons, while novel LVCs can continuously enter the language, they can be very difficult for both humans and computers to detect and delimit.

Such semi-productive constructions are generally very problematic for lexical resources such as VN, but also FrameNet and WordNet (Fellbaum, 1998), because all of these resources are somewhat static in nature, such that they are currently unable to reflect the possibility for speakers to use verbs in novel contexts that shift and extend their meanings. LVCs, like caused-motion constructions (e.g. *She blinked the snow off of her eyelashes*), are productive enough to be extremely problematic for coverage by a lexical resource (Hwang et al., 2010-b; Bonial et al., 2011). Fixed idiomatic expressions, which are not productive and undergo only morphosyntactic variation, can be stored as a single entry or lexical item, following a words with spaces approach (more flexible idiomatic constructions require a more general treatment). In contrast, the productivity and flexibility of LVCs (both syntactic flexibility and flexibility of adding elements such as determiners and modifiers) make this somewhat impractical. There are promising approaches for the automatic identification of non-frozen, variable idiomatic expressions (e.g. *blow one's own trumpet* and *toot one's own horn*) using measures of both syntactic and lexical fixedness (Fazly, Cook and Stevenson, 2009). Although these methods may also be effective for identifying even low frequency LVCs, they have not yet been applied to this problem. Thus, ideally the constraints on productivity and family resemblances of well-attested LVCs could be leveraged to make predictions about likely LVCs, without the need to exhaustively list each unique LVC.

With such information, VN could be augmented with probabilities that verbs will participate in certain types of constructions, regardless of whether this is an LVC or a coercive construction. Therefore, current work on VN includes efforts to use Hierarchical Bayesian Modeling (HBM) to capture patterns of verb behavior, and therefore statistical likelihoods that a given verb will participate in a given construction, including LVCs (Bonial et al., 2011). As additional corpora are modeled, the HBM, and in turn VN, can continue to evolve to capture the flexible, dynamic nature of language including semi-productive expressions like LVCs.

However, in the case of LVCs, understanding the likelihood for a verb to participate in this construction only addresses half of the problem. Although there are 'families' of semantically similar nouns that pair with a given light verb, there are seemingly idiosyncratic constraints concerning which light verbs pair with which eventive or stative noun, but statistical patterns could also be of assistance in making this prediction. Some of this information is conveniently provided by Sketch Engine.

5.1 Assistance from Sketch Engine

An examination of the Word Sketches of the common light verbs *do, give, have, make* and *take* firstly underscores the importance of including light usages in lexical resources, because they are very common. For example, in the English TenTen corpus of approximately 3.2 billion tokens, the second most frequent object of *do* is the eventive noun *job*, the top four most frequent objects of *give* are *rise, birth, notice, advice*, the second most frequent object of *have* is *effect*, the most frequent object of *make* is *decision*, and finally, the second most frequent object of *take* is *care*. The tendency for these verbs to pair with predicating nouns to form LVCs is quite clear from Sketch Engine, demonstrating the importance for such usages to be treated appropriately by lexical resources. While Sketch Engine can provide a wealth of information on what nouns are most likely to combine with a particular light verb to form an LVC, it cannot provide information on the semantic classes of nouns that often combine with a given light verb, and therefore can provide little assistance when it comes to detecting less frequent or novel constructions. Unfortunately, it is precisely such generalizations that could be most usefully incorporated into VN, therefore circumventing the need to simply list all attested LVC combinations.

With the aid of collocational tendencies from Sketch Engine, FrameNet can be used as a resource to predict other infrequent or even perhaps novel LVCs, by working under the assumption that if a frequent, attested LVC has a noun that falls into a particular frame, then it is likely that all noun members of that frame could potentially combine with the same light verb. For example, PropBank LVC annotations indicate that many eventive and stative noun collocates with *have* are nouns of mental activities and perception, e.g. *have knowledge, have a thought, have an understanding*. Sketch Engine also reflects this tendency with *have knowledge* as one of the most frequent collocates of *have* in the English TenTen corpus. The nouns of these LVCs are all found in FrameNet's Awareness frame. One could allow an automatic system to assume that any member of the Awareness frame could grammatically combine with *have* to form an acceptable LVC. To investigate the validity of this assumption, the Corpus of Contemporary American English (COCA) (Davies, 2008) was searched for each member of the Awareness frame in combination with *have* within a three word window. The results of this investigation are summarized in Table 1.

Similar searches of the Cogitation frame members and Purpose frame members, which also include nouns of frequent, attested LVCs like *have a thought* and *have the intention*, demonstrate that all of the noun members of these frames are also attested in COCA within light usages. These cursory findings demonstrate that each of the members of these frames have the potential to combine with *have* to create an attested LVC. However, these initial findings also include many false positives due to inevitable overlap with heavy senses and intervening material. For example *application* is a noun found in FrameNet's Purpose frame; *application* in its concrete sense frequently combines with *have* in its heavy, ownership sense: *I had the application on my desk*. Additionally, if the light verb *have* were replaced with a semantically similar verb, such as *possess* in these usages, it is likely that these too would work as LVCs; however, this requires further investigation.

It should be noted that not all of the potential combinations found in these frames would sound grammatical to all, or perhaps even most speakers. Thus, this process does not necessarily predict what would be acceptable LVCs. It simply would allow for computational systems to have a resource that essentially lists potential LVCs, and if and when these are actually used in a corpus, their semantics would be interpreted as likely LVCs instead of heavy usages of the verb. The problem of overlap with heavy senses of the same nouns should also be addressed through continued research using manual PropBank annotations of LVCs and HBM.

5.2 Incorporating Light Verb Resources

The challenge remains of how exactly to incorporate information on light verbs into VN's class structure. This is particularly difficult since VN's existing class membership assumes that event semantics stem primarily from verbs. Thus, it seems most appropriate for this information to exist in a supplementary resource to VN. When a verb is relatively frequently realized as a light verb, then this would be added as a sense when one searched for this verb in VN. Instead of this search taking one to a sense located in a VN class, however, selecting the light sense would provide information on the most common eventive and stative noun collocates of that light verb, along with links to the associated FrameNet frames. This information can currently be drawn from the manual PropBank annotations, and ideally in the future could be expanded through the aforementioned research using HBM. The collocational tendencies found in the smaller PropBank corpus can also be verified

Awareness Frame Members	Number of Instances	Example Usage
awareness	687	She **had** a fascinating **awareness** of the space around her.
comprehension	107	This suggests that students in our sample **had**, on average, higher **comprehension** in Spanish than in English.
conception	300	They **had** a different **conception** of what was going to happen.
consciousness	504	That night she **had** a new **consciousness** of the country, felt almost a new relation to it.
hunch	319	I **had** a **hunch** you were more than just a pretty face.
ignorance	103	But we, the art-beholders, **have** no such **ignorance**.
knowledge	4729	This study found that pet owners **had** a basic **knowledge** of rabies and the quarantine.
presumption	73	Americans have always **had** a **presumption** that you will not do your job.
suspicion	934	In my mind, I truly **had suspicion** that she had tried to take her own life on that cliff.
thought	4831	Acknowledge he **had thoughts** of leaving her.
understanding	2449	That much planning implies he **had** a clear **understanding** of his actions and he understood the consequences...

Table 1: COCA instances of *have* LVCs from FrameNet Awareness frame.

against those of Sketch Engine's larger corpora, and additional LVC combinations could also be discovered through a manual inspection of common light verb's collocations in Sketch Engine.

6 Conclusions and Future Work

This research generally demonstrates the efficacy of considering complementary lexical resources together, for frequently the information provided by such comparisons is greater than what can be gleaned by an individual resource alone. Specifically, Sketch Engine's Word Sketch and Thesaurus function can be extremely informative and useful in expanding and adding VN classes. The two resources are quite complementary in that VN makes important theoretical assumptions about syntax underlying semantics, and Sketch Engine simply reports syntactic and collocational information from large corpora, yet this information often leads to fruitful expansion of classes. In some senses, the very fact that Sketch Engine can be used so successfully to expand VN underscores the validity of Levin's hypothesis that syntax is a reflection of semantics.

Sketch Engine can also be useful in discovering common LVCs, and FrameNet can be leveraged to discover other likely LVC combinations based on the frequent existing LVCs. Although this has yet to be fully investigated, the Thesaurus function could also be used to find semantically similar nouns to those in attested LVCs, which could lead to the discovery of additional families of LVCs, in the same way that FrameNet frames could be used. The Thesaurus function could then potentially lead to suggestions for new candidates to add to FrameNet frames as well. Future work will also include an investigation of whether or not there is a systematic selection of nouns or noun classes that are compatible with specific light verbs. Of special interest on this topic would be whether or not more semantically general super-type nouns are more often compatible within LVCs as compared to more semantically specified subtypes (e.g. *take a walk* vs. **take a limp*).

With the help of these resources, VN can be expanded to include the relatively frequent, but difficult cases discussed here. Future work expanding LVC annotations in PropBank and discovering LVCs automatically using HBM will allow for VN to flexibly account for constructions like LVCs and coercive constructions, in which verbs can be used in novel and semantically distinct ways. Such flexibility will greatly improve currently static resources like VN and allow lexicons to more closely reflect what one might imagine a speaker's lexicon to be: dynamically updating through experience with novel lexical items in novel contexts.

Acknowledgments

We gratefully acknowledge the support of the National Science Foundation Grant NSF-IIS-1116782, A Bayesian Approach to Dynamic Lexical Resources for Flexible Language Processing. Any opinions, findings, and conclusions or recommendations expressed in this material are those of the authors and do not necessarily reflect the views of the National Science Foundation.

References

Claire Bonial, Susan Windisch Brown, Jena D Hwang, Christopher Parisien, Martha Palmer and Suzanne Stevenson. 2011. Incorporating Coercive Constructions into a Verb Lexicon. *Proceedings of the ACL 2011 Workshop on Relational Models of Semantics held in conjunction with ACL-2010*. Portland, Oregon.

Miriam Butt. 1995. *The Structure of Complex Predicates in Urdu*. Dissertation in Linguistics. CSLI Publications, Stanford.

M Davies. 2008-. *The Corpus of Contemporary American English (COCA): 425 million words*. Available online at http://www.americancorpus.org.

Afsaneh Fazly, Paul Cook and Suzanne Stevenson. 2009. Unsupervised type and token identification of idiomatic expressions. *Computational Linguistics*. 35(1): 61–103 Uppsala, Sweden.

Christiane Fellbaum (Ed.) 1998. *Wordnet: An Electronic Lexical Database*. MIT press, Cambridge.

Charles J Fillmore, Christoper R Johnson, and Miriam R L Petruck. 2002. Background to FrameNet. *International Journal of Lexicography*, 16(3):235–250.

Adele Goldberg. 2006. *Constructions at Work: The Nature of Generalization in Language*. Oxford University Press, New York.

J. Grimshaw and A. Mester. 1988. Light verbs and Theta-marking. *Linguistic Inquiry*, 19(2):205-232.

Charles Huang. 1992. Complex Predicates in Control. *Control and Grammar*, ed. Richard Larson, Sabine Iatridou, and Utpal Lahiri. 109-147. Kluwer Academic Publishers.

Jena D. Hwang, Archna Bhatia, Claire Bonial, Aous Mansouri, Ashwini Vaidya, Nianwen Xue and Martha Palmer. 2010-a. PropBank Annotation of Multilingual Light Verb Constructions *Proceedings of the Linguistic Annotation Workshop held in conjunction with ACL-2010.*. Uppsala, Sweden.

Jena D. Hwang, Rodney D. Nielsen and Martha Palmer. 2010-b. Towards a Domain Independent Semantics: Enhancing Semantic Representation with Construction Grammar. *Proceedings of Extracting and Using Constructions in Computational Linguistic Workshop held in conjunction with NAACL HLT 2010*. Los Angeles, CA.

Otto Jespersen. 1942. *A Modern English Grammar on Historical Principles*. Part VI: Morphology. Ejnar Munksgaard, Copenhagen.

E. Joanis, Suzanne Stevenson, and D. James. 2008. A general feature space for automatic verb classification. *Natural Language Engineering*. 14(3):337-367.

Adam Kilgarriff, Pavel Rychly, Pavel Smrz, and David Tugwell. 2004. The Sketch Engine. *Proceedings of EURALEX*. Lorient, France.

Karin Kipper, Anna Korhonen, Neville Ryant and Martha Palmer. 2008. A large-scale classification of English verbs. *Language Resources and Evaluation Journal*, 42:21–40

Anna Korhonen and T. Briscoe. 2004. Extended lexical-semantic classification of english verbs. *Proceedings of HLT/NAACL Workshop on Computational Lexical Semanticsl* Boston, Massachusetts.

Beth Levin. 1983. *English Verb Classes and Alternations: A Preliminary Investigation*. University of Chicago Press, Chicago.

Edward Loper, S. Yi, and Martha Palmer. 2007. Combining lexical resources: Mapping between PropBank and VN. *Proceedings of the Seventh International Workshop on Computational Semantics (IWCS-7)* Tilburg.

Tara Mohanan. 1994. *Argument Structure in Hindi*. CSLI Publications, Stanford.

Gerhard Nickel. 1978. Complex Verbal Structures in English. *Studies in Descriptive English Grammar* 63–83.

G. Nunberg, Ivan A Sag, and T. Wasow. 1994. Idioms. *Language* 70: 491–538.

Martha Palmer, Daniel Gildea, and Paul Kingsbury. 2005. The Proposition Bank: An annotated corpus of semantic roles. *Computational Linguistics* 31(1):71–106.

Martha Palmer. 2009. Semlink: Linking PropBank, VN and FrameNet. *Computational Linguistics* 31(1):71–106.

Sameer Pradhan, E. Hovy, M. Marcus, M. Palmer, L. Ramshaw and R. Weischedel. 2007. OntoNotes: A unified relational semantic representation. *Proceedings of the First IEEE International Conference on Semantic Computing(ICSC-07)*. Irvine, CA.

James Pustejovsky. 1995. *The Generative Lexicon*. MIT Press.

Sara Rosen. 1989. Argument Structure and Complex Predicates. Doctoral dissertation, Brandeis University.

R. Swier and Suzanne Stevenson. 2004. Unsupervised semantic role labeling. *Proceedings of the Generative Lexicon Conference, GenLex-09*. Pisa, Italy.

Annie Zaenen, C. Condoravdi, and D G. Bobrow. 2008. The encoding of lexical implications in VN. *Proceedings of LREC 2008*. Morocco

Primitives of Events and the Semantic Representation

Hongzhi Xu
The Department of CBS
The Hong Kong Polytechnic University
hongz.xu@gmail.com

Chu-Ren Huang
Faculty of Humanities
The Hong Kong Polytechnic University
churenhuang@gmail.com

Abstract

The event structure (aktionsart) is a widely discussed issue for the representation of verbal semantics in languages. However, there is still problems for the classification of verbs into state, activity, accomplishment, achievement and semelfactive. It is also not clear where are the differences of them embedded in terms of lexical, semantic or syntactic levels. In this paper, we will give a discussion on the primitives of events from an ontological point of view. We suggest that event types should be discussed in the usage level of language. Based on the Generative Lexicon theory, we provide a semantic representation of verbs which can give a better explanation how the semantics of verbs and the composition with their complements can determine the event type they denote.

1 Introduction

According to Vendler (1967), events can be divided into four classes: state, activity, accomplishment and achievement. Smith (1991) proposed a fifth class called semelfactive (instantaneous events), such as knock, kick. Some diagnostics are used to distinguish them. For example, states and achievements cannot appear in progressive aspect, while accomplishment and activities do. The so-called imperfective paradox is used to discriminate activity and accomplishment. For example, *he is running* entails that *he has run*, but *he is building a house* doesn't entail *he has built a house*. In addition, activities doesn't allow *in* time adverbial, while achievement does. For example, **he run in five minutes* is unacceptable, while *he built a house in one month is acceptable*.

Regardless of how many categories there are, it has been observed that the event type of verbs are affected by their complements, as discussed in (Dowty, 1991; Verkuyl, 1993; Tenny, 1994; Ritter and Rosen, 2000). For example, (1a) and (2a) denote activities, while (1b), (2b) and (2c) denote accomplishments. It seems that the discussion of event types has been mixed from the lexical level to the usage level of language. If a verb that has been classified as accomplishment can also express activities, then what is the purpose to do verb classification?

(1) a. He is eating sandwiches.
    b. He is eating a sandwich.

(2) a. He is running.
    b. He is running to school.
    c. He is running 1000 meters.

Degree achievement verbs, such as cool, strengthen as discussed in (Jackendoff, 1996; Hay et al., 1999) failed to be classified into the four categories as they take both *in* and *for* time adverbials as shown in (3). Some other verbs, such as eat, clean and water as discussed in (Harley, 1999) also have this problem as shown in (4) to (6). According to Hay (Hay et al., 1999), there is a telicity implicature for these verbs. Such implicature could be cancelled when taking *for* time adverbial. We agree with this explanation. However, we still need to know how pragmatic factors can give different interpretations.

(3) a. He cooled the soup in one minute.
    b. He cooled the soup for one minute.

(4) a. He ate in one minute.
    b. He ate for one minute.

(5) a. He watered the flower in one minute.
    b. He watered the flower for one minute.

(6) a. He cleaned the house in one hour.
    b. He cleaned the house for one hour.

Another problem of most of the previous discussion is that their analyses are language dependent and thus will not expose the insight of what events are from an ontological point of view. The imperfective paradox actually utilizes the meaning carried by the perfective aspect. However, it doesn't apply in Chinese. In Chinese, the perfective aspect is ambiguous in that it can denote both the start of a process, either an activity or an accomplishment, and the finishing of it. For example, *ta pao le* (he has run) means either he has finished running or he has started running. So we cannot say that *ta zai pao* (he is running) entails *ta pao le* (he has run). Similarly, *ta chi le na ge han bao* (he has eaten that sandwich) means either he ate the entire sandwich or he took some bites on it.

Even for English, the imperfective paradox test is also problematic. If we take *knit* for example, *he is knitting* entails *he has knitted*, and *he is knitting a sweater* doesn't entail *he has knitted a sweater*. It seems that *knit* qualifies both activity and accomplishment. Should we treat *knit* as polysemy? Actually, the difference of *knit* and *build* is that *knitting* itself can denote an action, while *building* always requires an object. According to the Generative Lexicon theory (Pustejovsky, 1995). The argument of verb *knit* has a default value, while *build* doesn't. So, the argument of *build* must be realized explicitly.

The evidence suggests that event type is affected by many factors, and to do event classification in the lexical level is difficult and not enough. On the other hand, it is more important to discuss which elements or parts of the meaning of verbs allow them to behave differently from each other, and is there any rules to follow in order to predict the behavior of verbs based on their semantic representation. In this paper, we will discuss the primitives of events from an ontological point of view. Within the GL framework, we will give a semantic representation for verbs which can predict the behavior when combined with different complements.

In Section 2, we will discuss different event types from an ontological point of view. In Section 3, we will present the primitives of events and show how these primitives can be combined together to produce different event types. In Section 4, we will discuss factors that affect event types and give the semantic representation for verbs, based on which we can make better prediction on what kind of events they can denote. Section 5 is the conclusion.

2 Ontological Event Types

Although the classification of verbs in terms of event types is difficult, the definitions of the Vendler's terms, namely state, activity, accomplishment and achievement, are quite clear. From now on, we will use his terms from ontological point of view which is independent on a specific language. The term *event* will be used to denote any kind of the four types. The term *process* will be used to denote activity and the first part of accomplishment without the final state as is used in GL theory (Pustejovsky, 1995).

Events are located in time axis. When talking about events, we always bear a reference time in mind, which is by default the speaking time. When we stand at different positions to a certain event in time axis, we will have to use different ways to describe it. On the other hand, we can describe an event from different perspectives, which will form different aspects. For example, we can describe the start point, end point and the instant state of any point between them. We can also describe the duration of an event, the duration from the start point to a middle point etc. This is how we understand and describe events with our language from an ontological point of view. We would like to claim that the perspectives to describe events are universal across languages, although may be realized in different ways. Let's discuss some examples in English as follows.

(7) He became angry just now.
(8) He started running at 9:00am.
(9) He will start building a house tomorrow.
(10) He stopped being angry when he got the money.
(11) He will stop running in an hour.
(12) He stopped building the house.
(13) He was angry just now.
(14) He was running from 9 to 10.
(15) He is building a house now.
(16) He has been angry for hours.
(17) He had been running for hours when you came.
(18) He has been building the house since last year.
(19) He was angry yesterday.
(20) He ran yesterday.
(21) He built the house last year.

In the above sentences, (7) to (9) describe the start of an event (state, activity or accomplishment), which is called inchoative for states and inceptive for activities and accomplishments. (10) to (12) describe the end of an event, which is called terminative or completive. (13) to (15) describe an instant state of the whole events. Note that, although (14) takes a durative time complement, it actually means that at each point in the interval it is true that he is running; (16) to (18) describe the duration from the start point to a reference time which is in the middle of the whole event duration. (19) to (21) describe three whole events. In other words, (19) is a bounded state; (20) is a bounded activity; (21) is a real accomplishment which implies that the final goal has been accomplished.

2.1 Activity and accomplishment

(14) and (15) both express an ongoing process. The difference is that there is a goal/target encoded in (15). However, syntactically, they behave the same. For example, they take time point or durative complements and don't take *for* and *in* time adverbials. In terms of truth condition, (14) and (15) are also similar. Although (15) include a goal which is carried by the object, the truth condition doesn't include the achievement of the goal. Otherwise, the truth value of (15) will be dependent on future which is not true considering that (15) can also be true even if he gave up building the house in future. In this sense, we argue that (14) and (15) denote the same kind of event from the ontological point of view.

2.2 Achievement and accomplishment

Achievements and accomplishments are different. Achievements are instantaneous, such as *arrive*, *die*, *kill*, *break* (inchoative), while accomplishments take a time duration. Some causative verbs behave similar to achievement verbs, such as *kill* and *break* (causative), e.g. they don't appear in progressive. However, they are different in that achievements are logically instantaneous. They describe pure changes of state, while causative verbs entail an action (Engelberg, 2001). Causative verbs, such as kill and break, can be treated as a special kind of accomplishment, where the process part is perceived as instantaneous (ter, 1995; Verkuyl, 1993). It is possible that some accomplishment verbs can denote instantaneous events. For example, *he ate a bug accidently* doesn't entail a noticeable process, as it is incompatible with progressive: **he is eating a bug accidently.*

Based on headedness theory by Pustejovsky (1995), *arrive* and *die* are right headed verbs with the left process shadowed. We suggest that the process are not encoded at all. For example, *he died* doesn't mean *he was killed.* The latter one certainly entails a cause which is not expressed explicitly. For the former one, it is similar to say that *he became dead,* which doesn't obviously entail a cause. We should not exclude the possibility that some verbs can denote pure change of state. An evidence for this claim can be observed from Chinese compound *sha si* (kill to death), composed by *sha* (kill) and *si* (dead/die/death). This shows that *sha* (kill) is an activity verb, which do have a goal to make something die. So, it is also possible to say *sha bu si* (kill not to death) meaning that one can try to kill someone but he may not die in the end.

The headedness theory is aimed to explain the causative/inchoative alternation phenomena. However, it is not intuitive in terms of human's perception of linguistic knowledge. We still need to test whether people notice the headedness when using different verbs. Although the principle of GL theory is to treat logical polysemy as unique while different meaning could be generated by some devices. We should not exclude the possibility that some verbs only describe a pure change of state in some context without any process encoded. We will discuss this issue further in the next section.

2.3 Activity and semelfactive

Semelfactives such as knock, kick, vibrate are actually a special kind of activity which is perceived as instantaneous and implies no change of state. Instantaneous verb should not appear in progressive aspect. However, this is not exactly true. For example, *he is kicking the tree.* In this case, it actually describes an activity with iterative sub events. Then, what is the difference between *kick* and *run*? Actually, *kick* is the lexicalization of one action, while *run* is the lexicalization of the whole iterative activity. For example, *he knocked the door twice* describes two individual knocks. But *he ran twice* only means that he performed two independent running activities, rather than two steps.

3 Primitives of Events

Generalizing the different event types we discussed above, we found two primitives: state and change of state. For state, the definition here is different from that of previous literatures. States can be further divided into two different types: static state and dynamic state. A static state is a property of an object with a specific value at a certain time. Dynamic state refers to the state of being in a process, such as (14) and (15). Borer (1996) also argued that the progressive expresses an event as a state. Actually, some phrases can also express such dynamic state, such as *he is at work*.

3.1 State

The homogeneity can differentiate the dynamic state from the static state. For dynamic state, there are always a series of sub events which can be described with different predicates. Dynamic state can be iterative (e.g. vibrating) or non-iterative (e.g. building a house). Formally, the static state and dynamic state can be represented as in (1) and (2).

$$static(e) \models \lambda_P[P(e) \wedge \forall_{e' \prec e}[P(e')]] \quad (1)$$

$$dynamic(e) \models \lambda_P[P(e) \wedge \exists_{e' \prec e} \exists_{P'}[P' \neq P \wedge P'(e')]] \quad (2)$$

3.2 Change of state

Change of state is then defined a change from one state to another as in (3). We can get four different kinds of changes of state: static-static, static-dynamic, dynamic-static, dynamic-dynamic. The static-static change refers to inchoative, such as *die* (alive to dead), *break* (unbroken to broken), *recognize* (unrecognize to recognize), *become red* (non-red to red). Static-dynamic change refers to inceptive, such as *start running*. The dynamic-dynamic change in real world is relatively rarely lexicalized. However, there do exist such kind of evets. For example, *he continued to read the book after washing clothes*. The dynamic-static change refers to terminative or completive, it usually describes an ending of an dynamic state, such as finish, end etc.

$$change(e) \models \lambda e_1 \lambda e_2[state(e_1) \wedge state(e_2) \wedge holds(e_1, t < time(e)) \wedge holds(e_2, t > time(e))] \quad (3)$$

3.3 Complex events and lexicalization

Based on the two primitives, we claim that some words in language describe pure states, and some describe changes of state. There are also words that can describe complex events that are made up of more than one primitive. For example, an accomplishment is made up of a bounded dynamic state and a final static state. The phrase *start up* describes a special kind of accomplishment that is made up of a bounded dynamic state and a final dynamic state. For example, *the machine started up and is working now*.

Theoretically, for a event that is made up of three states $state_0$, $state_1$ and $state_2$, there will be eight cases. If we also consider whether $state_0$ and $state_2$ are the same, then there will be another four cases. All the twelve cases are shown in Table 1. Some of the combination may not correspond to any words or some examples of real events. Theoretically, any combination is possible to be lexicalized if the combination denotes a whole meaningful event. In addition, the sub states in the combination may overlap. However, this is not the focus of this work and it is a different perspective to discuss event structure. The extended event structure in GL can deal with this problem very well.

3.4 The *in* and *for* time adverbials

The semantics of *in* and *for* time adverbials can be represented as (22) to (25). The difference of *in* and *at* is that, *in* describes the duration from a potential standing point to a future change of state, while *at* doesn't include the standing point information. Similarly, the difference of *for* and *at* for a state is that, *for* described the duration of the state, while *at* only describe a certain time point at which the state holds, but the duration information is not included.

For accomplishments and achievements, the *in* time adverbial actually modifies the duration from a reference time to the culminations of the events. For accomplishments, it is also possible to describe the dynamic state part. So, (24) and (25) also apply to the dynamic process of an accom-

combination	exemplar words	example setences
$s_0\_s_1\_s_2$	/	he fainted to death
$s_0\_s_1\_s_0$	faint	he fainted for a while
$s_0\_s_1\_d_0$	/	he got nervous before the examination/
$s_0\_d_0\_s_1$	build	he built a house
$s_0\_d_0\_s_0$	run	he ran for a while
$s_0\_d_0\_d_1$	/	the engine started up
$d_0\_s_0\_s_1$	/	he sat down after running
$d_0\_s_0\_d_1$	/	
$d_0\_s_0\_d_0$	pause	the match paused for a while
$d_0\_d_1\_s_0$	/	the car slowed down until stopped
$d_0\_d_1\_d_2$	/	the car slowed down
$d_0\_d_1\_d_0$	insert	they inserted an advertisment during the TV program.

Table 1: Complex events with three states. *s* is for static state, *d* is for dynamic state

plishment. For example, the perfective progressive in English actually works in this way, e.g. *he has been building a house for one month.*

In summary, the *in* time adverbial is related to change and focus on time duration from a reference time to it; the *for* time adverbial is related to state either static or dynamic. For a bounded durative state, there are two potential changes of state, start and end. So, we can predict that the *in* time adverbial can refer to both the start and the end. For example, *the class will start in ten minutes* and *the class will end in ten minutes* are both acceptable.

(22) [Change] will happen *in* [time duration].

(23) [Change] happens *at* [time point].

(24) [State] lasts *for* [time duration].

(25) [State] is true *at* [time point].

4 Semantic Representation of Events

As mentioned above, static state and dynamic state can be discriminated based on the homogeneity. Activity and semelfactive can be differentiated from Accomplishment and achievement based on whether they have an final change of state or not. Activity is different from semelfactive that it has a longer time duration. Accomplishment and achievement are different in that accomplishment include a dynamic state while accomplishment only describes a change of state and is thus logically instantaneous.

So, duration and change of state are two important factors to differentiate different event types. Duration information is actually embedded in the start time and end time of an event, which should be an external factor that is based on the time system. We can define functions such as *start_fn* to get the start time of an event. So, for semantic representation, we should only focus on the second factor. How change of state is expressed has been widely discussed in literatures, namely semantically or syntactically (e.g. resultatives). In this section, we will give a discussion on how meaning of verbs based on the two primitives and their arguments can affect the event types.

4.1 Semelfactive and activity

The semantic representation of *kick* is shown in (4). The semelfactive *kick* is the lexicalization of the predicate *kick_act*. However, *run_act* as shown in (6) is not lexicalized as *run*, which is the lexicalization of a series of *run_acts*, such as stepping as shown in (7). The progressive aspect of semelfactive verb *kick* denotes an activity with iterative sub events of *kick_acts* as in (5). Here, we introduce an operator $while(x)[y]$, which means that event *y* repeats until *x* becomes false. *x* actually encodes the conditions that control the process. The kicking event is controlled by the intention of the agent meaning that the agent performing the kicking act again and again until he doesn't want to. In this case, it is of the same event type as *running*.

$$\begin{aligned} kick\_act \models &\lambda e \lambda x \lambda y \exists z[animal(x) \wedge phy\_obj(y) \\ &\wedge foot(z) \wedge part\_of(z,x) \\ &\wedge touch(e,x,y,z)] \end{aligned} \tag{4}$$

he is kicking the door.

$$\models \exists e \exists x \exists y \exists w[human(x) \land door(y) \land proposition(w) \land while(w)[\exists e' \prec e[kick\_act(e', x, y)]]] \quad (5)$$

$$run\_act \models \lambda e \lambda x \lambda y \lambda z[animal(x) \land location(y) \land location(z) \land run\_step(e, x, y, z)] \quad (6)$$

$$run \models \lambda e \lambda x \exists w[animal(x) \land proposition(w) \land while(w)[\exists e' \exists y \exists z[location(y) \land location(z) \land run\_act(e', x, y, z)]] \quad (7)$$

He is running.

$$\models \exists e \exists x \exists w[human(x) \land proposition(w) \land \lambda w[run(e, x)](w)]] \quad (8)$$

The *run_act* is not elementary. The movements of arms and legs both could be treated as *run_acts*. However, by this definition, we can represent a non-iterative activity as an iterative one. For example, the process of building a house could also be represented as an iterative activity with a definition of *build_act*. However, this abstract concept could be implemented with more details when needed.

We should also note that we only describe the main part of the semantic representation to show how event primitives work. The difference of run and walk is not described in (7). But it is possible to add this information to it. For example, there must be some moment that both of the feet are over the ground for running, while no such moment should exists for walking. The difference of progressive and perfective is not described neither. As we have discussed, progressive only describe an instant state, which is a slice of the whole event. This means that the reference time is actually after the start of the process while before its end. In other words, the speaker noticed the happening of some instantaneous actions, e.g. kick_act, run_act etc.

4.2 Activity and accomplishment

Similar to *kick_act* and *run_act*, we can define *eat_act* as (9). Based on the while(x)[y] predicate, the final change of state of accomplishments actually gives another constraint in *x*. So, for event denoted by (11), the final disappearance of the sandwich ends the eating process. Basically, the verb *eat* denotes a human action which has a shadowed argument, e.g. food. When taking an explicit object, the default value of the shadowed argument is substituted with the new value through a λ conversion. This rule also applies to other activities verbs with such argument, such as knit.

$$eat\_act \models \lambda e \lambda x \lambda y[animal(x) \land phy\_obj(y) \land holds(existing(y), t < time(e)) \land holds(!existing(y), t > time(e)] \quad (9)$$

$$eat \models \lambda e \lambda x \exists y[human(x) \land phy\_obj(y) \land while(existing(y))[\exists e' \exists y'[eat\_act(e', x, y')]]] \quad (10)$$

He is eating a sandwich.

$$\models \exists e \exists x \exists y[human(x) \land sandwich(y) \land \lambda y[eat(e, x)](y)] \quad (11)$$

Similarly, we can give the semantic representation for *build_act* and *build*. The difference is that the condition for performing *build_act* is the existing rather than disappearance of the object. In addition, the object must be explicitly assigned.

Now, let's discuss the examples (1) and (2) repeated below. First, the resultatives (2b) and (2c) are explicit conditions that control the running process. This is how an activity verb can denote an accomplishment. (12) and (13) show how the external argument can cooperate with activity verb *run* and form an accomplishment. The qualia unification operation in GL can also explain (2b). However, it has a problem to explain (2c). On the contrary, the generic NP *sandwiches* in (1a) doesn't provide a quantity limitation that could control the eating action. In this way, an accomplishment verb can also denote activities.

(1) a. He is eating sandwiches.
 b. He is eating a sandwich.

(2) a. He is running.
 b. He is running to school.
 c. He is running 1000 meters.

He is running to school.

$$\models \exists e \exists x \exists y[human(x) \land school(y) \land \lambda w[run(e, x)](!at(x, y))] \quad (12)$$

He is running 1000 meters.

$$\models \exists e \exists x \exists w[human(x) \wedge distance(w) \\ \wedge \lambda w[run(e,x)](w < 1000m)]] \quad (13)$$

Finally, we come back to the examples from (3) to (6) repeated below. We agree with Hay (1999) that the telicity interpretation is give by pragmatic factors. We suggest that factor is actually encoded in the telic role of the verbs. For example, the telic role of *cool* is make something cool; the telic role of *eat* is to be not hungry; the telic role of *water* is to make something not dry; the telic role of *clean* is to make some place clean. The telic role is different from the formal role in that the purpose or function is not necessary to qualify the predict. Even though the purpose is not completely achieved for some reason, the process doesn't change meaning that it can be described with the same predicate. According to the Cooperative Principle (Grice, 1991), if the sentence *he watered the flower* is uttered, it should imply that the listener doesn't have to do it any more. Since, the implicatures could be cancelled, examples (26) to (29) are all acceptable.

(3) a. He cooled the soup in one minute.
b. He cooled the soup for one minute.

(4) a. He ate in one minute.
b. He ate for one minute.

(5) a. He watered the flower in one minute.
b. He watered the flower for one minute.

(6) a. He cleaned the house in one hour.
b. He cleaned the house for one hour.

(26) He cooled the soup, but it is still hot.

(27) He ate but still hungry.

(28) He watered the flower, but it is still dry

(29) He cleaned the house, but it is still dirty.

4.3 Achievement and accomplishment

Achievements as we suggested only denote changes of sate. The verb *arrive* could be represented as (14). Such verbs can appear in progressive as in (30) and (32). In our opinion, this should be an syntactic issue, i.e. expressing a near future event with progressive. So, the sentence (31) expresses the same meaning as (30).

$$arrive \models \lambda e \lambda x \exists y[human(x) \wedge location(y) \\ \wedge holds(!at(x,y), t < time(e)) \\ \wedge holds(at(x,y), t > time(e))] \quad (14)$$

(30) He is arriving.

(31) He will arrive soon.

There are two cases for collectives either in subject or object position. The first is that the verb requires collective subject or object, such as crowd, disperse etc. The second is that all the individuals in the collective are doing the same kind of event, such as (32). However, (32) is ambiguous, the first meaning is similar to (30), which express a forerunning stage. The second meaning is that every guest arrives one after another, which denotes an iterative event composed by a series of achievements. The meaning of (32) can be represented as (15).

(32) The guests are arriving.

$$\models \exists e \exists X \exists y[guest\_set(X) \wedge location(y) \\ \wedge while(\exists x \in X[!at(x,y)])[\\ \exists e' \prec e[arrive(e',x)]]] \quad (15)$$

4.4 Causative and accomplishment

Causative verbs such as kill and break are usually treated as instantaneous. For example, (33) also has similar interpretation to (30). However, they are different from pure change of state verbs. So, in progressive, they will have different interpretations. For example, the progressive in (33) can also refer to the action part, which for some reason takes a noticeable time duration. This interpretation is shown in (16). However, for the pure change of state verb arrive, there is no *arrive_act* defined.

(33) He is killing a dog.

$$\models \exists e \exists x \exists y[human(x) \wedge dog(y) \\ \wedge while(alive(y))[\\ \exists e' \prec e[kill\_act(e',x,y)]]] \quad (16)$$

Such causative verbs, when taking massive object, also have different interpretations. For example, (34) could have a similar interpretation as (33) or can be interpreted as (17) which is similar to (32).

(34) He is killing the bugs.

$$\begin{aligned} \models\ & \exists e \exists X \exists y[bug\_set(X) \wedge human(y) \\ & \wedge while(\exists x \in X[alive(x)])[\\ & \exists e' \prec e[kill(e', y, x)]]] \end{aligned} \tag{17}$$

5 Conclusion

In this paper, we discussed different event types from an ontological point of view. We have shown that the concept of event type should not exist in lexical level. Then, we presented two primitives based on which all different kinds of events could be composed. We also discussed factors that could affect the types of events and how one type of event could be changed into another. Finally, we give semantic representation for different kinds of verbs and exemplar events. It is shown that our representation can give a better prediction on event types verbs can denote.

Acknowledgments

The work is supported by a General Research Fund (GRF) sponsored by the Research Grants Council (Project no. 543810 and 544011).

References

Hagit Borer, 1996. *Morphological Interfaces*, chapter Passive without theta grids. Stanford: Center for the Study of Language and Information.

David Dowty. 1991. Thematic proto-roles and argument selection. *Language*, 67(3):547–619.

Stefan Engelberg. 2001. The semantics of the progressive. In *Proceedings of the 2001 Conference of the Australian Linguistic Society*, pages 1–8.

H.P. Grice. 1991. Logic and conversation. *Pragmatics: A Reader, New York*, pages 305–315.

Heidi Harley. 1999. Denominal verbs and aktionsart. *MIT Working Papers in Linguistics*, 35:73–85.

Jennifer Hay, Christopher Kennedy, and Beth Levin. 1999. Scalar structure underlies telicity in "degree achievements". In Tanya Matthews and Devon Strolovitch, editors, *Proceedings of Semantics and Linguistic Theory IX*, pages 127–144. Ithaca, NY: Cornell University.

Ray Jackendoff. 1996. The proper treatment of measuring out, telicity, and perhaps even quantification in english. *Natural Language and Linguistic Theory*, 1(4):305–354.

James Pustejovsky. 1995. *The Generative Lexicon*. Cambridge: The MIT Press.

Elizabeth Ritter and Sara Thomas Rosen, 2000. *Events as Grammatical Objects*, chapter Event structure and ergativity, pages 187–238. Stanford: Center for the Study of Language and Information.

Carlotta Smith. 1991. *The Parameter of Aspect*. Dordrecht: Kluwer Academic Publishers.

Carol Tenny. 1994. *Aspectual Roles and the Syntax-Semantics Interface*. Dordrecht: Kluwer Academic Publishers.

Meulen Alice G.B. ter. 1995. *Representing Time in Natural Language: The Dynamic Interpretation of Tense and Aspect*. Cambridge, MA: MIT Press.

Zeno Vendler. 1967. *NY: Linguistics in Philosophy Ithaca*. Cornell University Press.

Henk Verkuyl. 1993. *A theory of Aspectuality*. Cambridge: Cambridge University Press.

Generative Lexicon Theory and Linguistic Linked Open Data

Fahad Khan **Francesca Frontini** **Riccardo Del Gratta** **Monica Monachini** **Valeria Quochi**
Consiglio Nazionale delle Ricerche, Istituto di Linguistica Computazionale "A. Zampolli"
Via Moruzzi 1, Pisa, Italy
name.surname@ilc.cnr.it

Abstract

In this paper we look at how Generative Lexicon theory can assist in providing a more thorough definition of word senses as links between items in a RDF-based lexicon and concepts in an ontology. We focus on the definition of lexical sense in *lemon* and show its limitations before defining a new model based on *lemon* and which we term *lemonGL*. This new model is an initial attempt at providing a way of structuring lexico-ontological resources as linked data in such a way as to allow a rich representation of word meaning (following the GL theory) while at the same time (attempting to) re-main faithful to the separation between the lexicon and the ontology as recommended by the lemon model.

1 Introduction

The linked data movement aims to make it easier to publish and to use collections of data stored at different online locations by providing a standardized way of structuring, describing, and interlinking this data. One of the main tools in the linked data movement's arsenal is the Resource Description Framework (RDF)[1] a general purpose language which organises data on the basis of *subject-predicate-object* triples. These triples are used to link together data stored at different locations using Unique Resource Idenfiers. The RDF model also serves as the basis for Web Ontology Language (OWL)[2] a family of formal knowledge representation languages of varying degrees of expressivity developed for the purpose of building ontologies.

For the Language Resources and Technology (LRT) community the popularity of linked data makes it far easier to carry out its traditional aims of standardising, linking, and re-using linguistic data. This has led to a trend towards the conversion of existing lexicons using the RDF format and other linked data tools. It also opens up the way for a greater linking up of distributed lexical and ontological resources offering both greater access to the knowledge explicitly stated in a lexicon as well as increased possibilities for inferring new knowledge from associated ontologies (Smrž and Sinopalnikova, 2003).

In this paper we look at *lemon*, an increasingly popular RDF-based model for sharing lexical information online. We focus in particular on how *lemon* handles the link between the lexical entries contained in a lexicon and the associated semantic data in an ontology. We examine some of the shortcomings of *lemon* in this respect and suggest an altered version of *lemon*, *lemonGL*, which attempts to present a more accurate model of the interaction between lexical entries and their meanings. This model is based on Generative Lexicon theory (GL) which treats lexical senses as complex structured semantic objects which can enter into a range of generative semantic operations with other senses in order to generate meanings for linguistic expressions.

In the next section, Section 2.1 we look at the *lemon* view of senses, and argue that it leads to difficulties when it comes to modelling logical polysemy. In Section 2.2 we give a brief overview of the GL approach to word senses. In Section 3, we look at a previous example of the conversion of a GL inspired lexical resource, PAROLE-SIMPLE-CLIPS, using *lemon*, and explore some of the issues related to that conversion. We give a definition of *lemonGL* in Section 4. In the final section we present our conclusions.

[1] http://www.w3.org/RDF/
[2] http://www.w3.org/OWL/

2 *lemon* and GL

2.1 *lemon* senses and their limitations

lemon is a model that provides an RDF-based standard for publishing lexical data online (McCrae et al., 2011). As such it has fast gained both acceptance and widespread popularity within the LRT community[3]. At its heart *lemon* defines a set of core modules that help to describe the basic aspects of the entries in most lexicons such as those aspects relating to morphology, the phrase structure of complex expressions, and the syntactic frames associated with predicative lexical items. It also allows the addition of semantic information to any given lexical entry by mapping the entry to a concept in an ontology via an intermediate lexical sense object. This is all based on the idea of semantics by reference and entails a clear separation between the linguistic and ontological levels of a lexical resource as well as facilitating the "plugging-in" of different ontologies into the same lexicon – this turns out to be particularly useful when it comes to modelling the meanings of terms in different domains.

We now provide a brief overview of the theoretical basis for the *lemon* treatment of lexical senses and references as developed in (Cimiano et al., 2012) and as also presented in (McCrae et al., 2010).

Within the *lemon* framework, each lexical entry l in a *lemon* lexicon L can be mapped to an concept c in an ontology O via a *lemon* lexical sense object, $\sigma^{(l,c)}$. The definition of a *lemon* lexical sense object given in (Cimiano et al., 2012) presents three different, complementary, facets to each *lemon* word sense. These are as follows.

Firstly, a *lemon* sense object $\sigma^{(l,c)}$ can be viewed as representing "a subset of the uses of the lexical entry l in which l can be understood as meaning concept c", or in other words as a *disambiguated lexical entry*. So that for example given the lexical item $bank$, and a concept **bank** within an ontology where it is taken to mean something like an incline at the side of a body of water, we can view the sense object $\sigma^{(bank,\mathbf{bank})}$ as standing for the set of uses of the word $bank$ where it has a meaning corresponding to this geographical sense. Secondly, we can understand the sense object $\sigma^{(l,c)}$ as the "reification" of a pairing between the lexical entry l and the ontological element c where $\sigma^{(l,c)}$ is defined as *valid* if there exists evidence of at least one instance of the lexical item l being taken to mean c. Finally, $\sigma^{(l,c)}$ can also be seen as the hypothetical full meaning of the lexical entry l, such that if this full meaning were to be added to the ontology as a concept then it would be a subtype of c.

The foregoing tripartite definition of a lexical sense object seems to suggest that each time we are able to match the meaning of a lexical entry l to a concept c in an ontology we are also permitted to create a new *lemon* lexical sense object that will serve to mark this pairing of word and meaning. It is also clear that *lemon* sense objects only play a limited role at the intersection of a lexicon and an ontology and correspondingly carry very little structure (although as we will see there is provision in *lemon* for subsenses as well as for mappings between senses and representations of syntactic frames). All of which leaves us with a reasonably clear division of labour: the lexicon should contain all the morpho-syntactic data that relates to a lexical entry, whereas the ontology should contain most if not all of the "purely" semantic data associated with the entry, with *lemon* sense objects serving to map between these two layers.

This view of the sense relation between a lexical entry and an ontological concept can be seen however to lead to difficulties when it comes to modelling examples of logical polysemy. Following (Pustejovsky, 1995, 28) we define logical polysemy as any (syntactically realised) category-preserving semantic ambiguity where the different senses of a word have meanings that overlap or that otherwise clearly depend on one another. For example take the following two sentences.

- She walks through the door.
- She paints the door.

These sentences demonstrate that the noun *door* can be taken to mean either an aperture allowing passage (as in the first sentence) or a physical object occupying such an aperture (as in the second).

But then, according to the *lemon* model, given any ontology that distinguishes between these two concepts (i.e., between *door* as aperture and *door* as physical object) as c_1, c_2 respectively, and given a lexicon with an entry for *door* which we wish to map to the aforementioned ontology, there should be at least two distinct *lemon* sense objects

[3]See http://lemon-model.net/index.html for more details.

$\sigma^{(door,c_1)}$ and $\sigma^{(door,c_2)}$ mapping between the lexicon and the ontology. Indeed one could argue that even were there just one concept c in our ontology O representing the meaning of the word *door* in a vague enough way to cover both meanings of *door* then we would still be justified in creating at least two different sense objects since both of the instances of *door* given above represent different full hypothetical concepts though with the same reference, c, in O.

In other words the *lemon* model seems to necessitate what Pustejovsky calls a sense enumeration lexicon: that is a lexicon in which the multiple senses of each word are stored separately[4]. Pustejovsky argues in (Pustejovsky, 1995) that the sense enumerative approach to lexicon design is problematic precisely because it fails to capture several important aspects of the phenomena of logical polysemy. This inadequacy is addressed under three different heads in (Pustejovsky, 1995).

Firstly, the sense enumerative approach makes it extremely awkward to deal with the creativity of word use. For example an adjective like *fast* is able to appear in different, potentially novel, contexts and to have different (though related) meanings in each: *fast* in the phrase *a fast car* means something different from the use of *fast* in the phrase *a fast motorway*, which in turn has a different meaning from *fast* in *a fast programmer* or *a fast song*. Indeed the possibilities seem open ended, and a simplistic sense enumerative approach in which lexical sense entities are multiplied at every turn seems at the very least impracticable. Secondly, a basic sense enumerative approach fails to capture the relatedness, or in Pustejovsky's terms, the permeability of word senses. For example if we create a distinct sense apiece for the word $lamb$ when taken to mean a young sheep and when it is taken to mean the meat of a young sheep, respectively, then its hard to see how to relate these two senses under a basic sense enumerative approach. Certainly *lemon* sense relations like *equivalent, incompatible, narrower*, or *broader* fail to capture the close relationship between these two different meanings of $lamb$. Thirdly, verbs like *forget* can have different syntactic realisations each of which seem to require a separate sense.

All of this would tend to suggest that another, more nuanced approach to sense relations is in order – or at the very least it means that if a sense is to serve as an intermediary between a lexical item l and its meaning as a concept c then it might not be enough to regard the sense as merely a simple atomic pairing of a word and meaning.

One could argue however that rather than adding extra structure to the sense object there should be sufficient information within the ontology to derive c as a meaning for l, assuming that an already existing lexical sense pairing (l, c') exists, and that c can be somehow derived from c'. So that, for example, given the meaning of the lexical entry of *lamb* as a young sheep in the ontology and given other (commonsense) knowledge contained in the ontology representing the fact that the flesh of young sheep is edible and is commonly eaten by humans, it should be possible to derive the correct sense of lamb in the following sentence.

- I had some delicious lamb last night.

However, since most types of systematic polysemy are only semi productive[5] and since according to many (although by no means all) semantic theories, only limited aspects of commonsense or world knowledge are necessary for disambiguating most cases of logical polysemy, this would necessitate organising the concepts in an ontology in a particular (theory specific, linguistically motivated) way or, in some cases anyway, enriching the kinds of relations that can hold between senses. Thus we might include a relation between senses to represent the fact that they can take part in a systematic polysemic alternation (although, simply adding a polysemy relation between systematically related senses only partially solves the issue, as we would still lack the explanation of how the senses are related; i.e. what the specific dimensions of meaning involved are).

This strategy is problematic however for a number of reasons many of which relate to the fact that it seems to necessitate a certain sort of linguistically based organisation of our ontology in order to make efficient use of the information held therein; it thus very obviously blurs the distinction between what is contained in a lexicon and what is contained in corresponding ontologies. This strategy would also call for a major redefinition of the

[4] Although this might also entail that, for instance, so called complementary related senses are stored under a single entry.

[5] For instance even though the word for a young sheep and the word for the meat of a young sheep are the same in English and even though this is the case for many other animals it is not true of cows and beef.

role played by a *lemon* lexical sense object between a lexical entry l and a concept c so that it represents something along the lines of, say, the concept c's being a prototypical/common reading of l. In Section 3 we discuss an attempt to convert a GL inspired lexical resource PAROLE SIMPLE CLIPS with *lemon* using just this kind of strategy.

Another sort of strategy and one which we will discuss in some detail below is to give *lemon* senses additional structure so that as well as providing a link to a reference in an ontology they enable a more efficient access to particular kinds of "explanatory" information such as are necessary for disambiguating the meanings of polysemous words. This would effectively create an intermediate layer between the lexicon and the ontology and would have the benefit of retaining most of the rest of the *lemon* syntax as well as mimimizing our assumptions as to the structure of the ontology and thereby helping to maintain – at least to a substantial extent – the *lemon*-inspired lexicon-ontology distinction described above[6]. We will detail one potential theoretical foundation for this kind of approach in the next section. We present a model based on this strategy in Section 4.

2.2 The Generative Lexicon Approach

Generative Lexicon theory (GL henceforth) is a theory of lexical organisation that treats senses not as atomic units but instead as formal entities with a complex internal (conceptual) structure which can be described using four different levels of representation. These levels are as follows:

- The **argument structure** - An elaboration of the type and number of logical arguments associated with the entry, along with associated syntactic information;
- The **event structure** - A specification of the event structure associated with the entry;
- The **qualia structure** - A specification of the four qualia roles associated with the entry, see below;
- The **lexical inheritance structure** - The place of the lexical entry within a wider type system.

For each lexical entry GL foregrounds four different, representative, aspects of word meaning, the so called qualia roles, which along with a number of generative mechanisms are, or so the proponents of this approach would claim, sufficient to handle most cases of logical polysemy and creative sense modulation in context. These four qualia roles are regarded as being the modes of explanation for a lexical item and also as generalising the idea of verbal argument structure to apply to nominals, etc. They are defined as follows:

- The **formal**: that which specifies the hierarchical relations of an entity with other entities;
- The **constitutive**: that which specifies what an entity is made of, its relations with its various components;
- The **telic**: that which specifies the function or purpose of an entity;
- The **agentive**, that which specifies the origin of an entity, how it came about.

Pustejovsky (Pustejovsky, 1995) uses these four qualia roles (and the notion of a complex type) along with the information contained in the other representative levels in a lexical entry, as well as a number of generative semantic mechanisms such as type coercion and co-composition, to show how it is possible to disambiguate a variety of different kinds of logical polysemy without having to resort to the division of a word sense into separate senses for each shift in meaning such as is, as we have seen, characteristic of the sense enumerative approach. It is further argued in (Pustejovsky, 1995) that the kind of linguistic knowledge necessary for disambiguating instances of logical polysemy is distinct from the general common sense or pragmatic knowledge that is useful in, say, disambiguating instances of homonymous words such as *bank*, since in the former case rather than choosing between two or more different "contrastive" meanings we instead focus on diverse aspects of a single, complex meaning. This idea will play an important role in our proposed model.

As we noted above the knowledge contained in the qualia structure represents a set of basic building blocks for structuring and generating the concepts expressed by a word sense. The qualia structure can therefore be seen as the main interface to the knowledge of the world such as might be represented by an ontology. We will expand on this in what follows below.

[6]Although as we will see it does necessitate some level of reduplication of what is contained in the ontology.

3 Converting PAROLE SIMPLE CLIPS with *lemon*

In this section we briefly detail an attempt made in previous work to convert a GL based lexical resource, PAROLE SIMPLE CLIPS (PSC), into the RDF format using *lemon*; full details of the conversion are available at (del Gratta et al., 2013)[7]. PSC is a multi-layered Italian language lexicon built up within the framework of three successive projects: the EU-funded PAROLE (Ruimy et al., 1998) and SIMPLE (Lenci et al., 2000) and the Italian national project CLIPS. In particular, the conversion focused on the Italian SIMPLE lexicon, i.e., the lexical semantic layer of the PSC lexical database. As the model used by SIMPLE was strongly informed by GL its conversion is of particular interest for our discussion here.

Each lexical sense object or semantic unit (*USem* for short) in SIMPLE is described using the four different qualia roles, although in this instance the qualia roles are represented as binary relations between the USem in question and other USems in the SIMPLE semantic layer. These relations together comprise a so called *extended qualia structure*. This is a hierarchy of relations arranged at the top level under the four original qualia roles and structured in such a way as to build upon the notion of qualia structure found in the GL literature. For example, the USem corresponding to the semantic type *Vehicle* is associated with the agentive relation $created\_by$, the constitutive relations $made\_of$, has_as_part, and the telic relation $used\_for$; the formal role is given by the is_a relation.

The first part of the conversion of PSC was to define and build the top level ontology which had been described in the specifications of the project and used as a framework for the SIMPLE semantic layer encoding but which hadn't originally been implemented as a separate ontological resource (see (Toral and Monachini, 2007)). Next the SIMPLE lexical database, i.e., the set of USems and the relations which held between them, were converted using the *lemon* model. The main problem here was the fact that the USems in SIMPLE took part both in conceptual relations concerning the meaning and reference of their associated lexical entries, such as for example that a certain kind of tree produces a certain kind of fruit, as well as purely sense based relations such as synonymy. This all needed to be disentangled in order to maintain a separation between the lexicon and the ontology and to thus properly adhere to the philosophy of *lemon*.

Briefly, the solution adopted was to use *lemon* to model the purely lexical part of the resource and then to convert the semantic layer of SIMPLE into an OWL ontology (subsequently linked to the top level ontology). This meant that a new *lemon* lexical resource was created in which each lexical entry was related to its corresponding USem via the *lemon* sense relation. Each one of these USems was duplicated twice, once as a *lemon* sense object and once as an object which was then added to the ontology previously constructed.

This posed some interesting questions about the status of the qualia relations which were now fully transformed into ontological relations. While it is true that the qualia structure encodes knowledge about the world, the relations represented by the qualia structure present only a limited range of the kinds of commonsense knowledge that we might put in an ontology. How then is it possible to distinguish between those relations that are relevant for lexical semantics and those that are just part of encyclopedic knowledge (and which are therefore relevant to language understanding at a more pragmatic level)? The top level ontology in PSC was designed with a focus on structuring the semantic layer of a lexical resource and in fact its design closely follows the notion of qualia structure as found in the GL literature. Therefore there was no neccessity to try and separate out that part of the PSC ontology which dealt with "linguistic" knowledge from the rest. But things in general won't always be so straightforward: we may not be able in other situations to depend on such a closely "linguistic" structuring of ontological knowledge.

4 *lemonGL*

In this section we present *lemonGL* a RDF-based model that builds upon the *lemon* model by presenting a more nuanced version of lexical senses, one that falls in broadly line with the view presented in GL theory. *lemonGL* is an initial attempt at providing a way of structuring lexico-ontological resources as linked data in such a way as to make it easier to access those aspects of a lexical entry's meaning that best serve as modes

[7] The conversion is incomplete: so far only the nouns have been converted.

of explanation for that entry (according to GL theory) while at the same time (attempting to) remain faithful to the separation between the lexicon and the ontology as recommended by the *lemon* model. In what follows we will describe the *lemonGL* model and explain where it diverges from *lemon* before presenting an example to illustrate its use.

lemonGL differs from *lemon* essentially only in its definition of lexical senses and in the kinds of relations into which a lexical sense enters. In *lemonGL* a lexical sense object is still connected to a lexical entry via a *lemon* sense relation which can in turn link the lexical entry to a concept to an ontology that provides a meaning for the lexical entry. On the other hand, a *lemonGL* lexical sense object has a complex structure of its own, and each sense object can be related to an *ArgumentStructure* object via an *hasArgumentStructure* relation; to an *EventStructure* object via an *hasEventStructure* relation both of which are in turn related to *GLArgument* objects; and to a *QualiaStructure* object via a *hasQualia* relation. This *QualiaStructure* is related in its turn to a *Quale* object via the *hasAgentive, hasFormal, hasTelic* and *hasConstitutive* relations. These extra objects then provide a sort of middle layer, or an interface, between the lexical entry and the ontology that serves to isolate certain aspects of the entry's meaning as contained within the ontology.

Figure 1: A diagram of the *lemonGL* model.

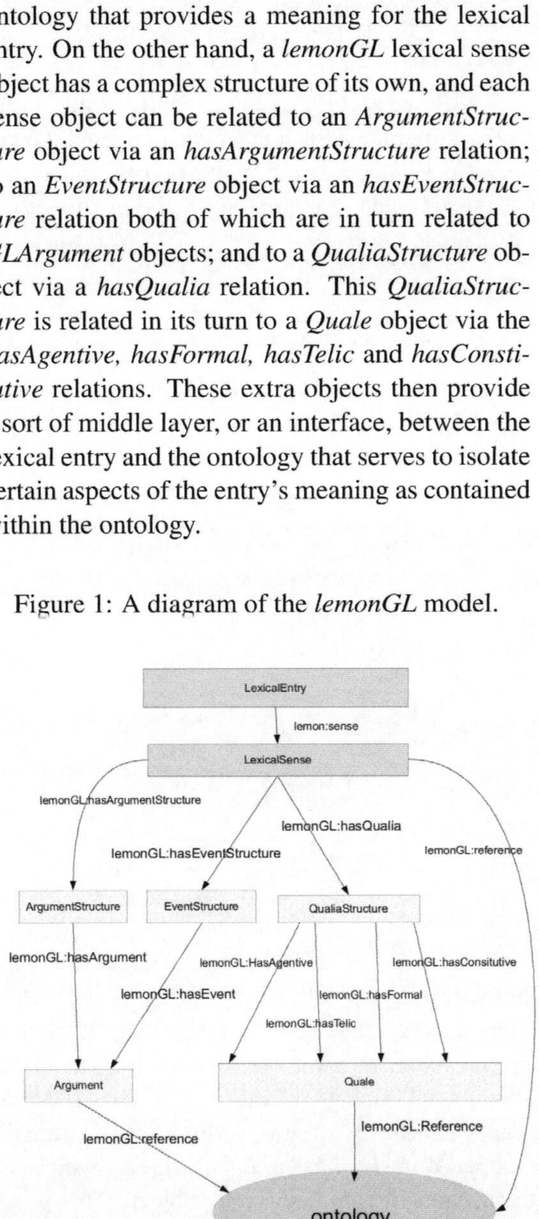

This might seem a little like overkill: if the meaning of a lexical entry l is determined by a concept c in an ontology O along with the network of relations that c enters into with other items in the ontology, then what is the purpose of transferring or duplicating a subset of this information into the lexicon? The answer is that it helps to preserve the division between the language specific information in the lexicon and the (relatively speaking) language independent conceptual information contained in the ontology.

As discussed above, in GL theory a word's qualia structure serves to specify the central modes of explanation associated with that word – as distinguished from other more general, common sense, one could say, more purely ontological, knowledge – and that the knowledge encoded in qualia structures is used in dealing with instances of logical polysemy. In fact one could argue that the qualia information is part of a lexical entry in the same way that a verbs argument structure is part of a verb's lexical information and that it therefore doesnt really belong in the ontology.

Another option would be for a separate, linguistically motivated ontology to hold this kind of knowledge which could then be somehow linked up with other ontologies, but this solution is uneconomical both from the theoretical and the practical point of view. Theoretically it would imply that human beings have a subset of their encyclopedic knowledge duplicated as part of their linguistic knowledge; practically speaking it would involve a lot of duplication of labour. With respect to the interaction between the linked data movement and the LRT community it seems necessary to be able both to easily access and to build upon the large amount of formalised knowledge that is currently becoming available online, while at the same time retaining the ability to set the boundaries as to what is relevant to lexical semantics. The *lemonGL* model then attempts to structure word senses in a way that maintains a Pustejovskian linguistic versus commonsense knowledge distinction.

We now present an example modelled using *lemonGL* to illustrate its potential use. We will be using RDF turtle syntax to present our example[8]. The example concerns the noun *wine* which we will represent with the following feature struc-

[8]http://www.w3.org/TeamSubmission/turtle/

ture[9].

$$\begin{bmatrix} \textbf{WINE} & & \\ \text{ARGS} & = & \begin{bmatrix} \text{ARG1} = x \\ \text{D-ARG1} = y \end{bmatrix} \\ \text{EVENTS} & = & \begin{bmatrix} \text{D-E1} = e \end{bmatrix} \\ \text{QUALIA} & = & \begin{bmatrix} \text{FORMAL} = liquid(x) \\ \text{AGENTIVE} = make(e, y, x) \end{bmatrix} \end{bmatrix}$$

Here the argument structure has two logical arguments, x and y and the event structure has one event argument e, all of which are found in the qualia expressions in the qualia structure: these arguments can be understood to play the same role as the bound variables x, y and e in the following lambda expression:

$$\lambda x \lambda y \lambda e[liquid(x) \wedge make(e, y, z)].$$

Only two of the qualia roles are instantiated. The first, the formal quale here expresses the fact that wine is a type of liquid using the *liquid* predicate; the second quale, by referring to the *make* predicate and the variables mentioned previously, to expresses the fact that there is a process of creation associated with each instance of a wine "entity".

In order to represent this feature structure using *lemonGL* we will first assume that our (OWL) ontology contains the following definitions.

```
:hasMadeObject  rdf:type owl:ObjectProperty ;
rdfs:range :Made_Object ;
rdfs:domain :Make_Event .
:hasMaker  rdf:type owl:ObjectProperty ;
rdfs:domain :Make_Event ;
rdfs:range :Maker .
:makes  rdf:type owl:ObjectProperty ;
rdfs:range :Made_Object ;
rdfs:domain :Maker .
:Made_Object rdf:type owl:Class .
:Make_Event rdf:type owl:Class .
:Maker rdf:type owl:Class .
:liquid rdf:type owl:Class .
```

The following lines of RDF structure the sense of the lexical entry for *wine* in the lexicon into an argument structure, an event structure and a qualia structure:

```
:wine rdf:type lemon:LexicalEntry ,
owl:NamedIndividual ;
lemon:sense [rdf:type lemon:LexicalSense ;
lemonGL:hasArgumentStructure :wine_arg_str;
lemonGL:hasEventStructure :wine_ev_str ;
lemonGL:hasQualia :wine_qua_str].
```

[9]The feature structure for *wine* is taken from (Pustejovsky, 1998). Also note that the OWL/RDF code used in the examples has been made up for the purpose of demonstration, and is not drawn from an existing resource. We have not so far converted any non trivial lexical resource into RDF using *lemonGL*.

We refer to the argument structure associated with the lexical sense of the entry for *wine* using the identifier $wine\_arg\_str$. We specify that the first argument associated with $wine\_arg\_str$ has the ontological type of $Made\_Object$, whereas the second argument has the ontological type of $Maker$.

```
:wine_arg_str rdf:type  Glemon:ArgumentStructure ,
owl:NamedIndividual ;
lemonGL:hasArgument
[lemonGL:reference ontology:Made_Object ] ,
[lemonGL:reference ontology:Maker] .
```

Next we specify that the ontological type of the event associated with the event structure of the sense object is a Make_Event.

```
:wine_ev_str rdf:type lemonGL:EventStrucuture ,
owl:NamedIndividual ;
lemonGL:hasEvent
[lemonGL:reference ontology:Make_Event ].
```

Finally we specify that the agentive role for the qualia structure associated with the sense object refers to a make relation in our ontology, and that the formal role has the ontological type of *liquid*.

```
:wine_qua_str rdf:type lemonGL:QualiaStructure ,
owl:NamedIndividual ;
lemonGL:hasAgentive
[lemonGL:reference ontology:makes] ;
lemonGL:hasFormal
[lemonGL:reference ontology:liquid ].
```

The following figure presents the example schematically:

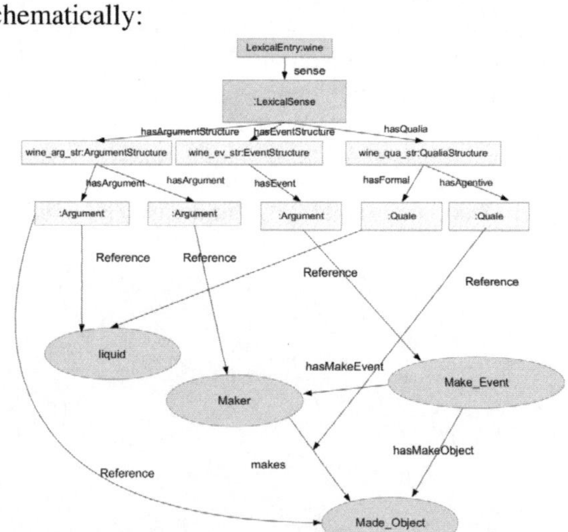

Even though we have somewhat altered the *lemon* framework, the changes we propose are far from drastic. Indeed, as is helpfully illustrated by the representation of the verb *to give* in the *lemon* cookbook (McCrae et al., 2010), *lemon* senses can have subsenses which can in turn be mapped onto *lemon Argument* objects which are themselves linked to a *Frame* object. This parallel between our GL-inspired representation of the noun *wine* in *lemonGL* and the representation of a verb like *give* in *lemon* is no surprise since, as we've described above, one of the motivations behind GL theory was to provide what is in essence an argument structure for nominals (Pustejovsky and Boguraev, 1993). On the other hand, as we have striven to show throughout this paper, the notion of sense in *lemon* stands in need of substantial revision and part of this means providing extra functionality for other part of speech categories.

5 Conclusion

In this paper we've tried to argue for a revised notion of a sense object in *lemon*, one that both makes it easier to model a range of important linguistic phenomena and that enables the practical implementation (to some extent) of an important and influential theory of lexical semantics. We plan to continue this work by using *lemonGL* to model existing lexical resources, developing the language further as the need arises, and also to investigate the extent to which *lemonGL* makes it easier to reason about such resources.

We have discussed the desirability of maintaining a separation between lexical and ontological knowledge. We believe by adding what is effectively an intermediary layer between the lexicon and the ontology we have created a model for lexical-ontological resources which preserves this separation as far as possible (by limiting what we can assume about the structure of the ontology) while still enabling us to handle the phenomena of logical polysemy.

To take a more general view, we feel that it is of the utmost importance, given the current popularity of LLOD as well as the great potential that it holds out, that the GL community become more active in the definition of the models that are defining the structure of LLOD lexicons and their connections to existing or new conceptual resources. In particular it is important that models that are too geared towards sense enumeration do not become predominant to the detriment of more realistic models of lexical semantics, and that the available lexicon representation schemes allow for the real complexity of lexical semantic relations to be fully represented.

References

Philipp Cimiano, John McCrae, Paul Buitelaar, and Elena Montiel-Ponsoda, 2012. *On the Role of Senses in the Ontology-Lexicon.*

Riccardo del Gratta, Francesca Frontini, Fahad Khan, and Monica Monachini. 2013. Converting the parole simple clips lexicon into rdf with lemon. *Semantic Web Journal (Under Review).*

Alessandro Lenci, Nuria Bel, Federica Busa, Nicoletta Calzolari, Elisabetta Gola, Monica Monachini, Antoine Ogonowski, Ivonne Peters, Wim Peters, Nilda Ruimy, Marta Villegas, and Antonio Zampolli. 2000. Simple: A general framework for the development of multilingual lexicons. *International Journal of Lexicography*, 13(4):249–263.

John McCrae, Guadalupe Aguado de Cea, Paul Buitelaar, Philipp Cimiano, Thierry Declerck, Asuncin Gmez Prez, Jorge Gracia, Laura Hollink, Elena Montiel-Ponsoda, Dennis Spohr, and Tobias Wunner, 2010. *The Lemon Cookbook.* http://lemon-model.net/lemon-cookbook.pdf.

John McCrae, Dennis Spohr, and Philipp Cimiano. 2011. Linking lexical resources and ontologies on the semantic web with lemon. In *Proceedings of the 8th extended semantic web conference on The semantic web: research and applications - Volume Part I*, ESWC'11, pages 245–259, Berlin, Heidelberg. Springer-Verlag.

James Pustejovsky and Branimir Boguraev. 1993. Lexical knowledge representation and natural language processing. *Artif. Intell.*, 63(1-2):193–223.

James Pustejovsky. 1995. *The Generative Lexicon.* MIT Press, Cambridge, MA.

James Pustejovsky. 1998. The semantics of lexical underspecification.

N. Ruimy, O. Corazzari, E. Gola, A. Spanu, N. Calzolari, and A. Zampolli. 1998. The european le-parole project: The italian syntactic lexicon. In *Proceedings of the First International Conference on Language resources and Evaluation*, pages 241–248.

Pavel Smrž and Anna Sinopalnikova. 2003. Present-day lexical knowledge bases - what they are and what they need. In *Proceedings of the Eight International Symposium on Social Communication*, pages 100–105, Santiago de Cuba. Center of Applied Linguistics of the Santiago de Cuba's branch of the Ministry of Science, Technology and the Environment.

Antonio Toral and Monica Monachini. 2007. Simple-owl: a generative lexicon ontology for nlp and the semantic web. In *Workshop of Cooperative Construction of Linguistic Knowledge Bases, 10th Congress of Italian Association for Artificial Intelligence.*

Disambiguation of Basic Action Types through Nouns' Telic Qualia

Irene Russo, Francesca Frontini, Irene De Felice,
Fahad Khan, Monica Monachini
ILC CNR / Via G. Moruzzi 1, 56124 Pisa
{irene.russo,francesca.frontini,irene.defelice,
fahad.khan,monica.monachini}@ilc.cnr.it

Abstract

Knowledge about semantic associations between words is effective to disambiguate word senses. The aim of this paper is to investigate the role and the relevance of telic information from SIMPLE in the disambiguation of basic action types of Italian HOLD verbs (*prendere*, 'to take', *raccogliere*, 'to pick up', *pigliare* 'to grab' etc.). We propose an experiment to compare the results obtained with telic information from SIMPLE with basic co-occurrence information extracted from corpora (most salient verbs modifying nouns) classified in terms of general semantic classes to avoid data sparseness.

1 Introduction

Word senses emerge in lexicographic practice as the result of splitting strategies depending on context of use, syntagmatic patterns and perceived semantic similarity. Lexicographers share working assumptions (e.g. the concrete sense is encoded before the abstract sense of a lemma) on the way to structure glosses. The induction of word senses from corpus co-occurrences, as in the Corpus Pattern Analysis effort (Hanks 2008), has an impact on the definition of how many different senses are available and, with the focus on general semantic classes of nouns involved for example as objects in verbal contexts, the path toward sense induction is made fully empirical.

Since word senses are not metaphysical objects but depend on dedicated tasks that require them (Kilgarriff 1997), other operative principles are possible. In this paper we present a manually annotated dataset relative to basic Italian action verbs that have been partitioned in basic action types when the action described in the sentence was analysed in terms of body movements involved. This split among senses can't be unequivocally aligned with lexical resources such as WordNet (Moneglia et al. 2012) and, even if the induction from corpora examples implies that the syntagmatic structure is important, the guiding motivation in segmenting the meaning concerns salient differences in the action performed by the agent for the sake of basic action modelling in robotics.

In this dataset a central role is assigned to nouns denoting concrete objects and as a consequence the task of basic action type classification focuses on nouns and the information attached to them that could help in disambiguation.

In word sense disambiguation tasks different sets of features have been tested in order to understand which are the most relevant for classifying senses. Among these features, there are PoS and syntactic information, collocations (or selectional preferences), thematic roles, semantic associations between words in terms of taxonomic relations (e.g. *chair, furniture*), events (e.g. *chair, sitting*), topic (e.g. *bat, baseball*), head argument relations (e.g. *dog, bite*). (Agirre and Martinez 2001) reviewed these features, discovering that collocations and semantic associations are the most useful (and manually annotated corpora are the best source to acquire them).

The aim of this paper is to investigate the role and the relevance of telic information from SIMPLE (Ruimy et al. 2003) in the disambiguation of basic action types of Italian HOLD verbs (*prendere*, 'to take', *raccogliere*, 'to pick up', *pigliare* 'to grab' etc.). We propose an experiment (see 5) to compare the results obtained with telic information from SIMPLE with basic co-occurrence information extracted from corpora (most salient verbs modifying nouns) classified in terms of general semantic classes to avoid data sparseness.

2 ImagAct Basic Action Types: Bottom-up Derivation of Verbs Senses

Action verbs are among the most informative elements in a sentence: the concepts they codify have a great relevance in human life and they are the most frequent elements in speech (Moneglia and Panunzi, 2007). In our everyday experience, the kind of actions we can carry out is almost endless but, given that every human language tends towards economy of expression, the number of action verbs we use is always somehow restricted. So we adopt the same verbs to denote different types of events: for example, the verb "to take" in (1) *John takes a present from a stranger* means "to receive, to accept"; but in (2) *John takes Mary the book* it means "to bring"; in (3) *John takes the pot by the handle* it simply means "to grasp"; finally, in (4) *John takes Mary to the station* it means "to conduct, to accompany". Furthermore, every language manifests a different behaviour in segmenting human experience into its proper action verbal lexicon. For this reason, the examples just cited can't be translated with a single Italian verb: (1a) *John prende un regalo da uno straniero*; (2a) *John porta il libro a Maria*; (3a) *John prende la tazza dal manico*; (4a) *John porta Maria alla stazione.* But we expect that, in a given language, similar events will be referred to by using the same verb: so "to take" will apply also to *John takes the children to school/his wife to the cinema*, similarly to (4); we also expect this tendency to be found in other languages, as is the case for "portare" in *John porta i bambini a scuola/sua moglie al cinema*, similar to (4a). In the ImagAct framework these coherent sets of similar events are referred to as action types. Verbs which extensionally denote more than one action types (as "to take") are named general verbs.

Since written corpora tend to abound in abstract verbs or verbs used in their abstract senses, the best way to study action verbs' actual variation is in spontaneous speech, i.e. in transcribed spoken corpora. The ImagAct project focuses on high frequency action verbs (approximately 600 lexical entry) of Italian and English, which represent the basic verbal lexicon of the two languages. All occurrences of these verb were retrieved, respectively from a collection of Italian spoken corpora (C-ORAL-ROM; LABLITA; LIP; CLIPS), and from the BNC-Spoken; linguistic contexts of each occurrence were then standardized and reduced to simple sentences as those reported above (1-4).

Once the ImagAct corpus was created, as a first step, annotators made a distinction between the metaphorical and phraseological usages (e.g. *John takes Mary to be honest*) from proper occurrences of action verbs (e.g. *John takes the glass*); then, they grouped the occurrences into action types, keeping granularity to its minimal level, so that each type contained a number of instances referring to similar events (*John takes the glass/the umbrella/the pen* etc.). This procedure was accomplished through a web based annotation interface and was standardized in the specifications of the ImagAct project. Finally, one best example was chosen (or more than one, if the verb had more than one possible syntactic structure) from all standardized sentences of each type, and it was then associated to a video to exemplify the action type.

To obtain a parallel corpus, all English standardized instances assigned to a type have been translated into Italian, and vice versa; the possibility of translating all instances of a type into another language, using only one verb, assures the coherence of that type. In the very last phase, a mapping between English and Italian action types has been conducted onto the same set of scenes. The validation of basic action types is going on also for Chinese and in the future other languages will be involved in this procedure. Crosslinguistic comparison between languages highlights coarse-grained distinctions between word senses (Resnik and Yarowsky 1998); as a consequence we expect that the extension to more languages will make the basic action types more general and less dependent on a specific language.

The result of the procedure described above is a set of short videos, each one corresponding to an action type and showing simple actions (e.g. a man taking a glass on a table), by which a user can access the English/Italian best examples chosen for that type (*John takes the glass/John prende il bicchiere*) and all the standardized sentences extracted from corpora that have been assigned to that type; these videos show the actual use of the verb when referring to a specific type of action. Also, a user can access this data by lemma: for example, searching for the verb "to take", he will be presented with a number of scenes, showing the different action types associated to that verb, with their related information. Scenes, and their associated best examples, represent the variation of all action verbs considered and constitute the ImagAct ontology of action. This ontology is not only inherently inter-linguistic, having been derived through an inductive process from corpora of different languages, but also takes into account the intra-linguistic and inter-linguistic variation that characterizes action verbs in human languages.

3 GL Co-Composition and ImagAct General Verbs

Pustejovsky (1995) defines co-composition as a semantic property of a structure in which both a predicate and its argument(s) contribute functionally to the meaning of an expression, so that the semantic contribution of the argument(s) of the predicate is greater than can be accounted for on a strictly compositional analysis of meaning. We can then view certain verbs as being lexically underspecified in the sense that the arguments of these verbs play a significant role in ascertaining the full meaning of the verb in context. The classic example of co-compositionality as given in Pustejovsky (1995) involves the verb "bake" which can be understood in at least two distinct senses, a "change of state" sense as in sentence (5) and a "creation" sense as in sentence (6):

(5) John baked the potato.
(6) John baked the cake.

This can be understood as an example of logical polysemy since, although "bake" has a slightly different meaning in each of the two sentences (5) and (6), these meanings are somehow closely related. It's not hard to find other examples in which co-compositionality is clearly evident and where the meaning of a verbal predicate in context, including the type of action to which it might refer, is heavily dependent on the type and meaning of its arguments. So that for example the following two sentences refer to two different action types for the Italian verb *prendere* in ImagAct:

(7) *Marco prende la mela.* ('Marco takes the apple')
(8) *Marco prende la mela dall'albero.* ('Marco picks the apple from the tree').

One could argue that those action verbs which best fit the definition of lexical underspecification as given above should also be regarded as "general" verbs in the ImagAct sense. Each general verb is associated with a finite set of action types, which are themselves determined by the different kinds of objects to which the actions referred to by the verb might apply. If an action verb is underspecified, it can be said to lack one determinate meaning which might provide a clear prototypical example of the kinds of actions to which it refers, so that a verb like "to open" or "to take" is "vague" enough to be associated with a number of distinctive action types in its primary non-metaphorical usages, whereas a verb like "to knife" or even "to eat" can plausibly be associated with only one type of action: this is at least the viewpoint taken up the ImagAct project (www.imagact.it). Thus, ImagAct could be viewed as an important lexical resource for the analysis of the phenomena of co-composition at least to the extent that it pertains to the class of action verbs.

4 Enriching HOLD Verbs' Sentences with Semantic Information from SIMPLE

A disambiguation task performed on manually annotated data involving action types has a practical application, considering that these data will be analysed in the on-going ModelAct project for human-robot interaction and modeling of actions. However, the results have also theoretical implications because the way the senses have been individuated is peculiar and the kind of meanings classified (verbs' senses referring to concrete actions) can change the expectations about the most relevant/useful knowledge source for disambiguation. In this paper we mainly use semantic associations knowledge from SIMPLE to disambiguate between basic action types.

The Italian component of the ImagAct dataset contains at the moment 744 verbs and 1358 basic action types, for a total of 26233 standardized sentences. The intra-linguistic mapping between basic action types to discover local equivalence between verbs is in progress. In this paper we focus on a semantically coherent verbs' class, that of Levin's HOLD verbs (Levin 1993) (*to clasp, to clutch, to grasp, to grip, to handle, to hold, to wield*), corresponding to Italian verbs *acchiappare, afferrare agguantare, pigliare, prendere, raccattare, raccogliere, stringere, tenere.* Looking at basic action types of these verbs, we find several equivalence *(Marco piglia lo yogurt dal frigorifero/ Marco prende il prodotto dalla busta*) that will be grouped in the disambiguation experiment (see 5).

We extract from SIMPLE the telic information about the objects of the HOLD verbs.

We decided to use SIMPLE because of great amount of structured encyclopedic knowledge it contains. SIMPLE is largely based on Pustejovsky's Generative Lexicon (GL) theory. GL theory posits that the meaning of each word in a lexicon can be structured into components, one of which, the qualia structure, consists of a bundle of four orthogonal dimensions.

These dimensions allow for the encoding of four separate representative aspects of the meaning of a word or phrase: the formal, namely that which allows the identification of an entity, i.e., what it is; the constitutive, what an entity is made of; the telic, that which specifies the function of an entity; and finally the agentive, that which specifies the origin of an entity. These qualia structures play an important role within GL in explaining for example, the phenomena of polysemy in natural languages. SIMPLE itself is actually based on the notion of an extended qualia structure, which as the name suggests is an extension of the qualia structure notion found in GL. Thus, there is a hierarchy of constitutive, telic, and agentive relations that can hold between semantic units. SIMPLE contains a language independent ontology of 153 semantic types as well as 60k so called "semantic units" or USems, representing the meanings of lexical entries in the lexicon. SIMPLE also contains 66 relations organized in a hierarchy of types and subtypes all subsumed by one of the four main qualia roles:

- FORMAL (is-a)
- CONSTITUTIVE, such as ACTIVITY produced-by
- TELIC, such as INSTRUMENTAL used-for
- AGENTIVE, such as ARTIFACTUAL caused-by

4.1 Manual annotation of affording properties

Since HOLD verbs selected are the most generic verbs involving actions done with hands, a manual annotation has been done on each sentence in terms of affording properties of the objects (Gibson 1979).

As additional information we annotated the properties of the objects denoted by lemmas that afford grasping. These properties are defined by the type of grasping the object afford. We created these categories adopting a bottom-up approach, by looking at all the possible objects of primary verbs and identifying a minimum set of common features among them.

One-Hand_Grasp: this is a property of objects that can be grasped using only one hand. The size of two of the object's dimensions (length, width or thickness) must not exceed the maximum span of a hand with at least two fingers bent in order to grasp and hold something. E.g.: "Johs takes the lighter". The agent's control over the grasped object is maximum.

Two-Hands_Grasp: this property is still related to the object size and qualifies objects that cannot be grasped without necessarily using two hands. Note this kind of grasp is not specifically directed to any of the object's parts. E.g.: "John takes the board". Also in this case, the agent's control over the grasped entity is very high, also with animates (when they can be taken and hold with two hands, as in "The nurse takes the baby from the incubator").

Grasp_by_part: this property is proper of big objects (i.e., whose size exceed the maximum span of a hand) that, even so, can be perfectly controlled by agents using only one hand thanks to a handle. Handle refers here to any part of an object specifically designed to afford grasping (like a handle of a handbag). This property is also shown by objects with dimensions bigger than a hand size, especially all animate entities, that have no designed handles, but that still can be grasped and hold simply using one hand: the grasp will be directed to one of their parts, the one (usually hand, arm) that better allows grasping for its suitability in size with hands (but note that in these cases agent's control over the grasped entity is much less strong). These parts are often explicitly mentioned for their relevance for action (especially if there are many possible graspable parts in the same entity, as in "John takes Mary by her hand/her leg/her arm"), for they are not predetermined, as designed handles are.

Grasp_with_instrument_container: this is the main property of entities (mainly substance and mass entities) which humans cannot directly control without using some other object, because of their fluid consistency and because of the absence of a solid, tangible, definite shape contour. For example, water and other liquids cannot be grasped without a container, as a bottle or a glass. Because it is impossible for humans to grasp these entities without a recipient, explicit reference to the container is often omitted (as in "John takes the water for the dog from the faucet": it is implicitly understood that he uses a bowl), and in some cases is even lexicalized, as demonstrated by the fact that some objects can accept a quantified form, as in "John takes two beers out of/from the fridge" (= bottles of beer). In this example, the grasping event properly involves the solid container, but is semantically referred to the content. This kind of polysemy (container/content), which originates from metonymic processes, is quite regular and widespread in languages: this can be easily understood considering that, for humans, contents are usually much more salient than containers.

Additional information: sometimes, objects shape, dimensions and constituency do not suffice to predict how humans actually grasp them. For this reason, we annotated some objects with two affording properties. This mainly concerns objects that can be grasped with one hand, but that usually are grasped with an instrument (that in turn can be grasped with one or two hands). For example, *zucchini, potatoes, meat* and other foods (as in "John takes the zucchini/the meatball from the tray"), can be grasped directly by hands, but usually we prefer to use a fork (grasped with one hand). So, for *zucchini*, when intended as [food], we annotated both one_hand_grasp and one_hand_instrumental_grasp. Another case in which we annotated two affording properties is when an object is one_hand_graspable, but it has a part specifically designed for grasping (as for scissors or pacifiers). In this case, we annotated both one_hand_graspabable and grasp_by_part.

5 Disambiguation of HOLD Verbs Basic Action Types: a First Experiment

Our starting dataset comprises 1419 sentences and 29 basic action types. Some sentences were doubled because the telic qualia in SIMPLE for several nouns has more than one entry. At the end we have 1573 instances to classify. We performed a ten-fold cross validation experiment with the implementation provided in WEKA (Hall el al. 2009) of Support Vector Machine algorithm (called SMO) since results from the literature WSD on benchmark data show that support vector machines (SVMs) yield models with one of the highest accuracies.

The features for this experiment are:

- manually annotated information about the semantic class of nouns in WordNet 3.0 (SCN in Table 1):
  - o *libro* ('book') → artifact
  - o *caramelle* ('candies') → cibo
- annotation on the affording properties of objects as described in 4.1 (AffP in Table 1).
- values encoded for Telic qualia in SIMPLE, manually disambiguated for each noun and reported as Boolean values for each of the 23 verbs' abstract semantic classes in SIMPLE (as Cause_Constitutive_Change in the following example) (SIMPLE in Table 1):

  Matteo prende il coltello. 'Matteo takes the knife'
  knife **UsedFor** tagliare ('to cut')

  tagliare is Cause_Constitutive_Change
- SIMPLE semantic classes of most salient verbs that precede the target noun in itTenTen, a web corpus of 3.1 billion tokens, accessible through APIs provided by sketchengine.co.uk . These data have been extracted as word sketches (Kilgarriff et al. 2004) and as a consequence report on selectional preferences that are among the most useful features in WSD (see Introduction) (itTenTen in Table 1). We found out that this pattern extracts content similar to telic qualia and for this reason we compare telic information and word sketches in this experiment.

We also perform disambiguation experiment on a version of the dataset with grouped action types (i.e. 14) composed by 1577 sentences because we found equivalence between several types. Baseline assigns each sentence to the most common action type (75.3% for AllBT, the dataset with all the basic action types, and 84% for GroupedBT, the dataset with grouped action types).

The results are reported in Table 1.

	AllF	SCN	AffP	SIMPLE	itTenTen
AllBT	81.6%	77%	76%	77.4%	80.5%
GroupedBT	89.7%	86.9%	85.7%	87.6%	90.2%

Table 1: Accuracy for basic action types disambiguation with different set of features

The best result is obtained on the grouped basic action types dataset, with 0.88 as precision and 0.90 as recall. For this dataset information extracted from SIMPLE have a small negative impact on the accuracy while for the dataset with all the action types it contributes to improve the result. Affording properties are not very relevant for disambiguation: even if the affordances of objects are known from psychological studies as a relevant feature in action learning, the annotation proposed is probably not the best way to represent this knowledge.

6 Conclusions and Future Work

Knowledge about semantic associations between words is effective to disambiguate word senses. Distributional models of word meanings represent this information providing a vector-based representation of most frequent words in context. We extracted this information from SIMPLE, a rich lexical resource that provide essential information about objects' typical uses in the telic qualia. The three most salient verbs that have as object the target nouns in ImagAct sentences have been extracted from a large web corpus. To avoid data sparseness SIMPLE complex ontology that label verbs with coarse-grained semantic classes have been used. The results show that qualia information is useful for disambiguation but enriching it with salient data from corpus improves the accuracy.

As future work we want to enrich the ImagAct dataset with information from other qualia in SIMPLE (i.e. formal, constitutive and agentive) and from other resources, such as dictionary's glosses, ontologies for actions, distributional data from different corpora with the aim to find the best set of features for the disambiguation of basic action types. As a collateral project, we plan to find additional salient values for nouns' qualia structure through patterns in corpora.

References

Agirre, E. Martinez, D. (2001), Knowledge sources for word sense disambiguation. In Proceedings of International Conference on Text, Speech and Dialogue (TSD'2001) Selezna Ruda, Czech Republic.

Gibson, J. J. (1979). The Ecological Approach to Visual Perception. Boston: Houghton Mifflin.

Hall, M. Eibe Frank, Geoffrey Holmes, Bernhard Pfahringer, Peter Reutemann, Ian H. Witten (2009); The WEKA Data Mining Software: An Update; SIGKDD Explorations, Volume 11, Issue 1.

Hanks, Patrick. (2008). "Mapping meaning onto use: a Pattern Dictionary of English Verbs". AACL 2008, Utah.

Levin, B. (1993), "English Verb Classes and Alternations: A Preliminary Investigation." In: The University of Chicago Press.

Kilgarriff, A.; Rychly, P.; Smrz, P.; Tugwell, D. (2004). 'The Sketch Engine'. Proceedings Euralex. Lorient.

Kilgarriff, A. (1997), "I don't believe in word senses" Computers and the Humanities 31: 91-113.

Moneglia, M., Alessandro Panunzi, Gloria Gagliardi, Monica Monachini, Irene Russo (2012), Mapping a corpus-induced ontology of action verbs on ItalWordNet. Global Wordnet Conference 2012.

Pustejovsky, J. (1995), The Generative Lexicon. MIT Press, Cambridge, MA.

Resnik, P., Yarowsky, D. (1998) Distinguishing Systems and Distinguishing sense: new evaluation methods fot WSD. Natural Language Engineering.

Ruimy, N, M. Monachini, E. Gola, N. Calzolari, M.C. Del Fiorentino, M. Ulivieri, and S. Rossi (2003), A computational semantic lexicon of italian: SIMPLE. Linguistica Computazionale XVIII-XIX, Pisa, pages 821–64.

Class-based Word Sense Induction for dot-type nominals

Lauren Romeo
Universitat Pompeu Fabra
Roc Boronat, 138
Barcelona (Spain)
lauren.romeo@upf.edu

Héctor Martínez Alonso
University of Copenhagen
Njalsgade, 140
Copenhagen (Denmark)
alonso@hum.ku.dk

Núria Bel
Universitat Pompeu Fabra
Roc Boronat, 138
Barcelona (Spain)
nuria.bel@upf.edu

Abstract

This paper describes an effort to capture the sense alternation of dot-type nominals using Word Sense Induction (WSI). We propose dot-type nominals generate more semantically consistent groupings when clustered into more than two clusters, accounting for literal, metonymic and underspecified senses. Using a class-based approach, we replace individual lemmas with a placeholder representing the entire dot type, which also compensates for data sparsity. Although the distributional evidence does not motivate an individual cluster for each sense, we discuss how our results empirically support theoretical proposals regarding dot types.

1 Introduction

In this article, we propose a Word Sense Induction (WSI) task to capture the sense alternation of English dot types, as found in context. *Dot type* is the Generative Lexicon (GL) term to account for a noun that can denote at least two senses as a complex semantic class (Pustejovsky, 1995). Consider the noun *England* in the following example from the American National Corpus (ANC) (Ide and Macleod, 2001) as an illustration.

(1) (a) Manuel died in exile in 1932 in *England*.
 (b) *England* was being kept busy with other concerns.
 (c) *England* is conservative and rainy.

In this example, (1a) shows the *literal* sense of England as a location, while (1b) demonstrates the *metonymic* sense of England as an organization. Dot types also allow for both senses to be simultaneously active in a predicate, as in example (1c). All proper names representative of geopolitical entities, for instance, demonstrate this type of class-wide sense alternation, which is defined as *regular polysemy* (Apresjan, 1974).

Copestake (2013) emphasizes the relevance of distributional evidence in tasks regarding phenomena characteristic to regular polysemy, such as underspecification, because it incorporates frequency effects and is theory-neutral, requiring only that examples cluster in a way that mirrors their senses.

Thus far, underspecification in dot types has been formalized in the linguistic theory of lexical semantics, but has not been explicitly studied using WSI. Kilgariff (1997) claims that word senses should be *"construed as abstractions over clusters of word usages"*. Following this claim, our strategy employs WSI, which aims to automatically induce senses of words by clustering patterns found in a corpus (Lau et al., 2012; Jurgens, 2012). In this way, we hypothesize that dot-type nominals will generate semantically more consistent (i.e. more homogeneous, cf. Section 5) groupings if clustered into more than two induced senses.

This paper is organized as follows: we discuss related work (Section 2); elaborate upon our use of WSI and methodology employed (Section 3 and Section 4), as well as present results obtained; we discuss our results (Section 5) and conclude with final observations and future work (Sections 6 and 7).

2 Related Work

Natural Language Processing (NLP) tasks that exploit distributional information are based on the Distributional Hypothesis (Harris, 1954). However, Pustejovsky and Ježek (2008) claim that only using distributional data cannot explain the variation of linguistic meaning in language, while Markert and Nissim (2009) refer to the challenges of dealing with regular polysemy as the different senses of polysemous words present obstacles due to varied use in context. Along this line, the empirical work of Boleda et al. (2012) showed that the skewed sense distribution of many words makes it difficult to distinguish evidence of a class from noise, presenting a challenge to model the relations between senses. When their machine-learning experiments reached the upper bound set by the inter-encoder agreement in their gold standard, they concluded that in order to improve the modelling of polysemy there is a need to shift from a type to a token-based (word-in-context) model (Schütze, 1998; Erk and Padó, 2008). Hence, we employ a token-based model in our experiments.

In our approach, we propose an unsupervised task using WSI to capture the sense alternation of dot types, using distributional evidence from corpus data. Our results will be noisier than supervised approaches, such as those of Markert and Nissim (2009), Nissim and Markert (2005) and Nastase et al. (2012), but we make use of a much larger amount of data and thus should suffer from less sparsity. The related experiment by Rumshisky et al. (2007) uses verbal arguments as features, while we use only a five-word context window.

2.1 Word Sense Induction

As stated above, our main goal is to use WSI to capture the sense alternation of dot types in context. WSI methods, based on the distributional information available in corpus data, employ unsupervised means to induce senses using contexts of indicated target words without relying on hand-crafted resources (Manandhar et al., 2010).

Distributional Semantic Models (DSM) provide the groundwork for WSI. A DSM, also known as a Word Space Model (Turney and Pantel, 2010), attempts to describe the meaning of words by characterizing their usage over distributional patterns, i.e. their context. Each word is represented by a numeric vector positioned in a space where vectors for words that appear in similar contexts are closer to each other. Sense induction is achieved by building a DSM over a large corpus and clustering the contexts into induced senses.

In recent years, WSI has been used with success for different tasks such as: novel sense detection (Lau et al., 2012), community detection (Jurgens, 2011) and graded sense disambiguation (Jurgens, 2012), among others. Jurgens (2011) previously employed WSI to discover overlaps in the distributional behavior of words in order to identify multiple senses with success. However, that work was not inclusive to any specific phenomenon of polysemy. Our objective is to cluster dot-type nominals according to their distributional evidence in context, using WSI to characterize the behavior of these nouns.

3 Method

We use WSI to computationally assess the predicational behavior of dot types. To do this, we employ a WSI system to induce senses from a large corpus (in our case UkWaC cf. Section 3.2). We then cluster dot-type nominals into the different induced k-solutions and evaluate the WSI model using a dot-type sense-annotated corpus to measure how well the induced senses map to human-annotated data.

3.1 Data

The dot-type sense-annotated corpus (Martínez Alonso et al., 2013) provides examples for each of the following dot types:

1. Animal/Meat (ANIMEAT): *The chicken ran away* vs. *the chicken was delicious.*
2. Artifact/Information (ARTINFO): *The book fell* vs. *the book was boring.*
3. Container/Content (CONTCONT): *The box was red* vs. *I ate the whole box.*
4. Location/Organization (LOCORG): *England is far* vs. *England starts a tax reform.*
5. Process/Result (PROCRES): *The building took months to finish* vs. *the building is sturdy.*

To evaluate our clustering, we made use of the aforementioned sense-annotated corpus as a gold standard. The corpus provides senses that have been obtained by majority voting with a theory-compliant back-off strategy (see Martínez et al., 2013 for a detailed description). Each section of the sense-annotated corpus[1] is a block of 500 sentences with one dot-type headword the annotators had to disambiguate. The authors do not make a distinction between sense alternations that are based on physical contiguity (CONTCONT) from temporal contiguity (PROCRES). We use their data as provided.

The gold standard includes nouns annotated as literal, metonymic or underspecified. Each dataset

[1] We obtained the data from MetaShare at http://metashare.cst.dk/repository/search/?q=regular+polysemy

Dot type	$\overline{A_o}$	α
ANIMEAT	0.86	0.69
ARTINFO	0.48	0.12
CONTCONT	0.65	0.31
LOCORG	0.72	0.46
PROCRES	0.50	0.10

Table 1: Averaged observed agreement ($\overline{A_o}$) and Krippendorf's alpha (α)

has a different average observed agreement and Krippendorf's α coefficient (cf. Poesio and Artstein, 2008), as shown in Table 1.

The variation in agreement for each dataset was strong, which is a sign of the difficulty of each annotation task. For instance, LOCORG is easier to annotate than ARTINFO, which is reflected in its higher agreement. Another relevant characteristic of the gold standard is that there is also an imbalance of frequency between the annotated senses of each dot type. For instance, it resulted that ANIMEAT was annotated with more literal readings and PROCRES was annotated with more metonymic readings. Figure 1 provides the distribution of senses between each dot type studied in this article.

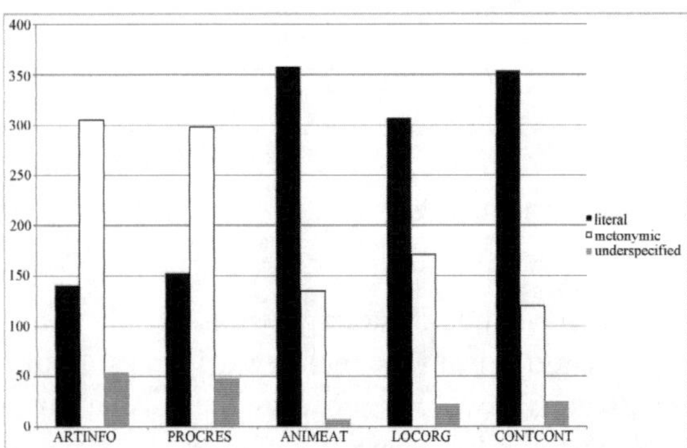

Figure 1: Distribution of senses between classes

3.2 Preprocessing

For our experiments we used the UkWaC corpus (Baroni et al., 2009) to fit our WSI models. After lemmatizing, lowercasing and removing all punctuation from the corpus, we extracted a random sample of 60 million words (2.8 million sentences) where each sentence was at least five tokens long. We did not remove stop words from the corpus as we expect the interaction between stop words (e.g. articles, prepositions, etc.) and dot-type nominals to represent strong distinguishing features between different interpretations of a dot type, along the lines of Rumshisky et al. (2007).

In our experiments, we assume that words of the same class behave similarly. Thus, our intent is to induce the same senses for all the words of a given semantic class, making our approach class-based.

To group the occurrences of all words of a given dot type, we replaced their occurrences with a placeholder lemma that represents the entire dot type (*animeatdot, artinfodot, contcontdot, locorgdot, procresdot*). For instance, the lemmatized examples (2a) and (2b) with the words *paris* and *london* become the sentences in the examples (2c) and (2d).

(2) (a) whilst i be in **paris** in august i decide to visit the catacomb
(b) you can get to both **london** station on the **london** underground
(c) whilst i be in **locorgdot** in august i decide to visit the catacomb
(d) you can get to both **locorgdot** station on the **locorgdot** underground

Replacing individual lemmas by a placeholder for the overall class yields results similar to those obtained by building prototype distributional vectors for a set of words once the DSM has been calculated (cf. Turney and Pantel (2010) for more on prototype vectors of a semantic class). Our take, however, is a preprocessing of the corpus to assure we infer senses directly for the placeholder lemmas. In this way, we avoid having to reconstruct overall class-wise senses from the inferred senses for each individual lemma.

Regular polysemy is a class-wide phenomenon (cf. Section 1), hence we expect that all lemmas in a dot type will predicate their senses in a similar manner—in similar contexts, e.g. headed or followed by the same prepositions. Thus, the placeholders represent the entire dot type as well as provide the added benefit of circumventing the effects of data sparseness, especially for evaluation purposes. For instance, in our data there are some lemmas (eg. in ANIMEAT: *anchovy, yak, crayfish*) that only appear once in the gold standard, limiting evaluation power. The placeholder reduces the impact this may have on evaluation by considering each individual lemma as a member of the entire dot type that its placeholder represents.

This replacement method is not exhaustive because we strictly replace the words from the test dataset by their dot-type placeholder and, for instance, plenty of country and city names are not replaced by *locorgdot* as they were not considered target nouns in the annotation task.

3.3 Applying WSI

Our WSI models were built using the Random Indexing Word Sense Induction module in the S-Spaces package for DSMs (Jurgens and Stevens, 2010) employing the UkWaC corpus, as described in Section 3.2. Random Indexing (RI) is a fast method to calculate DSMs, which has proven to be as reliable as other word-to-word DSMs, like COALS (Rohde et al., 2009). In DSMs, words are represented by numeric vectors calculated from the occurrence of words in a n-word window around a target word. The similarity between words is measured by means of the cosine of the vectors that represent them.

We induced the senses for the placeholder dot-type lemmas (*locorgdot*, *animeatdot*, and so on), using the following k values to see how the senses are clustered when considering a coarse (k=2; literal and metonymic), a medium (k=3; literal, metonymic, underspecified) and a finer-grained amount of induced senses (k=6), along the lines of Markert and Nissim (2009).

In WSI, instead of generating one vector for each word, each word is assigned k vectors, one for each induced sense. These induced vectors are obtained by clustering the occurrences of a selected word into k senses. The features used to cluster the contexts into senses were the words found in a window of five, both to the left and the right of the target word. For each of the three values of k, we fit a model using K-means clustering and a model using Spectral Clustering (Cheng et al., 2006), for a total of 6 models. The output of the system is a DSM where each vector is one of the k-induced senses for the placeholder dot-type lemmas.

3.4 Assigning word senses

The S-Spaces API permits the calculation of a vector in a DSM for a new, unobserved example. For each sentence in the test data, we isolated the placeholder to disambiguate and we calculated the representation of the sentence within the corresponding WSI model using the specified 5-word context window.

Once the vector for the sentence was obtained, we assigned the sentence to the induced sense representing the highest cosine similarity for each model (cf. Table 2 in Section 4 for evaluation).

4 Results

To determine the success of our task for each class, sense representation and k value, we consider the information-theoretic measures of *homogeneity*, *completeness* and *V-measure* (Rosenberg and Hirschberg, 2007). These three measures compare the output of the clustering with a gold standard (as described in Section 3.1) and provide a score that can be interpreted in a manner similar to precision, recall and F1, respectively.

Homogeneity determines to which extent each cluster only contains members of a single class, while completeness determines if all members of a given class are assigned to the same cluster. Both the homogeneity and completeness scores are bounded by 0.0 and 1.0, with 1.0 corresponding to the most homogeneous or complete solution, and can be interpreted in a manner similar to precision and recall.

V-measure is the harmonic mean of homogeneity and completeness, used to evaluate the agreement of two independent assignments on the same dataset. Values close to zero indicate two label assignments that are largely inconsistent, while values close to one indicate consistency. Much like F1, the V-score indicates the best trade-off between homogeneity and completeness.

	DATASET	HOM	COM	V-ME
k=2	ANIMEAT	0.0031	0.0030	0.0030
	ARTINFO*	**0.0097**	**0.0128**	**0.0110**
	CONTCONT*	0.0067	**0.0075**	0.0071
	LOCORG*	0.0013	0.0016	0.0015
	PROCRES	0.0005	0.0007	0.0006
k=3	ANIMEAT	0.0055	0.0033	0.0041
	ARTINFO*	0.0214	0.0191	0.0201
	CONTCONT*	0.0291	0.0197	**0.0235**
	LOCORG*	**0.1070**	**0.0788**	**0.0908**
	PROCRES*	0.0051	0.0044	0.0047
k=6	ANIMEAT*	0.0379	0.0139	0.0204
	ARTINFO*	0.0253	0.0140	0.0180
	CONTCONT*	**0.1008**	0.0442	**0.0615**
	LOCORG*	**0.1096**	**0.0540**	**0.0724**
	PROCRES*	0.0166	0.0085	0.0112

Table 2: Results of clustering solutions for each class in terms of homogeneity **(HOM)**, completeness **(COM)** and V-measure **(V-ME)**

Table 2 presents the results for each clustering solution (k=2, k=3 and k=6) using K-means clustering. The highest values are shown in bold. It is to be expected that the higher-agreement datasets provide higher homogeneity results because their annotations are more consistent. However, we can see that the performance does not necessarily correlate with agreement as ARTINFO is the dataset that fares best in the k=2 solution, yet it has a very low alpha (α=0.12). In this way, we can say that the homogeneity score for low-agreement datasets will be lower because low-agreement annotations are less reliable due to their lower internal consistency.

In addition, performance (measured in V-measure) improves as k increases. For instance, CONTCONT has the 2nd highest V-measure in the k=3 solution and in the k=6 solution. LOCORG yielded the 4th highest V-measure in k=2 and the highest V-measure in both the k=3 and the k=6 solutions.

We compare our system against a random baseline. This is because the customary one-in-all and all-in-one baselines are not useful in our scenario as they are meant to evaluate adaptative clustering and we use fixed values of K. We do not report the baseline scores because they are not informative. However, we mark the datasets that surpassed those scores with a star (*) in Table 2.

Although our system is unable to beat the random baseline for PROCRES in k=2 and ANIMEAT for k=2 and k=3, we do beat the baseline for each dot type in k=6.

The low performance in ANIMEAT is due to the lower proportion of underspecified senses in the dataset (cf. Figure 1). We attribute the low performance of PROCRES to the complexity of the sense distinction of this dot type. Thereby, we doubt the validity of this particular dataset for WSI.

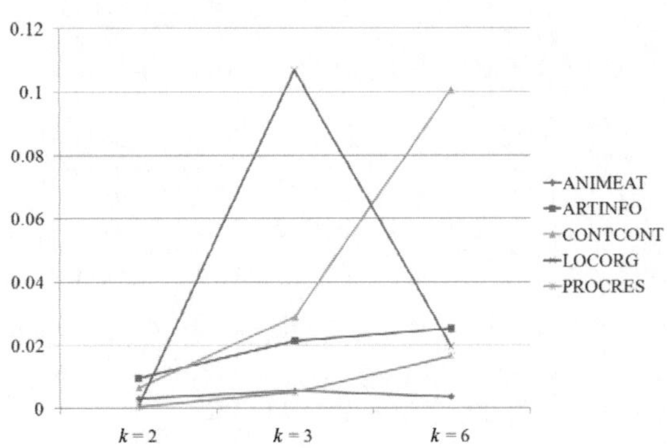

Figure 2: Homogeneity scores for each clustering solution

Figure 2 demonstrates the difference of homogeneity between the clusters, depending on the number of induced senses (k-value). LOCORG and ANIMEAT, on one hand, demonstrate a higher homogeneity score in k=3 while they demonstrate a lower homogeneity score for k=6. CONTCONT, ARTINFO, PROCRES, on the other hand, gain homogeneity with the increase of k.

5 Discussion

The main objective of this experiment is to capture the sense alternation of dot types by computational means. We hypothesize that dot types will generate semantically more consistent groupings if clustered into more than two clusters. To test this, we employ a WSI system to induce the senses and subsequently cluster dot-type nominals into three different k solutions (k=2, k=3, k=6), as detailed in 3.3.

5.1 Inducing two senses

The k=2 solution attempts to mirror a literal vs. metonymic partition between the senses of each dot type. The classes ANIMEAT, CONTCONT and LOCORG are composed of more literal senses while the other two are mostly metonymic (cf. Figure 1). Although there is an a priori difference in the proportion of literal, metonymic and underspecified senses for each class, we assume the UkWaC and test data to have similar distributions of literal and metonymic senses for each dot type. This assumption is congruent with Rumshisky et al. (2007), who claim an asymmetry in the way dot types are used in general.

Overall, the clusters produced in k=2, on one hand, are representative of the asymmetry of the gold standard, i.e. the classes that contain more literal senses, according to our gold standard, yield clusters composed of a higher ratio of literal senses. On the other hand, the underspecified senses tend to spread between both clusters for each class. In this way, the underspecified sense does not represent a homogeneous group, rather it clusters with both the literal and metonymic senses, thereby exhibiting properties of each of the two induced senses.

We observed, for instance, the underspecified senses of ARTINFO occurred often with an "of" PP-phrase, a strong feature for the clustering of examples into a metonymy-dominated sense cluster while the underspecified examples that were objects of verbs such as *keep* or *see* were clustered alongside the literal examples. In this way and along the lines of Pustejovsky and Ježek (2008), we can concur that these verbs tend to trigger a literal (artifactual) reading as they typically describe actions that require some sort of physical entity.

We next increase the K to k=3, a solution that also considers the underspecified sense.

5.2 Inducing three senses

The goal of the k=3 clustering solutions is to cluster each of the three proposed senses of the dot type (literal, metonymic and underspecified) into clusters representative of their respective senses.

The middle row in Table 2 presents the results obtained in the k=3 solution. Our expectation for this solution would have had each gold-standard annotated sense assigned to its corresponding induced sense cluster (literal, metonymic or underspecified). However, we noticed a tendency for the underspecified sense to cluster with the induced sense that contains a higher ratio of the most frequent annotated sense of a given class, either literal or metonymic. Despite the fact that the distributional information for the underspecified sense was not strong enough to spawn a separate cluster, it demonstrates behavior characteristic of the more frequent sense for each dot type, as indicated by the gold standard (cf. Figure 1).

The k=3 solution for the dot types ANIMEAT and LOCORG separates the literal and the metonymic senses, yet the underspecified senses are distributed between all three clusters. In this case, the more frequent sense of the gold standard is split between two clusters, while the remaining cluster is composed of the less frequent sense. The underspecified sense is spread among all three clusters, as illustrated in the confusion matrices provided in Table 3.

	ANIMEAT			LOCORG		
	L	M	U	L	M	U
c=0	110	51	3	62	69	8
c=1	127	43	1	151	17	5
c=2	121	41	3	94	85	9

Table 3: k=3 solutions for ANIMEAT and LOCORG dot types

In Table 4, we observed that the articles *the* and *a* were the most frequent components of the contexts that contributed to the clustering of clusters c=1 and c=2, respectively, for ANIMEAT. On one hand, the importance of the article as a feature reflects that the mass/count distinction is a key component in the sense alternation of some instances of regular polysemy (such as ANIMEAT). In this way, these very formalized constructs that are required for a certain interpretation can help to more easily partition the clusters as they represent grammatical criteria for interpretation. On the other hand, we can also see the importance of a given token in context in the case of LOCORG. For LOCORG, in c=1 and c=2, the most frequent components that contribute to each cluster are prepositions (*in* and *to*, respectively).

	ANIMEAT	LOCORG
c=0	*and, animeatdot, of, a, for,with, the, fish, in, to*	*the, of, and, to, a, in, that, time, it, for*
c=1	*the, of, and, in, a, to, is, that, animeatdot, with*	*in, the, and, to, a, of, that, is, it, for*
c=2	*a, of, to, in, that, or, is, with, for, from*	*to, and, from, a, locorgdot, the, that, with, for, is*

Table 4: Top 10 most frequent words per c used in k=3 for ANIMEAT and LOCORG dot types

The very frequent preposition *in* seems to favor the literal (*location*) reading for LOCORG that appears in c=1. In c=2, the most important preposition is *to*, which indicates a directionality that can be both topological or more abstract, giving to the introduced noun the role of experiencer or beneficiary in the predicate, for instance. However, this preposition does not necessarily coerce a metonymic or a literal sense, which becomes apparent in the balanced composition of the senses of LOCORG in c=2.

The placeholders also appear as important features for their respective dot type among all the grammatical words. We observed that other animals are mentioned when predicating the ANIMEAT dot type (see Table 4). The noun *fish* was not replaced by its placeholder as it does not appear in the gold standard data but is one of the few nouns in the top 10 words for each cluster. We comment upon the effect of our use of a limited selection of lemmas in this task in Section 7.

Overall, the distributional evidence used in the k=3 solution is again not strong enough to motivate an individual cluster for each sense, indicating the underspecified senses may not be as lexically homogeneous as the other two. This is because they have properties of both senses of a given dot type, supporting the assumption that the underspecified sense is formed by the union of both the literal and metonymic senses (Pustejovsky, 1995). However, under the assumption that more fine-grained patterns may indicate underspecified reading, we attempted a k=6 solution to differentiate between senses with a larger K.

5.3 Inducing six senses

The k=6 solution was proposed to uncover fine-grained sense distinctions between a given dot type (Markert and Nissim, 2009). We observed, namely in CONTCONT, ANIMEAT and PROCRES, that the resulting clusters demonstrate a higher V-measure than their k=2 and k=3 counterparts, but this is a consequence of a higher homogeneity expected from an increased k-value. On one hand, the less homogeneous clusters in k=3 are more prone to be split into at least two smaller yet more homogeneous clusters in k=6. On the other hand, the more homogeneous clusters in k=3 were mostly preserved in k=6, as the senses that pertain to it remained identifiable in its own separate cluster. This demonstrates that, although disperse, the resulting clusters contain stable elements that are representative of a given sense.

The k=6 solution is thus a further refinement of k=3 into more fine-grained induced senses. The results for k=6 still reflect the challenges of the task and the variation of the sense composition of dot-type nominals, i.e. they occur predominantly in one sense and the distributions of their underspecified senses largely overlap with the distribution of the literal and metonymic senses.

6 Conclusions

In this work, our objective was to use WSI to capture the sense alternation of dot types. Although our system surpassed the random baseline for all dot types in k=6, the V-measure of the induced-sense clustering solutions demonstrates that our method was not able to isolate the literal, metonymic and underspecified senses. Our results do not imply an absolute distinction between the senses of a dot type.

The skewedness in sense distributions of the dot types in the gold standard (cf. Figure 1) has an impact on the quality of our results. This can be attributed to a preference of a dot type to be selected for more often as one sense over the other in a given context, along the lines of Rumshisky et al. (2007).

The lower-agreement datasets (cf. Table 1; CONTCONT, PROCRES) increase in homogeneity with the increase of K (see Table 2), suggesting that more difficult-to-annotate dot types have more variation and thus cluster better in a higher K.

The differences between the contexts of the senses were still not strong enough to motivate separate clusters for each individual sense. This is in line with Markert and Nissim (2009) and Boleda et al. (2012) which refer to the difficulty of dealing with different forms of regular polysemy as a factor that limits conclusion power. It is also in line with Pustejovksy and Ježek (2008), as our analysis provided distributional evidence considering only 5-word window contexts, which do not reflect modulations that a given dot type may undergo due to its occurrence in context. We leave the refinement of features for future work (see Section 7).

7 Future Work

In many cases the clustering solutions appear to be governed by a particular syntactic or lexical context (i.e. a dependent PP in the case of the metonymic-dominated cluster of ARTINFO), denoting its resulting sense through a specific context. Moreover, our DSM only calculated relations between lemmas. However, we are aware, for instance, that the plural number is an informative feature for the count/mass alternation (Gillon, 1992), which is parallel to many instances of regular polysemy (Copestake, 2013).

As we use 5-word contexts to induce and subsequently cluster our senses, we do not capture all the contextually complex phrases or gating predicates, coordinated co-predications, and vague contexts that can cause underspecified predications. However, our results depend not only on an accurate induction of the senses in context, but also on the reliability of the test set (see Table 1).

We also consider that we now have a baseline which provides information with regard to the sense relations of a given dot type, as per our analysis based on the results of our WSI task. Thereby, we can use a DSM for a WSI that takes into account syntactic role of each token to compare results.

Finally, the placeholder lemmas replace all the lemmas in the gold standard, as indicated in Section 3.2. The selection of lemmas that we replace restricts the class-based WSI because of its small sample size. We should expand these lists with more lemmas, so the distribution of the semantic class can be less biased by the choice of lemmas.

Acknowledgements

This work was funded with the support of the SUR of the DEC of the Generalitat de Catalunya and the European Social Fund, by the European Commission's 7th Framework Program under grant agreement 238405 (CLARA) and by SKATER TIN2012-38584-C06-05.

References

M. Baroni, S. Bernardini, A. Ferraresi, and E. Zanchetta. 2009. The wacky wide web: A collection of very large linguistically processed web-crawled corpora. *Language Resources and Evaluation*, 43(3):209–226.

G. Boleda, S. Schülte im Walde, and T. Badia. 2012. Modeling regular polysemy: A study of the semantic classification of catalan adjectives. *Computational Linguistics*, 38(3):575–616.

D. Cheng, R. Kannan, S. Vempala, and G. Wang. 2006. A divide-and-merge methodology for clustering. *ACM Transactions on Database Systems (TODS)*, 31(4):1499–1525.

A. Copestake. 2013. Can distributional approached improve on goold old-fashioned lexical semantics? In *IWCS Workshop Towards a Formal Distributional Semantics*.

Katrin Erk and Sebastian Padó. 2008. A structured vector space model for word meaning in context. In *Proceedings of the Conference on Empirical Methods in Natural Language Processing*, pages 897–906. Association for Computational Linguistics.

B.S. Gillon. 1992. Towards a common semantics for english count and mass nouns. *Linguistics and Philosophy*, 15:597–639.

Z. Harris. 1954. Distributional structure. *Word*, 10(23):146–162.

N. Ide and C. Macleod. 2001. The american national corpus: A standardized resource of american english. In *Corpus Linguistics*, pages 274–280.

D. Jurgens and K. Stevens. 2010. Measuring the impact of sense similarity on word sense induction. In *First workshop on Unsupervised Learning in NLP (EMNLP 2011)*.

D. Jurgens. 2011. Word sense induction by community detection. In *6th ACL Workshop on Graph-based Methods for Natural Language Processing (Text-Graphs 6)*.

D. Jurgens. 2012. An evaluation of graded sense disambiguation using word sense induction. In **SEM First Joint Conference on Lexical and Computational Semantics*.

A. Kilgariff. 1997. I dont believe in word senses. *Computers and the Humanities*, 31:91–113.

J.H. Lau, P. Cook, D. McCarthy, D. Newman, and T. Baldwin. 2012. Word sense induction for novel sense detection. In *13th Conference of the European Chapter of the Association for Computational Linguistics (EACL)*.

S. Manandhar, I.P. Klapaftis, D. Dligach, and S. Pradhan. 2010. Task 14: Word sense induction and disambiguation. In *15th International Workshop on Semantic Evaluation (ACL)*, pages 63–68.

K. Markert and M. Nissim. 2009. Data and models for metonymy resolution. *Language Resources and Evaluation*, 43(2):123–138.

H. Martínez Alonso, B. Sandford Pedersen, and N. Bel. 2013. Annotation of regular polysemy and underspecification. In *51st Meeting of the Associatation for Computation Linguistics (ACL 2013)*.

V. Nastase, A. Judea, K. Markert, and M. Strube. 2012. Local and global context for supervised and unsupervised metonymy resolution. In *Proceedings of the 2012 Joint Conference on Empirical Methods in Natural Language Processing and Computational Natural Language Learning*, pages 183–193. Association for Computational Linguistics.

M. Nissim and K. Markert. 2005. Learning to buy a renault and talk to bmw: A supervised approach to conventional metonymy. In *International Workshop on Computational Semantics (IWCS2005)*.

J. Pustejovsky and E. Ježek. 2008. Semantic coercion in language: Beyond distributional analysis. *Italian Journal of Linguistics*.

J. Pustejovsky. 1995. *The Generative Lexicon*. Oxford University Press, Oxford.

D. Rohde, L. Gonnerman, and D. Plaut. 2009. An improved model of semantic similarity based on lexical co-occurrence. *Cognitive Science*.

A. Rosenberg and J. Hirschberg. 2007. V-measure: A conditional entropy-based external cluster evaluation measure. In *Conference on Empirical Methods in Natural Language Processing (EMNLP 2007)*.

A. Rumshisky, V. Grinberg, and J. Pustejovsky. 2007. Detecting selectional behavior of complex types. In *4th International Workshop on Generative Approaches to the Lexicon*.

H. Schütze. 1998. Automatic word sense discrimination. *Computational linguistics*, 24(1):97–123.

P.D. Turney and P. Pantel. 2010. From frequency to meaning: Vector space models of semantics. *Journal of Artificial Intelligence Research*, 37:141–188.

Mixing in Some Knowledge: Enriched Context Patterns for Bayesian Word Sense Induction

Rachel Chasin
MIT CSAIL
Cambridge, MA
rchasin@mit.edu

Anna Rumshisky
Department of Computer Science
University of Massachusetts, Lowell, MA
arum@cs.uml.edu

Abstract

Bayesian topic models have recently been shown to perform well in word sense induction (WSI) tasks. Such models have almost exclusively used bag-of-words features, and failed to attain improvement by including other feature types. In this paper, we investigate the impact of integrating syntactic and knowledge-based features and show that both parametric and non-parametric models consistently benefit from additional feature types. We perform evaluation on the SemEval2010 WSI verb data and show statistically significant improvement in accuracy ($p < 0.001$) both over the bag-of-words baselines and over the best system that competed in the SemEval2010 WSI task.

1 Introduction

The resolution of lexical ambiguity in language is essential to true language understanding. It has been shown to improve the performance of such applications as statistical machine translation (Chan et al., 2007; Carpuat and Wu, 2007), and cross-language information retrieval and question answering (Resnik, 2006). Word sense induction (WSI) is the task of automatically grouping the target word's contexts of occurrence into clusters corresponding to different senses. Unlike word sense disambiguation (WSD), it does not rely on a pre-existing set of senses.

Much of the classic bottom-up WSI and thesaurus construction work – as well as many successful systems from the recent SemEval competitions – have explicitly avoided the use of existing knowledge sources, instead representing the disambiguating context using bag-of-words (BOW) or syntactic features (Schütze, 1998; Pantel and Lin, 2002; Dorow and Widdows, 2003; Pedersen, 2010; Kern et al., 2010).

This particularly concerns the attempts to integrate the information about semantic classes of words present in the sense-selecting contexts. Semantic roles (such as those found in PropBank (Palmer et al., 2005) or FrameNet (Ruppenhofer et al., 2006)) tend to generalize poorly across the vocabulary. Lexical ontologies (and WordNet (Fellbaum, 2010) in particular) are not always empirically grounded in language use and often do not represent the relevant semantic distinctions. Very often, some parts of the ontology are better suited for a particular disambiguation task than others. In this work, we assume that features based on such ontology segments would correlate well with other context features.

Consider, for example, the expression "to deny the visa". When choosing between two senses of 'deny' ('refuse to grant' vs. 'declare untrue'), we would like our lexical ontology to place 'visa' in the same subtree as approval, request, recognition, commendation, endorsement, etc. And indeed, WordNet places all of these, including 'visa', under the same node. However, their least common subsumer is 'message, content, subject matter, substance', which also subsumes 'statement', 'significance', etc., which would activate the other sense of 'deny'. In other words, the distinctions made at this level in the nominal hierarchy in WordNet would not be useful in disambiguating the verb 'deny', unless our model can select the appropriate nodes of the subtree rooted at the synset 'message, content, subject matter, substance'. Our model should also infer the associations between such nodes and other context relevant features that select the sense 'refuse to grant' (such as the presence of ditransitive constructions, etc.)

In this paper, we use the topic modeling approach to identify ontology-derived features that can prove useful for sense induction. Bayesian approaches to sense induction have recently been shown to perform well in the WSI task. In particular, Brody and Lapata (2009) have adapted the Latent Dirichlet Allocation (LDA) generative topic model to WSI by treating each occurrence context of an ambiguous word as a document, and the derived topics as sense-selecting context patterns represented as collections of features. They applied their model to the SemEval2007 set of ambiguous nouns, beating the best-performing system in its WSI task. Yao and Van Durme (2011) used a non-parametric Bayesian model, the Hierarchical Dirichlet Process (HDP), for the same task and showed that following the same basic assumptions, it performs comparably, with the advantage of avoiding the extra tuning for the number of senses.

We investigate the question of how well such models would perform when some knowledge of syntactic structure and semantics is added into the system, in particular, when bag-of-words features are supplemented by the knowledge-enriched syntactic features. We use the SemEval2010 WSI task data for the verbs for evaluation (Manandhar et al., 2010). This data set choice is motivated by the fact that (1) for verbs, sense-selecting context patterns often most directly depend on the nouns that occur in syntactic dependencies with them, and (2) the nominal parts of WordNet tend to have much cleaner ontological distinctions and property inheritance than, say, the verb synsets, where the subsumption hierarchy is organized according how specific the verb's manner of action is.

The choice of the SemEval2010 verb data set was motivated by the fact that SemEval2007 verb data is dominated by the most frequent sense for many target verbs, with 11 out of 65 verbs only having one sense in the combined test and training data. All verbs in the SemEval2010 verb data set have at least two senses in the data provided. The implications of this work are two-fold: (1) we confirm independently on a different data set that parametric and non-parametric models perform comparably, and outperform the current state-of-the-art methods using the baseline bag-of-words feature set (2) we show that integrating populated syntactic and ontology-based features directly into the generative model consistently leads to statistically significant improvement in accuracy. Our system outperforms both the bag-of-words baselines and the best-performing system in the SemEval2010 competition.

The remainder of the paper is organized as follows. In Section 2, we review the relevant related work. Sections 3 and 4 give the details on how the models are defined and trained, and describe the incorporated feature classes. Section 5 describes the data used to conduct the experiments. Finally, in Section 6, we describe the evaluation methods and present and discuss the experimental results.

2 Related Work

Over the past twenty years, a number of unsupervised methods for word sense induction have been developed, both for clustering contexts and for clustering word senses based on their distributional similarity (Hindle, 1990; Pereira et al., 1993; Schütze, 1998; Grefenstette, 1994; Lin, 1998; Pantel and Lin, 2002; Dorow and Widdows, 2003; Agirre et al., 2006).

One of the recent evaluations of the state of the art in word sense induction was conducted at SemEval2010 (Manandhar et al., 2010). The participant systems focused on a variety of WSI improvements including feature selection/dimensionality reduction techniques (Pedersen, 2010), experiments with bigram and cooccurrence features (Pedersen, 2010) and syntactic features (Kern et al., 2010), and increased scalability (Jurgens and Stevens, 2010).

Following the success of topic modeling in information retrieval, Boyd-Graber et al. (2007) developed an extension of the LDA model for word sense disambiguation that used WordNet walks to generate sense assignments for lexical items. Their model treated synset paths as hidden variables, with the assumption that words within the same topic will share synset paths within WordNet, i.e. each topic will be associated with walks that prefer different "neighborhoods"of WordNet. One problem with their approach is that it relies fully on the integrity of WordNet's organization, and has no way to disprefer certain segments of WordNet, nor the ability to reorganize or redefine the senses it identifies for a given lexical item.

Brody and Lapata (2009) have proposed another adaptation of the LDA generative topic model to the WSI task. Text segments that contain instances of the target word are treated as documents in the classical IR setup for the LDA. The target word's senses are then similar to the hidden topics and are associated with a probability distribution over context features.

LDA assumes that each instance has been produced by a process that generates each of its context features by picking a sense of the target word from a known set of senses and then picking a feature for the context based on a sense-specific underlying probability distribution over context features. Importantly, the same prior distribution is assumed for all the features of an instance. However for many feature classes, for example, words vs. part-of-speech tags, this is false. Thus these algorithms do not immediately adapt well to being given features from many classes.

Brody and Lapata (2009) used part-of-speech and word n-grams as well as syntactic dependencies in addition to bag-of-words features, and used a multi-layer LDA model to handle the different classes separately in different "layers", bringing them together when necessary in a weighted combination. Their best model, however, showed very similar performance to the LDA model using only bag-of-words features. Yao and Van Durme (2011) reproduced some of their LDA experiments using HDP, a non-parametric model that induces the number of topics from data, over bag-of-words context representation.

3 Methods

We applied the LDA model (Brody and Lapata, 2009) and the the HDP model (Yao and Durme, 2011) over a set of features that included populated syntactic dependencies as well as knowledge-enriched syntactic features. Note that unlike the model proposed by Boyd et al (2007), which relies fully on the on the pre-existing sense structure reflected in WordNet, under this setup, we will only incorporate the relevant information from the ontology, while allowing the senses themselves to be derived empirically from the distributional context patterns. The assumption here is that if any semantic features prove relevant for a particular target word, i.e. if they correlate well with other features characterizing the word's context patterns, they will be strongly associated with the corresponding topic.

In reality, the topics modeled by LDA and HDP may not correspond directly to senses, but may represent some subsense or supersense. In fact, the induced topics are more likely to correspond to the sense-selecting patterns, rather than the senses per se, and quite frequently the same sense may be expressed with multiple patterns. We describe how we deal with this in Section 6.1.

3.1 Model Description

The LDA model is more formally defined as follows: Consider one target word with M instances and K senses, and let the context of instance j be described by some set of N_j features from a vocabulary of size V. These may be the words around the target or could be any properties of the instance. LDA assumes that there are M probability distributions $\theta_\mathbf{j} = (\theta_{j1}, \theta_{j2}, \ldots, \theta_{jK})$, with θ_{jk} = the probability of generating sense k for instance j, and K probability distributions $\phi_\mathbf{k} = (\phi_{k1}, \phi_{k2}, \ldots, \phi_{kV})$, with ϕ_{kf} = the probability of generating feature f from sense k. This makes the probability of generating the corpus where the features for instance j are $f_{j1}, f_{j2}, \ldots, f_{jN_j}$:

$$P(\text{corpus}) = \prod_{j=1}^{M} \prod_{i=1}^{N_J} \sum_{k=1}^{K} \theta_{jk} \phi_{k f_{ji}}$$

The goal of LDA for WSI is to obtain the distribution $\theta_{\mathbf{j}^*}$ for an instance j^* of interest, as this gives each sense's probability of being picked to generate some feature in the instance, which corresponds to the probability of being the correct sense for the target word in this context.

The corpus generation process for HDP is similar to that of LDA, but obtains the document-specific sense distribution (corresponding to LDA's θ_j) via a Dirichlet Process whose base distribution is determined via another Dirichlet Process, allowing for an unfixed number of senses because the draws from the resulting sense distribution are not limited to a preset range. The concentration parameters of both Dirichlet Processes are determined via hyperparameters.

3.2 Model Training

LDA

Our process for training an LDA model uses Gibbs sampling to assign topics to each feature in each instance, utilizing GibbsLDA++ (Phan and Nguyen, 2007). Initially topics are assigned randomly and during each subsequent iteration, assignments are made by sampling from the probability distributions resulting from the last iteration. Following the previous work in applying topic-modeling to WSI, we use hyperparameters $\alpha = 0.02, \beta = 0.1$ (Brody and Lapata, 2009). We train the model using 2000 iterations of Gibbs sampling (GibbsLDA++ default). To obtain θ for an instance of interest, the inference mode initializes the training corpus with the assignments from the model and initializes new test documents with random assignments. We then run 20 iterations of Gibbs sampling on this augmented corpus. 5 models are trained for each target using the same parameters and data. This is done to reduce the effect of randomization in the training algorithms on our results. Although the randomization is also present in the inference algorithms and we do not perform more than one inference run per model.

HDP

The HDP training and inference procedures are similar to LDA, but using Gibbs sampling on topic and table assignment in a Chinese Restaurant Process. We use Chong Wang's program for HDP (Wang and Blei, 2012) running the Gibbs sampling for 1000 iterations during training and another 1000 during inference (the defaults), and using the hyperparameters suggested in previous work (Yao and Durme, 2011) of $H = 0.1, \alpha_0 \sim Gamma(0.1, 0.028), \gamma \sim Gamma(1, 0.1)$.

This software does not directly produce θ values but instead produces all assignments of words to topics. This output is used to compute

$$\theta_{jk} = \frac{\text{count(words in document j labeled k)}}{\text{count(words in document j)}}.$$

Since new topics can appear during inference, we smooth these probabilities with additive smoothing using a parameter of 0.02 to avoid the case where all words are labeled with unseen topics, which would make prediction of a sense using our evaluation methods impossible.

4 Features

We used three types of features: bag-of-words with different window sizes, populated syntactic features, and ontology-populated syntactic features. Instead of using a multi-layered LDA model, we attempt to mitigate the effects of using multiple classes of features by choosing extra features whose distributions are sufficiently similar to the bag-of-words features. We describe these classes in more detail below.

Preprocessing done on the data includes: (1) tokenization, (2) identifying stopwords, (3) stemming tokens, (4) detecting sentence boundaries, (5) tagging tokens with their parts of speech, and (6) obtaining collapsed dependencies within sentences including the target words. For tokenization, sentence boundary detection, and part-of-speech tagging, we use OpenNLP (OpenSource, 2010). We remove the stop words and stem using the Snow ball stemmer. For collapsed syntactic dependencies we use the Stanford Dependency Parser (Klein and Manning, 2003).

Bag of Words Following previous literature (Brody and Lapata, 2009), we use a 20 word window (excluding stopwords) for BOW features. In our experiments, a smaller window size failed to produce better performance.

Ontology-Based Populated Syntactic Features To capture syntactic information, we use populated dependency relations. We populate these relations with semantic information from WordNet (Miller et al., 1990) as follows. For each syntactic dependency between the target word and the context word, we locate all synsets for the context word. We then traverse the WordNet hierarchy upwards from each of these synsets, and include a feature for each node

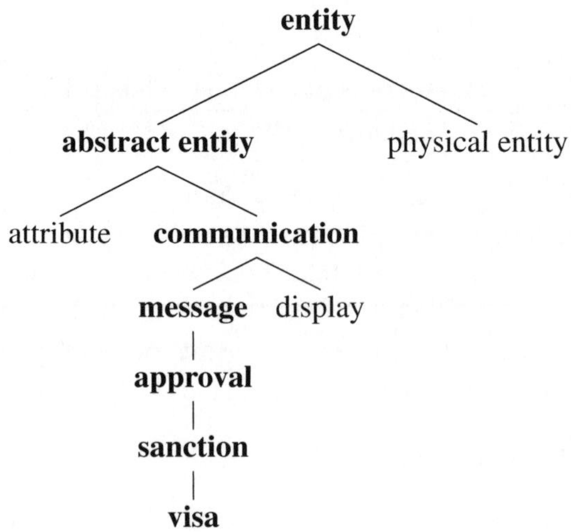

Figure 1: WordNet hierarchy path for "actor".

we visit. We use collapsed relations produced by the Stanford Dependency Parser (Klein and Manning, 2003).

For example, consider the path up the hierarchy for the word "visa", given in Figure 1. If the noun "visa" is found in direct object position of the target verb, traversing the tree to the root would produce features such as *noun-approval_dobj*, etc.

5 Data

We evaluate our methods on the 50 verb targets from the SemEval2010 dataset. The evaluation data is split into 5 mapping/test set pairs, with 60% for mapping (2179 instances) and 40% for testing (1451 instances). Each split is created randomly and independently each time, and 3354 out of 3630 instances appear in a test set at least once.

We train our topic models on unlabeled data from SemEval2010, which contains a total of 162,862 instances for all verbs. The targets "happen" and "regain" have the most and fewest instances with 11,286 and 266 respectively. We use this data to train our topic models. We limit each target to 50,000 instances for training HDP models, in order to maintain reasonable processing time.

6 Results

We show the comparisons of our systems with (1) the most-frequent-sense (MFS) (MFS in the mapping set predicted for all instances in the test set), (2) BOW baseline models, and (3) the best-performing system from SemEval2010. Since HDP performs better overall, we chose the HDP model to experiment with syntactic and ontological features. For completeness, we include results for the WordNet-populated syntactic features with the LDA model.

6.1 Evaluation Measures

Following the established practice in SemEval competitions and subsequent work (Agirre and Soroa, 2007; Manandhar et al., 2010; Brody and Lapata, 2009; Yao and Durme, 2011), we conduct supervised evaluation. A small amount of labeled data is used to map the induced topics to real-world senses; for a description of the method see (Agirre and Soroa, 2007). The resulting mapping is probabilistic; for topics $1, \ldots, K$ and senses $1, \ldots, S$, we compute the KS values

$$P(s|k) = \frac{\text{count(instances predicted k, labeled s)}}{\text{count(instances predicted k)}}.$$

Then given θ_{j^*}, we can make a better prediction for instance j^* than just assigning the most likely sense to its most likely topic. Instead, we compute

$$\text{argmax}_{s=1}^{S} \sum_{k=1}^{K} \theta_{j^*k} P(s|k),$$

the sense with the highest probability of being correct for this instance, given the topic probabilities and the KS mapping probabilities.

The supervised metrics traditionally reported include precision, recall, and F-score, but since our WSI system makes a prediction for every instance, we report accuracy throughout this section.

6.2 Cross-Validation

We use cross-validation on the mapping set to select the best system configuration. We use leave-one-out or 50-fold cross-validation, whichever has fewer folds for a given target word. The system configurations that we compare vary with respect to the following: (1) topic modeling algorithm (HDP or LDA), (2) included feature classes (bag-of-words with different window sizes, populated syntactic features, ontology-populated syntactic features), and (3) number of topics (i.e. senses) for the LDA model. The best configuration is then tested on the

Configuration	CV acc.
HDP, 20w +WN1h	**72.5%**
HDP, 20w +WN1h-limited	70.8%
HDP, 20w +Synt	71.3%
HDP, 20w (baseline)	**69.7%**
LDA, 5 senses, 20w +WN1h	71.2%
LDA, 5 senses, 20w	71.2%
LDA, 12 senses, 20w +WN1h	72.2%
LDA, 12 senses, 20w	70.2%

Table 1: Cross-validation accuracies using the SemEval2010 mapping sets.

evaluation data. Table 1 shows cross-validation results for some of the relevant configurations on the SemEval2010 dataset.

Since the evaluation data has 5 different mapping sets, one for each 60/40 split, we do cross-validation on each and average the results. We perform this process for each of our 5 trained models and again average the results.

The best HDP configuration outperforms the LDA configurations with low numbers of topics. This configuration combines the 20 closest non-stopwords bag-of-words (20w) with WordNet-populated syntactic dependencies (+WN1h) and achieves 72.5% accuracy. We evaluate two other configurations using HDP as well: 20w +WN1h-limited, which is 20w +WN1h minus those features from WordNet within 5 hops of the hierarchy's root; and 20w +Synt, which is the 20 closest non-stopwords bag-of-words plus syntactic dependencies 1 hop away from the target word populated with the stemmed token appearing there. As shown in Table 1, WordNet-based populated features do introduce some gain with respect to the syntactic features populated only at the word level. Interestingly, removing the top-level WordNet-based features, and therefore making the possible restrictions on the semantics of the dependent nouns more specific, does not lead to performance improvement.

Each topic produced by the model is a distribution over all feature types, and is comprised by a mix of bag-of-words and ontology-populated syntactic features. Each node on the path from a given synset to the root generates its own ontological feature, so when many nodes that activate the same sense have a common hypernym, that hypernym is likely to "float to the top" - become more strongly associated with the corresponding topic.

To illustrate this, consider the following two senses of the verb 'cultivate': "prepare the soil for crops" and "teach or refine". Topic 1 generated by the HDP 20w +WN1h model corresponds to the first sense and is associated with examples about cultivating land, earth, grassland, waste areas. Topic 5 generated by the same model corresponds to the second sense and is associated with examples about cultivating knowledge, understanding, habits, etc. One of the top-scoring features for Topic 1 is *location_dobj* which corresponds to the direct object position being occupied by one of the 'location' synsets, with direct hyponym nodes for 'region' and 'space' contributing the most. For topic 5, *cognition_dobj* is selected as one of the top features, with direct hyponyms for 'ability', 'process', and 'information' contributing the most.

In this best configuration, HDP produces an average of 18.6 topics, far more than the number of real-world senses. We investigated the possibility that its improvement over LDA might be due to this larger number of topics, testing the same feature combination on LDA with 12 topics. This does produce a similar accuracy, 72.2%, and the simpler bag-of-words features with 12 topics yield an accuracy drop to 70.2%, similar to the drop seen between HDP 20w +WN1h and HDP 20w.

6.3 Evaluation Set Results

For the five SemEval2010 test sets, senses are assigned slightly differently than in cross-validation. Instead of averaging over five models trained per target, for each instance, we predict the sense assigned by the majority of these models.

Table 2 shows the comparison of the configuration with the best cross-validation accuracy (HDP, 20w +WN1h) against the following: (1) MSF baseline, (2) the baseline bag-of-words model (3) the results obtained on this data set by the best-performing SemEval2010 system using supervised evaluation, Duluth-Mix-Narrow-Gap from the University of Minnesota Duluth (Manandhar et al., 2010). The HDP model with knowledge-enriched features obtains the best accuracy of 73.3%. For comparison, we also show results for the LDA model with 12 topics that performed well in cross-validation.

System	Accuracy
MFS	66.7 %
HDP, 20w +WN1h	**73.3%**
HDP, 20w (baseline)	71.2%
LDA, 12 senses, 20w +WN1h	72.5%
LDA, 12 senses, 20w	71.1%
Duluth-Mix-Narrow-Gap	68.6%

Table 2: Test set accuracies, SemEval2010 verbs

The improvements obtained by the best configuration are statistically significant by paired two-tailed t-test, treating each of the 3354 distinct test instances as separate samples. We consider a system's prediction on one such instance to be the sense it predicted in the majority of the test sets in which the instance appears. Significance levels are as follows:

- The best HDP configuration (20w +WN1h) vs. Duluth-Mix-Narrow-Gap: $p < 0.0001$
- The best HDP configuration (20w +WN1h) vs. HDP 20w: $p < 0.001$
- 12-sense LDA configuration 20w +WN1h vs. Duluth-Mix-Narrow-Gap: $p < 0.0001$
- 12-sense LDA configuration 20w +WN1h vs. 12-sense LDA 20w: $p < 0.05$.

7 Conclusion

We have presented a system that uses an adaptation of two Bayesian topic modeling algorithms to the task of word sense induction. Both the parametric and the non-parametric versions, when enriched with WordNet-based populated syntactic features, outperform the baseline bag-of-words models as well as the current state of the art in the WSI task for verbs. The next step for this system is an improved integration of knowledge-based features that would not require assuming a similar distribution on different feature types.

References

Eneko Agirre and Aitor Soroa. 2007. Semeval-2007 task 02: Evaluating word sense induction and discrimination systems. In *Proceedings of the Fourth International Workshop on Semantic Evaluations (SemEval-2007)*, pages 7–12.

Jordan Boyd-Graber, David Blei, and Xiaojin Zhu. 2007. A topic model for word sense disambiguation. In *Proceedings of the 2007 Joint Conference on Empirical Methods in Natural Language Processing and Computational Natural Language Learning (EMNLP-CoNLL)*, pages 1024–1033.

Samuel Brody and Mirella Lapata. 2009. Bayesian word sense induction. In *Proceedings of the 12th Conference of the European Chapter of the Association for Computational Linguistics*, EACL '09, pages 103–111, Stroudsburg, PA, USA. Association for Computational Linguistics.

M. Carpuat and D. Wu. 2007. Improving statistical machine translation using word sense disambiguation. In *Proc. of EMNLP-CoNLL*, pages 61–72.

Y. S. Chan, H. T. Ng, and D. Chiang. 2007. Word sense disambiguation improves statistical machine translation. In *Proc. of ACL*, pages 33–40, Prague, Czech Republic, June.

B. Dorow and D. Widdows. 2003. Discovering corpus-specific word-senses. In *Proceedings of the 10th Conference of the European Chapter of the Association for Computational Linguistics*, pages Conference Companion pp. 79–82, Budapest, Hungary, April.

Christiane Fellbaum. 2010. Wordnet. *Theory and Applications of Ontology: Computer Applications*, pages 231–243.

David Jurgens and Keith Stevens. 2010. Hermit: Flexible clustering for the semeval-2 wsi task. In *Proceedings of the 5th International Workshop on Semantic Evaluation*, pages 359–362, Uppsala, Sweden, July. Association for Computational Linguistics.

Roman Kern, Markus Muhr, and Michael Granitzer. 2010. Kcdc: Word sense induction by using grammatical dependencies and sentence phrase structure. In *Proceedings of the 5th International Workshop on Semantic Evaluation*, pages 351–354, Uppsala, Sweden, July. Association for Computational Linguistics.

Dan Klein and Christopher D. Manning. 2003. Accurate unlexicalized parsing. In *Proceedings of the 41st Annual Meeting on Association for Computational Linguistics - Volume 1*, ACL '03, pages 423–430, Stroudsburg, PA, USA. Association for Computational Linguistics.

Suresh Manandhar, Ioannis Klapaftis, Dmitriy Dligach, and Sameer Pradhan. 2010. Semeval-2010 task 14: Word sense induction & disambiguation. In *Proceedings of the 5th International Workshop on Semantic Evaluation(SemEval)*, pages 63–68, Uppsala, Sweden, July. Association for Computational Linguistics.

George A. Miller, Richard Beckwith, Christiane Fellbaum, Derek Gross, and Katherine Miller. 1990. Wordnet: An on-line lexical database. *International Journal of Lexicography*, 3:235–244.

OpenSource. 2010. Opennlp: $http : //opennlp.sourceforge.net/$.

Martha Palmer, Daniel Gildea, and Paul Kingsbury. 2005. The proposition bank: An annotated corpus of semantic roles. *Computational Linguistics*, 31(1):71–106.

P. Pantel and D. Lin. 2002. Discovering word senses from text. In *Proceedings of ACM SIGKDD02*.

Ted Pedersen. 2010. Duluth-wsi: Senseclusters applied to the sense induction task of semeval-2. In *Proceedings of the 5th International Workshop on Semantic Evaluation*, pages 363–366, Uppsala, Sweden, July. Association for Computational Linguistics.

Xuan-Hieu Phan and Cam-Tu Nguyen. 2007. Gibbslda++: A c/c++ implementation of latent dirichlet allocation (lda).

P. Resnik. 2006. Word sense disambiguation in NLP applications. In E. Agirre and P. Edmonds, editors, *Word Sense Disambiguation: Algorithms and Applications*. Springer.

J. Ruppenhofer, M. Ellsworth, M. Petruck, C. Johnson, and J. Scheffczyk. 2006. *FrameNet II: Extended Theory and Practice*.

H. Schütze. 1998. Automatic word sense discrimination. *Computational Linguistics*, 24(1):97–123.

Chong Wang and David M. Blei. 2012. A Split-Merge MCMC Algorithm for the Hierarchical Dirichlet Process, January.

Xuchen Yao and Benjamin Van Durme. 2011. Nonparametric bayesian word sense induction. In *Graph-based Methods for Natural Language Processing*, pages 10–14. The Association for Computer Linguistics.

Informativeness Constraints and Compositionality

Olga Batiukova
Spanish Philology Department
Autonomous University of Madrid
Cantoblanco, Madrid, Spain
volha.batsiukova@domain

James Pustejovsky
Computer Science Departament
Brandeis University
Waltham, Massachusetts, USA
jamesp@cs.brandeis.edu

Abstract

In this paper we examine the role that compositional mechanisms and lexical semantics play in the determination of *informativeness* at the phrasal and clausal level. While the computation of the "relevance" of an utterance is largely determined by pragmatic factors (such as quantity), we argue that phrasal informativeness can, in many cases, be computed compositionally and independently of pragmatics. To illustrate this, we focus on the well-documented contrast between predicative and derived participial modificational constructions in English (*build a house* results in well-formed sentences, while **a built house* does not). In our analysis, informativeness within an NP is computed in terms of minimal model generation (Blackburn and Bos, 2008), using the semantics associated with the qualia of the head noun; that is, modification is informative whenever a qualia value is not satisfied in all models.

1 Introduction

This paper studies the contrast in acceptability of certain past participle-noun (PP-N) modification constructions and their corresponding verb-noun predicates (V-N), as illustrated in (1):

(1) a. buy a ticket vs. *a bought ticket
b. eat a sandwich vs. *an eaten sandwich
c. feel sympathy vs. *a felt sympathy
d. give an answer vs. *a given answer
e. hear a noise vs. *a heard noise
f. make a mistake vs. *a made mistake
g. play the piano vs. *a played piano
h. read the newspaper vs. *a read newspaper
i. win the prize vs. *a won prize
j. write a book vs. *a written book
k. see the movie vs. *a seen movie

This is surprising, given the semantic similarity between verb argument selection and the corresponding modification operation. For example, both elements in the pairs below are well-formed.

(2) a. paint a house vs. a painted house
b. spill the milk vs. the spilled milk
c. poison the food vs. poisoned food

The question immediately arises as to why such a distinction in grammaticality should exist, as well as what the constraints affecting the well-formedness of these constructions might be. This topic has been approached from two different perspectives in the literature, which we review briefly before presenting our proposal: (a) an aspect-based approach; and (b) a pragmatically-determined informativeness approach.

According to the aspect-based approach (argued for in Bresnan (1995), Langacker (1991), Valin (1990), Embick (2004)), a PP-N construction is grammatical if the participle denotes the resultant state of the verb from which it is derived. However, most unacceptable combinations in (1) meet this requirement: they are either achievements (*given answer, made mistake*) or accomplishments (*bought ticket, eaten sandwich, written book*).

Grimshaw and Vikner (1993) introduce an additional requirement in their study of obligatory adjuncts in passives: each of the subevents of the event structure of the verb has to be identified by an argument. The only overt argument of PP-N constructions is usually the theme, which is involved in both subevents if the event is complex (e.g., *the ruined shirt* is an accomplishment composed of a process and a resultant state, both of which are related to *shirt*). Creation predicates are one exception, because the theme is related to the resultant state only (the object does not exist until the event is completed). This is why a second element, an adjunct, is needed to identify the process subevent, e.g., *an expertly written book*.

Under this assumption, in the rest of the examples in (1) one argument should be enough to guarantee the acceptability of the construction, which is obviously not what we get.[1] Grimshaw

[1] See Jung (1997) and Ackerman and Goldberg (1996) for a detailed criticism of aspect-based approaches.

and Vikner (1993) do mention an alternative approach to this issue in the conclusion of their study, where they suggest that the obligatory adjunct phenomenon is a matter of satisfying the requirement that one 'say something'.[2] This 'say something' requirement has been interpreted in Jung (1997) as a general *pragmatic* condition on presupposition and assertion in passives: "The predicate must assert more than what is presupposed by the subject". As definite NP subjects bear an existential presupposition, the reference to their creation violates the *Say Something Condition. Any* adjunct providing new information will qualify as compulsory in this situation. Compare the examples in (3):

(3) a. *A house* was built / * *This house* was built / *This house* was built *to our specification.*
b. *A picture* was taken / * *This picture* was taken / *This picture* was taken *to my liking.*

Following similar assumptions, the account by Ackerman and Goldberg (1996) is also pragmatically motivated. It is based on the Gricean maxim of Quantity ('make your contribution as informative as required for the current purposes of exchange; do not make your contribution more informative than is required') and Horn's R-principle ('make your contribution necessary; say no more than you must') (Levinson (2000) and Horn (1996)). They claim that "adjectival past participles (APP) can only occur if they are construable as predicating an informative state of the head noun referent". This claim is based on two constraints:

1. **Non-redundancy constraint**: If the referent of the head noun, N, implies a property P as part of its frame-semantic or encyclopedic knowledge, then the APP is not allowed to simply designate P; it must be further qualified.
2. **Paradigmatic Informativeness constraint**: An APP phrase is not felicitous if it is based on a superordinate level verb which contrasts with semantically more specific predicates (troponyms).

The non-redundancy constraint clearly accounts for cases in (1): all the newspapers are meant to be read, sympathy only arises when it is felt somehow, and so on. The addition of an adverb (4), an adjectival or nominal modifier ((5) and (6)), as well as certain morphological elements (derivational affixes, as in (7)) makes the property denoted by the participle more specific and renders the whole construction informative:

(4) a. *bought ticket vs. {recently / illegally / their already / the most} bought ticket
b. *eaten sandwich vs. {quickly / half / partially} eaten sandwich
c. *felt sympathy vs. {suddenly / heart / deep / instantly} felt sympathy
d. *given answer vs. {previously / frequently / commonly / the above} given answer
e. *heard noise vs. {barely / abnormally / repeatedly} heard noise
f. *made mistake vs. {stupidly / easily / often / widely} made mistake
g. *played piano vs. {beautifully / passionately / badly / gently} played piano
h. *read newspaper vs. {carefully / widely / the most} read newspaper
i. *won prize vs. {easily / rightly / fraudulently} won prize
j. *written book vs. {well / poorly / engangingly / intelligently / newly / vividly} written book
k. *seen movie vs. {last / little / never before / rarely} seen movie

(5) a. *manufactured aircraft vs. {contemporary / American} manufactured aircraft
b. *published books vs. {recent / foreign} published books

(6) a. ??trained people vs. science-trained people
b. *shaped fish vs. angle-shaped fish

(7) ??arranged rendezvous vs. pre-arranged rendezvous

The Paradigmatic Informativeness constraint is designed to explain the cases in (8), where a verb denoting a particular manner of performing the action is preferred to the less specific superordinate verb:

(8) a. **cut meat* vs. *sliced / chopped meat*
b. **told secret* vs. *disclosed / confessed secret*
c. **given funds* vs. *donated / sacrificed funds*

Note, however, that some of these examples are odd even if we add adverbial modifiers:

(9) a. ?quickly told secret
b. ?recently given funds
c. ?secretly taken shirt

While both constraints proposed in Ackerman and Goldberg (1996) seem to be on the right track, the notions they are based on (frame-semantic and encyclopedic knowledge) are left rather vague. Many things can be ascribable to encyclopedic knowledge. As for frame-semantic content, this can extend to an unrestricted repertoire of specific semantic and situational parameters (roles and otherwise). This vagueness and unrestrictedness makes it difficult to formalize both constraints and how to apply them .

In a move to remedy this vagueness, Goldberg and Ackerman (2001) propose a more general requirement for modification and predication constructions: they must be informative in the conversational context. One way the utterance can be informative is by containing a focus (provided by negation, modality, tense, aspect, adjunct, indefinite subject, etc.) that conveys something non-presupposed.

(10) a. The house was built.
b. The house was not built. NEGATION
c. The house {should/might} be built. MODALITY

[2] D. Pesetsky, p.c.

d. The house {will be / has been} built. TENSE/ASPECT
e. The house was built {last year}. ADJUNCT
f. A house has been built. INDEFINITE

As the adjectives and participles in modification constructions have less linguistic information associated with them than verbs (there is neither tense nor modality, and the array of aspectual interpretations is very limited), it is more difficult to provide a focus for a successful assertion (relative acceptability is indicated by '$>$'):

(11) a. #This house was built. > #a built house
b. #That book was read. > #the read book
c. #The television progam was watched. > #the watched program

While we acknowledge that much of the "informativeness" of lexical choice in an utterance can be determined only after most contextual variables are already fixed, we argue that there are *compositional aspects* to the calculation of informativeness that have not been adequately appreciated.

In the remainder of the paper, we show that a significant part of what is called "informativeness" can be accounted for compositionally. Following Konrad (2004) and Blackburn and Bos (2008), we utilize minimal model generation as part of the compositional computation, where we assume that a linguistic expression should be *consistent* within a discourse and *informative* relative to what is known. In model-theoretic terms, *consistent* means 'satisfied in at least some models or situations' (cf. the formal definition in the next section). Within the compositional construction of an utterance itself, we can compute consistency as type satisfaction (Pustejovsky, 2013), as assumed within typed functional languages. An expression is informative on the other hand, if it is 'not satisfied in all models and with all assignments'. Our treatment of informativeness is based on the semantics provided by the *qualia*, a structured representation of the meaning parameters encoded by lexical items (Pustejovsky, 1995): that is, whenever a qualia value is not attested in all possible situations involving a given expression (i.e. not satisfied in all models), the expression will be judged informative. We outline the basic ideas behind this approach in the section below.

2 General Hypothesis and Predictions

Our starting assumption relates to the definition of semantic predication and argument selection. We believe that the contrast in acceptability between predication and modification constructions involving the same elements (cf. the examples in (1)) can be better accounted for if we assume that both constructions are instances of semantic predication. The main difference is that in a V-N construction the verb is the predicate projecting the argument structure, imposing selectional requirements on its arguments, while in a modification construction the noun is the head, yet it projects its argument structure as well. A brief motivation of this step is in order.

Verbs and deverbal nominals are traditionally considered as prototypical relational items bearing the predicative force: they select for certain kinds of elements (arguments) compatible with them, which complete and specify their meaning. Chomsky (1993), Goldberg (1998), Dowty (1979), Croft (2005), among others, assume a verb-centered bias toward how arguments are identified in the phrase and sentence, be they verbs or relational nouns.

As is well known, the Generative Lexicon focuses to open up the channel of relation identification and argument selection through the introduction of non-verb based argument associations, i.e., the *Qualia Structure roles* associated with the nouns constituting arguments and adjuncts in the sentence. The four parameters encoded in the Qualia Structure are AGENTIVE (factors involved in the origin or creation of entities and events, such as *build* for *house*), CONSTITUTIVE (internal constituency of the whole, such as constituent parts of material entities), FORMAL (the distinctive features of entities, such as spatial orientation, size, shape, dimensionality, color, etc., and the taxonomic relations, e.g., a *house* is a *building*), and TELIC (purpose and function of entities and events, such as *reading* for *book*).

The Qualia Structure can be regarded as similar in many respects to the Argument Structure for verbs. In a fashion similar to Argument Structure realization, the Qualia roles do not need to be expressed overtly in order to be accessible for interpretation. Just as the verb *eat* presupposes that its direct object denote a kind of food even when not overtly expressed, nouns may encode "hidden" relations along with unexpressed arguments; e.g., the relation of inalienable possession denoted by the noun *hand*, as being a part of a *body*, to mention just one of the syntactically relevant semantic relationships. Artifactual nominals, in addition, refer to the event which brought them about and to the activity they are meant for: e.g., *house* presupposes a creation event, as well as a functional value associated with its purpose.

As we anticipated at the end of the previous section, qualia are crucially involved in the compositional calculation of consistency and informativeness of linguistic expressions. A consistent utterance describes a realizable situation, that is, representable as a first-order formula satified in at least some models. All the arguments must be consistent with the predicate, in the sense of "semantically compatible" (e.g., *male* is consistent with the semantics of the noun *bachelor*, while *married* is not). This applies to both arguments (in the strict sense of the term) and adjuncts. Inconsistent combinations should not be present in natural data. Informative utterances are a subset of consistent utterances, whose denotation is ruled out in at least some situations. Hence, while both *male* and *funny* are consistent with *bachelor*, only *funny bachelor* is an informative phrase, since not all bachelors are funny.

In typed functional languages, consistency is defined as *type satisfaction*: the argument must have the type required by the predicate or function. In GL, four predicative compositional mechanisms have been identified: *type matching* or *pure selection*, *accommodation*, *coercion by introduction* and *coercion by exploitation* (Pustejovsky, 2011; Asher and Pustejovsky, 2013). *Type matching* takes place when the type required by the verb is directly satisfied by the argument (e.g. *read a book*: *book* is $phys \bullet info$ and *read* is $phys \bullet info \rightarrow (e \rightarrow t))$.[3] *Accommodation* allows combining a predicate with an argument whose hypernym satisfies its selectional requirements through type inheritance (e.g. *the beer spoiled*: *spoil* is phys$\otimes_T \tau$ $\rightarrow$*t*, and it can be combined with *beer*: $liquid \otimes_T drink$, because $liquid \subseteq phys$ and $drink \subseteq \tau$). *Coercion* mechanisms are activated when the type a function requires is imposed on the argument type. In these cases, the qualia act as type shifting operators, allowing an expression to satisfy new typing environments through *introduction* or *exploitation*. In *enjoy a coffee*, for example, both mechanisms are consecutively activated: *enjoy* needs a direct object typed as *event*, and *coffee* must first be wrapped with the type *event* through introduction (*coffee*:event), and afterwards the value in the telic role of *coffee* is exploited to turn it into *coffee:drink* event.

To make our computation of consistency and informativeness more explicit, we adopt a strategy of *model generation* (Blackburn and Bos, 2008; Konrad, 2004).[4] The consistency of an expression, $\lambda x[F(x)](A)$, after function application of F over A, can be checked by determining whether the set of first-order formulas resulting from the application are satisfiable (i.e., there is a model $\mathcal{M}$ corresponding to this set). The informativeness of a function application can be similarly defined: a function application, $\lambda x[F(x)](A)$, is informative if and only if the set of first-order formulas resulting from the application is not satisfied in all models, $\mathcal{M}_i$.

We are now in position to take a closer look at the informative contribution of consistent arguments to the semantics of the resulting expression. Clearly, *non-required* arguments (adjuncts) are always informative, since they contribute additional information not deducible from the predicate meaning. *Required* arguments are a necessary part of the logical form of the predicate, but they may be left unexpressed in syntax for different reasons, due to anaphoric binding for example. Here we are interested in required arguments whose semantic content is incorporated in the predicate, i.e. the *default* arguments of the classical GL (Pustejovsky, 1995). These arguments can only appear when their denotation is informative with respect to the head, i.e., when there is a model and assignment where the resulting expression is not true. When uninformative, they are left unexpressed or *shadowed* by the predicate.

Shadowed arguments are assigned a very general interpretation, which has the same level of specificity of the semantic type imposed by the predicate. For instance, the default argument of *eat* is interpreted out of context as 'something eadible' (indefinite and non-specific) rather than a specific kind of food, and the default way of coming into being of *a sheep* is *to be born* rather than *cloned*.

The asymmetry in informativeness-determined acceptability of V-N predicative constructions and PP-N modification constructions emerges when the nominal argument is required by the verb and is informative with respect to it, but the verb (its

[3]The following notation is used in this paragraph: τ and T refer to the telic role, and $\bullet$ (the dot) and $\otimes$ (the tensor) are type constructors. The dot builds the *dot objects*, such as *book* above, and the tensor introduces agentive and telic information to the head type to derive artifactual types, e.g. *beer*.

[4]We discuss the details of the mechanism elsewhere, Pustejovsky and Batiukova (forthcoming).

participial form) is a default argument of the noun, and it fails to be informative: *eat a sandwich* is informative because many other things can be eaten (i.e., *sandwich* is more specific than the type selected by *eat*, which is FOOD). At the same time, *eaten sandwich* is uninformative because all the sandwiches are meant to be eaten: *eat* is the default argument (or *default telic*, in terms of qualia) of *sandwich*, it is uninformative with respect to the nominal head and therefore must be shadowed.

Even though the semantic mechanisms underlying predication and modification are different, we suggest that the same compositional principles are at play as far as consistency and informativeness of the argument with respect to the syntactic head is concerned. Predication is typically viewed as function application, whereby the predicate is applied to an argument in order to obtain a truth value. In the classical GL, modifying adjectives have been analyzed as typed functions applied to a particular quale of the head noun by means of *selective binding* or *subselection*. For example, *good* targets specifically the event description encoded in the telic role, and *long* can refer to one of the dimensions of a physical object or to the duration of the event referred to in one of the qualia of the head noun:

(12) a. *good teacher*: a teacher who teaches well; *a good knife*: a knife that cuts well
b. *long shadow*: a shadow having greater extension than usual; *long vowel*: a vowel whose pronunciation has a certain duration

Modifications introduced in recent versions of the theory suggest that the selectional mechanisms involved in verbal constructions can be applied to adjectival modification as well. In both kinds of constructions, type adjustment is guided by the *Head Typing Principle*, according to which the typing of the head must be preserved in any composition rule (Asher and Pustejovsky, 2013).

In both modification and predication constructions, the argument must be informative with respect to the syntactic head, hence the degree of informativeness of the construction is crucially determined by the mechanism involved in the combination of both elements: *type matching* gives rise to expressions with a very low degree of informativeness (which can even be zero or nonexistent), since the semantics of the argument is largely included in the meaning of the predicate. The compositional mechanisms of *accommodation* and *introduction* are always informative, the former less than the latter, since the argument is basically a subtyped version of the required type. As far as coercion is concerned, *introduction* is always informative, since the argument is wrapped with a new type, not entailed by argument's semantics. Note that *exploitation* is never inherently informative, since the semantic content is entailed by the argument's semantics.

From what has been said in this section, we can make the following generalizations and predictions, which will be tested in the following sections:

- The degree of informativeness of the PP-N combinations must be determined compositionally: the same modifier can be redundant or informative depending on the semantics of the head noun.
- Acceptable PP-N combinations cannot refer to the default qualia values of the head noun, such as physical parameters or internal constituency of the denoted entity. In addition, artifact-denoting nouns should not be compatible with modifiers referring to default function or origin.
- Whenever a priori uninformative PP-N combinations appear in natural data, this is due to the intervention of one of the rescue mechanisms: (1) the *default informative mechanism* is the contrastive reading, which presupposes a binary partition of the set of discourse elements (e.g. a BUILT *house* as opposed to non-existent or partially built houses)[5] and (2) the presence of an additional modifier attached to the construction, as in (4).

3 Source of data

The data analyzed in this study were extracted from the enTenTen12 corpus (using Word Sketch, cf. Kilgarriff et al. (2004)) and supplemented by introspective data. The search queries were defined for past participles followed by a noun. Two types of sequences were filtered out in the initial and the final position, respectively: the auxiliary *have*, to discard the present perfect forms, and postponed nouns, which give rise to compounds (as in *associated e-mail address*). Two types of forms were obtained this way: adjectival and participial deverbal *-ed* forms (e.g., *baked, broken, employed, seen*, etc.), and denominal adjectival forms ending in *-ed*, which will be referred to as *pseudo-participles*: *winged* (as in *winged aircraft*), *sanded* (as in *sanded dust*), etc. The decision of including deverbal adjectives along with true participles was motivated by the fact that the

[5] A reviewer points out that the possibility of contrastive interpretation for uninformative constructions indicates that pragmatics ultimately determines whether an expression is informative or not. We believe that this is not the case, since lexical semantics and pragmatics operate on different levels: pragmatics can not explain why certain word combinations (e.g. *eated sandwich*) are uninformative, because it has no access to the internal structure of words, but it can make them acceptable in context by expanding the universe of discourse (e.g. by including the non-consumed sandwiches therein).

limit between these two categories is not clearly defined in many cases. As a matter of fact, the same item in a similar distribution was classifed in enTenTen12 as a past participle in some instances and as an adjective in others (cf. *illustrated*, *damaged*, *introduced*, etc.). We also included the denominal derivatives, since the exact categorial nature of the prenominal modifier is not crucial for us. The main goal is to identify the constraints on informativeness operating in modification constructions.

In this study we compare nouns differing with respect to two sets of features, *natural / artifactual* and *count / mass*: *water, dust, sand* (natural, mass), *wine* (artifact, mass), *tree* (natural, count), *aircraft* (artifact, count). A total of 3350 PP-N pairs were extracted for *tree*, 777 for *sand*, 1241 for *dust*, 9350 for *water*, 3098 for *aircraft* and 7743 for *wine*. The annotation of the extracted pairs involved judging the grammaticality of the PP-N constructions without additional modifiers (of the kind illustrated in (4)-(7)), annotating the PP modifiers as default and non-default, and identifying the qualia roles they bind. For space reasons, only a small sample of all the attested PP-N combinations is explicitly referred to in what follows. We are particularly interested in the behavior of the PPs that bind one of the qualia roles, in order to test the hypothesis of *qualia informativeness* as formulated above: the modifier can not refer to the default qualia values of the head unless subtyped or given a contrastive reading.

4 Qualia Informativeness: Formal and Constitutive

All the nouns in our sample are compatible with PPs referring to the distinguishing physical properties of the denoted entities, whenever these properties are not default. *Colored* and *shaped* refer to a default attribute of most physical objects, therefore they need to be subtyped to be informative:

(13) a. *(deeply / garnet / beautifully) colored wine
b. *(naturally / white, brightly) colored sand
c. *(red / mud / orange / non-) colored dust
d. *(green / brightly / unusually) colored tree
e. *(white / vibrantly / oddly) colored aircraft
f. *(nicely / strangely / beautifully) shaped tree

If there is no modifier, *colored* is interpreted as 'artificially or unusually colored' for natural entities (*sand*, *dust*, and *tree*). This is the only possible interpretation of *colored water*, too, but for a different reason: *water* lacks the color attribute, therefore it is always informative.

(14) a. For this you may need colored sand
b. small quantities of what looks like colored dust
c. consider buying a colored tree and decorating it with dazzling lights
d. Allow each egg to stay in the colored water for increasingly more time

The same can be said about PPs referring to the internal constituency of both naturals and artifactuals: default constitutive attributes are shadowed unless subtyped:

(15) a. *(suitably / properly / similarly / specially / ADS-B) equipped aircraft
b. *(wide / narrow) bodied aircraft
c. *(full / light / heavy) bodied wine [6]
d. *(large / goof / coarse) grained sand
e. *(un- / well / strongly / firmly) rooted tree
f. *(thickly / fully / sparsely /low) branched tree

The default argument can only appear unmodified if it yields a contrastive interpretation. The following example, for instance, can only be interpreted as 'branched tree as opposed to trees without branches':

(16) in the shape of a branched tree

Combinations with non-default constitutives are informative, hence acceptable: not all aircrafts have wings (e.g. the helicopters do not) and not trees have leafs (e.g. coniferous trees do not).

(17) a. winged aircraft
b. leafed tree

5 Qualia Informativeness: Agentive

Markedness for origin and function is a prominent part of the lexical semantics of artifactuals as opposed to natural types: artifacts are entities created with a specific purpose or as a result of a purpose-driven activity. The default agentive value encoded in the lexical entry of artifactual nominals must be further specified in order to yield an informative construction:

(18) a. *(poorly / locally / well / excellently / sustainably / your own) made wine[7]
b. *(mass / commercialy / exclusively / locally) produced wine
c. *(Soviet / commercially) made aircraft
d. *(newly / technically /recently / fully) developed aircraft
e. *(commercially / domestically) produced aircraft

The same holds for metonymic interpretations, as in (19): strictly speaking, wine does not grow, but the grapes do (i.e., *grown* does not bind the agentive of *wine* directly, but through consecutive applications of *exploitation* of the agentive: wine is made of grapes or grape juice, which in turn come into existence by the process of growing).

(19) *(locally / organically) grown wine

[6] When applied to *wine*, *bodied* does not refer to its internal structure or ingredients. Rather, it describes the taste.

[7] *Made wine* can refer to a specific kind of alcoholic beverage, different from wine.

When the participle describes a specific, non-default way of creating the artifact, the combination is informative:

(20) Grahm defines this as a crafted wine.

Unlike artifacts, natural kinds are underspecified for origin. However, it can be referred to explicitly with the same restrictions as for artifacts.

(21) a. air-born dust
b. melted water
c. *(farm / seed / field / container) grown tree [8]

When naturally-occurring entities are produced artificially, the reference to origin becomes informative (by the mechanism of *introduction*, which always generates informative combinations, as argued in section 2):

(22) a. {manufactured / produced} sand
b. produced water
c. {ready / badly} made tree
d. {created / planted} tree

6 Qualia Informativeness: Telic

Following our hypothesis stated above, the activity associated with the telic quale of an object, when used in the PP-N construction, should be (modally) uninformative relative to the head.

(23) a. *(locally) eaten meat
b. *(rarely) driven car
c. *(seldom) watched film

We can account for this by constructing a minimal modal model, capturing the modal subordination inherent in the Telic value. Minimal model construction can reflect the modal subordination inherent in the telic role, following Blackburn and Bos (2008).[9] Informally, this says that the bare participial modifiers in (23) are uninformative, relative to the minimal modal models generated from the telic values for each of the respective head nouns. According to this analysis, artifact-denoting nouns in general should not be compatible with default telic arguments. Again, the prediction seems to be borne out, as seen in (24).

(24) a. *(commonly / widely / most often) drunk wine
b. *(remotely / carelessly / frequently / previously) flown aircraft

Natural kinds are underspecified for function (the telic role). However, they can be routinely recategorized to refer to some kind of conventionalized use, as seen in *drinking water*, *eadible fruit*, etc. These combinations are possible due to *qualia introduction*, and hence their informativeness. In (25), *used water* and *used sand* are interpreted as 'used before for human activity, not clean'. *Used tree*, in turn, refers to the Christmas tree when there is no modifier:

(25) a. The used water is fed back into the source for reheating.
b. There is potential for used sand to contain toxic or harmful ingredients.
c. Make it a resolution this new year to keep your used tree out of a landfill.

Our hypothesis predicts an inverse relationship between the degree of lexical-semantic specificity of different groups of nominals and the range of modifiers they are compatible with: since the artifactual types have more lexical-semantic information associated with them than the naturals, they are expected to reject a greater number of modifiers due to the informativeness constraint. This prediction can be tested statistically by calculating what percentage of PP-N combinations require an additional modifier in order to be informative. Although a much larger data sample is needed to get reliable results, we can say that this prediction is borne out for the six nominals examined here. The percentage of PP-N pairs with an additional modifier is higher when the head is an artifactual type: *tree*-31.43%, *sand*-31.02%, *dust*-22.08%, *water*-19.05%, *aircraft*-44.19%, *wine*-34.94%.

7 Conventionalized Attributes

A significant portion of what we know about events and their associated participants is not encoded linguistically (i.e., it does not affect the syntactic behavior of lexical items) and is not directly encoded in the lexical structures (the argument structure, the event structure or the qualia structure). Some aspects of such information, however, may be prominent both cognitively and statistically. This is what is called *conventionalized attributes* in Pustejovsky and Jezek (2008) or *Generalized Event Knowledge* in a recent trend in psycholinguistics (McRae and Matsuki, 2009). Here are some examples:

(26) a. *(moderately) priced wine
b. *(high / top) rated wine
c. *(full / heavy / light) bodied wine
d. *(strategically / conveniently) placed tree
e. *(well / professionally / badly) maintained aircraft

These attributes seem to behave similarly to true arguments: whenever a conventionalized attribute is entailed by the semantics of the head noun, it must be shadowed unless subtyped.

8 Data Summary

The following tables summarize the cases discussed in sections 4-6, with some additional corpus examples added for illustrative purposes. Even though only a small sample of all the analyzed data is reflected here, the validity of the overall predicted pattern has been confirmed in a thorough manual data analysis: default modifiers can

[8] This example is acceptable without modifier if *grown* refers to the size of the tree rather than to its origin.

[9] See Pustejovsky and Batiukova (forthcoming) for more details.

only appear without an adjunct when the sentence has a contrastive reading or as a consequence of coercion by introduction.

The following types of modifiers are included in the second column for all the qualia roles ('F/C' means 'formal/constitutive', 'A' 'agentive', and 'T' 'telic'): modified defaults, unmodified defaults with a contastive or coerced interpretation, and non-default subtyped modifiers.

Qualia	PP Modifier	Examples
F/C	Modified default	*colored, shaped, rooted, branched, formed, headed, crowned*
	Contr./C-E default	*colored, branched, curved*
	Subtyped	*leafed, unrooted*
A	Modified default	
	Contr./C-E default	*grown, made, created, planted, cultivated, cloned*
	Subtyped	
T	Modified default	
	Contr./C-E default	*used, harvested*
	Subtyped	

Table 1: *Tree*

Qualia	PP Modifier	Examples
F/C	Modified default	*colored, grained*
	Contr./C-E default	*colored*
	Subtyped	*bleached*
A	Modified default	
	Contr./C-E default	*manufactured, produced, excavated, eroded, obtained*
	Subtyped	
T	Modified default	
	Contr./C-E default	*used*
	Subtyped	

Table 2: *Sand*

Qualia	PP Modifier	Examples
F/C	Modified default	*colored*
	Contr./C-E default	*colored*
	Subtyped	*embedded, sanded, tinged, petrified*
A	Modified default	
	Contr./C-E default	*generated, manufactured*
	Subtyped	*air-born*
T	Modified default	
	Contr./C-E default	
	Subtyped	

Table 3: *Dust*

Qualia	PP Modifier	Examples
F/C	Modified default	
	Contr./C-E default	*colored, scented, flavored, atomized, crystallized*
	Subtyped	
A	Modified default	
	Contr./C-E default	*produced, harvested, extracted*
	Subtyped	*melted*
T	Modified default	
	Contr./C-E default	*used, utilized, ingested*
	Subtyped	

Table 4: *Water*

9 Conclusion

The goal of this paper has been to prove that the notion of informativeness (traditionally ascribed to the pragmatic domain and not sufficiently formalized before in the literature) can be accounted for compositionally at the phrasal and clausal level, and that the degree of informativeness of a given expression can be calculated by combining the model generation strategy with some of the basic notions of GL: first and foremost, the values provided by the qualia structure, as well as the GL typology of arguments (including *default* and *shadowed*). We suggested that, for a construction to be acceptable, it must be *consistent* (realizable in at least some situations) and *informative* (not satisfied in at least some situations). The contribution of an argument to the construction is only informative if it does not refer to an inherent property of the syntactic head (be it a verb, as in predicative constructions, or a noun, as in modification constructions); in terms of *qualia informativeness*, it must not refer to default qualia values of the syntactic head. We also proposed that the degree of informativeness of a given construction is crucially determined by the compositional mechanism involved in its derivation, and ranked the type satisfaction mechanisms accordingly: introduction is the most informative one, and type matching and exploitation are zero informative. We showed that this approach is borne out by corpus data by examining naturally occurring PP-N combinations.

Qualia	PP Modifier	Examples
F/C	Modified default	*colored, equipped, bodied, shaped*
	Contr./C-E default	
	Subtyped	*winged, twin-engined, armed*
A	Modified default	*made, developed, produced, constructed, manufactured, created*
	Contr./C-E default	*manufactured*
	Subtyped	
T	Modified default	*used, flown, operated, utilized*
	Contr./C-E default	*used, utilized*
	Subtyped	

Table 5: *Aircraft*

Qualia	PP Modifier	Examples
F/C	Modified default	*colored, bodied*
	Contr./C-E default	*aromatized*
	Subtyped	
A	Modified default	*made, produced, grown, created, farmed, harvested*
	Contr./C-E default	
	Subtyped	*crafted*
T	Modified default	*drunk, consumed*
	Contr./C-E default	
	Subtyped	

Table 6: *Wine*

Ongoing research elaborates on the formal details of the mechanism outlined in this paper and extends its application to a wide range of linguistic phenomena whose properties are determined by the general informativeness requirement.

Acknowledgments

The contribution by Olga Batiukova was partially financed by the Ministry of Economy and Competitiveness of Spain under Grant No. FFI2012-33807.

References

F. Ackerman and A.E. Goldberg. 1996. Constraints on adjectival past participles. In A.E. Goldberg, editor, *Conceptual Structure, Discourse and Language*, pages 17–30. CSLI Publications.

N. Asher and J. Pustejovsky. 2013. A type composition logic for generative lexicon. In *Advances in Generative Lexicon Theory*, pages 39–66. Springer.

P. Blackburn and J. Bos. 2008. Computational semantics. *THEORIA. An International Journal for Theory, History and Foundations of Science*, 18(1).

J. Bresnan. 1995. Lexicality and argument structure.

N. Chomsky. 1993. *Lectures on government and binding: The Pisa lectures*, volume 9. Walter de Gruyter.

W. Croft. 2005. Logical and typological arguments for radical construction grammar. *Construction Grammars: Cognitive grounding and theoretical extensions*, pages 273–314.

D. Dowty. 1979. *Word meaning and Montague grammar: The semantics of verbs and times in generative semantics and in Montague's PTQ*, volume 7. Springer.

D. Embick. 2004. On the structure of resultative participles in english. *Linguistic Inquiry*, 35(3):355–392.

A.E. Goldberg and F. Ackerman. 2001. The pragmatics of obligatory adjuncts. *Language*, 77(4):798–814.

A. Goldberg. 1998. Semantic principles of predication. *Discourse and Cognition: Bridging the Gap, CSLI Publications, Stanford University, Stanford, CA*, pages 41–54.

J. Grimshaw and S. Vikner. 1993. Obligatory adjuncts and the structure of events. In E. Reuland and W. Abraham, editors, *Knowledge and language*, volume II, pages 145–159. Kluwer Academic Publishers, Dordrecht.

L. Horn. 1996. Presupposition and implicature. *The handbook of contemporary semantic theory*, pages 299–319.

Y. Jung. 1997. Obligatory adjuncts. *Texas Linguistic Forum*, 38:161–171.

A. Kilgarriff, P. Rychlỳ, P. Smrž, and D. Tugwell. 2004. The sketch engine. In *Proceedings of the Eleventh EURALEX International Congress. Lorient, France: Universite de Bretagne-Sud*, pages 105–116.

K. Konrad. 2004. *Model generation for natural language interpretation and analysis*, volume 2953. Springer.

R. Langacker. 1991. *Foundations of Cognitive Grammar*. Stanford University Press.

S. Levinson. 2000. *Presumptive meanings: The theory of generalized conversational implicature*. The MIT Press.

K. McRae and K. Matsuki. 2009. People use their knowledge of common events to understand language, and do so as quickly as possible. *Language and linguistics compass*, 3(6):1417–1429.

J. Pustejovsky and O. Batiukova. forthcoming. Compositionality and information.

J. Pustejovsky and E. Jezek. 2008. Semantic coercion in language: Beyond distributional analysis. *Italian Journal of Linguistics*, 20(1):175–208.

J. Pustejovsky. 1995. *Generative Lexicon*. Cambridge (Mass.): MIT Press.

J. Pustejovsky. 2011. Coercion in a general theory of argument selection. *Linguistics*, 49(6):1401–1431.

J. Pustejovsky. 2013. Type theory and lexical decomposition. In *Advances in Generative Lexicon Theory*, pages 9–38. Springer.

R. Van Valin. 1990. Semantic parameters of split intransitivity. *Language*, 66:221–260.

Extended Generative Lexicon

Sumiyo Nishiguchi
School of Management, Tokyo University of Science
500 Shimokiyoku, Kuki-city, Saitama 346-8512, Japan
nishiguchi@rs.tus.ac.jp

Abstract

This paper proposes an elaboration of the Generative Lexicon (GL) in Pustejovsky (1995) based on a survey of BCCWJ (2009). I manually classified the Japanese NP_1-*no* NP_2 "NP_1's NP_2" construction in accordance with semantic relations between the two nominals. The result indicates the need for the expansion of GL for computing the meaning of the NP_1-*no* NP_2 construction by incorporating *referential module*, as I call, that predicates temporary location, time, and manner of the referent. For example, in *ima-no nihon* "the present Japan," *ima-no* modifies the time of the event argument in the referential module.

1 Generative Lexicon Theory

Generative Lexicon (GL) is a theory proposed in Pustejovsky (1995). GL reduces lexical ambiguity and avoids multiple lexical entries by allowing semantic type-shifts based on the detailed lexical information. For example, instead of considering *book* as lexically ambiguous, the Qualia Structure enables semantic type-shifting of *book*; this provides means for solving a type-mismatch between *finish* and *a book* in (1b).

(1) a. Sue finished reading a book.

b. Sue finished a book.

Most likely, the meanings of (1a) and (1b) are alike; (1a) expresses the action more explicitly than (1b), that is, Sue finished reading a book according to a highly probable reading. The correct interpretation of (1b) that Sue finished reading a book, rather than swallowing a book or something else, is obtained by means of the lexical knowledge that books are made to be read—the purpose or the telic role of the book is to have its readers. The reading activity contains an event argument inside and the agent of the event argument is realized as the sentential subject *Sue*.

Such "purpose" or TELIC role is encoded in the lexical knowledge in GL (Pustejovsky 1995). According to Pustejovsky who based his theory on Moravcsik (1975), the following four qualia that originate from Aristotle's concept of matters represent four inherent properties of the referent.

(2) **CONSTITUTIVE** part-whole relation, material, weight

FORMAL orientation, magnitude, shape, dimensionality, color, position, ontological category

TELIC purpose, function

AGENTIVE origin, creator, artifact, natural kind, causal chain

2 Problems with Deriving Possessive Relations

In formal semantics, Pustevjosky's qualia structure has been applied for deriving possessive relations by means of the type-shifting mechanism. Vikner and Jensen (2002) type-shift the possessor noun using one of the qualia roles to explain the meaning of the genitive phrases following Partee (1997).

Possessive relations are ambiguous in both English and Japanese. For example, there is more than one interpretation for *Tanaka-no hon* "Tanaka's book." *Tanaka's book* may refer to the book that *Tanaka* owns or the book that *Tanaka* wrote (Barker 1995, 87).

In view of such ambiguity, Langacker (1993) considers ownership to be the prototypical meaning of the possessive construction and other relations to be the instantiations. Partee (1997) assumes two syntactic types for *John's* depending on whether or not the following noun is inherently relational.

According to Partee, if the following noun is a non-relational common noun (CN) such as *car*, *John's* composes with *car* which is a regular (e, t) type predicate, namely, a function from individuals to truth-values (Montague 1973), and the relation between *John* and *car* is contextually supplied as shown in (3a).

On the contrary, when *John* is followed by inherently relational nouns such as *brother*, *employee*, and *enemy*, which are $(e, (e, t))$ type with an extra argument slot (a function from individuals to another function from individuals to truth-values), the relation between *John* and his brother in *John's brother* inherits kinship from the two-place predicate *brother* in (3b). (4) exemplifies the computation related to another relational noun, *friend*.

(3) a. Free R type:

Syntax: [John's]$_{NP/CN}$

Semantics: λQλP[NP'(λz [∃x[∀y[[Q(y) ∧ R(y)(z)] ↔ y = x] ∧ P(x)]])]

b. Inherent relation type: inherited from relational nouns:

Syntax: [John's]$_{NP/TCN}$ (TCN: transitive common noun)

Semantics: λRλP[NP'(λz [∃x[∀y[R(z)(y) ↔ y = x] ∧ P(x)]])]

(4) Syntax: [[John's]$_{NP/TCN}$[friend]$_{TCN}$]$_{NP}$

Semantics: λRλP[John'(λz.∃x[∀y[R(z)(y) ↔ y = x] ∧ P(x)]](friend-of')

= λP[John's(λz.∃x[∀y[friend-of'(z)(y) ↔ y = x] ∧ P(x)]]

If we apply Partee's theory to Japanese examples, most of the possessive relations are unpredictable, and there is no way to disambiguate the contextually supplied relation R.

Vikner and Jensen (2002) apply the qualia structure of the possessee noun and type-shift the possessee noun into a relational noun. For example, *John's poem*, that is, a possessive + CN, can be interpreted as the poem that John composed because the internal semantic structure of *poem* contains an *author-of* relation, which is the agentive role. According to Vikner and Jensen (2002), the meaning-shifting operator Q_A raises a one-place holder *poem* in (5a) into a two-place holder as in (5b). The type-shifted *poem* can now combine with the possessive NP, which has a uniform type $((e, (e, t)), ((e, t), t))$, so that the authorship relation is inherited from NP *poem*, and R is no longer a free variable.

(5) a. $[\![poem]\!]$ = λx.[poem'(x)]

b. Q_A(poem) = λxλy[poem'(x) ∧ compose'(x)(y)]

Similarly, *the girl's teacher* can be explained by their mechanism. The purpose of teachers is to teach; therefore, the TELIC role of teachers is to teach someone. Now, the telic quale in the qualia structure of *teacher* raises the semantic type of a common noun *teacher* into the one of a relational noun as given in (6). *Teacher* is always someone's teacher so that *teacher* is a function from individuals to another function from individuals to truth-values.

(6) a. $[\![teacher]\!]$ = λx.teacher'(x)

b. Q_T(teacher) = λxλy[teacher'(x) ∧ teach'(y)(x)]

Such a mechanism has dramatically reduced the ambiguity of possessive relations.

3 Limit to GL

Table 1 manually classifies the 3030 examples containing the *NP*$_1$-*no NP*$_2$ "*NP*$_1$-GEN *NP*$_2$" construction in Japanese, such as *Fuji-no rendora* "a soap opera by Fuji TV," according to the semantic relations between the two noun phrases. The examples were sorted out of the core data of the *Yahoo! Chiebukuro* portion of BCCWJ (2009) by using ChaKi.NET 1.2β.

The survey indicates that the qualia structure plays an important role in disambiguating the meaning of the genitive marker *no* in Japanese. 29% of all instances are examples that *NP*$_1$ *selectively binds*, or modifies the qualia structure of the lexical meaning of the *NP*$_2$. For example, *Fuji-no rendora* "a soap opera by Fuji TV" is a soap opera *created* by Fuji TV, i.e., the agentive relation between the Fuji TV and a soap opera substitutes the relation between the two. In *windows-no CM* "TV commercial for the Windows," the CM is for the Windows; therefore, the meaning of *no* inherits the telic role of CM. In *Gandamu-no kao* "the

Table 1: Distribution of Semantic Patterns of NP_1-*no* NP_2 Construction

selective binding of qualia in NP_2	886	0.292409241
NP_2 is a relational noun	777	0.256435644
NP_2 is a deverbal noun	445	0.146864686
NP_1 is adjectival property	395	0.130363036
referential module modification of NP_2	244	0.080528053
NP_1 is a quantifier	152	0.050165017
possession	45	0.014851485
demonstratives	32	0.010561056
NP_1 is a deverbal noun	24	0.007590759
NP_1 is theme of deadjectival NP_2	23	0.007306226
adverb	6	0.001980198
selective binding of qualia in NP_1	1	0.000330033
total	3030	1

face of Gundam," the face is part of the Gundam robot (constitutive quale). *Shikaku* in *shikaku-no katachi* "square shape" describes the shape (formal role modification).

(7) a. Fuji-no rendora
Fuji TV-GEN soap
"the soap opera by Fuji TV"

b. $[\![Fuji - no\_rendora]\!]$ = λe,x[soap(x) & AGENTIVE = [make_act(e) & agent(e) = FujiTV & theme(e) = x]]

Crucially, the survey demonstrated that the GL needs to be expanded to include not only inherent properties but also referential descriptions, because 8% of the data involved the modification of the temporary elements, such as location, time, and manner of the referent of NP_2 (e.g., *Operaza-no Kaijin* "Phantom of the Opera", that is, Phantom *in* the Opera) (Nishiguchi 2012) . As the relation between the Phantom and the Opera does not involve any of the inherent qualia structure—Phantom of the Opera was not born in the Opera (agentive), the Phantom is not made for the Opera (telic), the Phantom is not any part of the Opera (constitutive), or does not form any shape of the Opera (formal), none of the relations among the qualia structure Pustejovsky (1995) cannot substitute for the relation between the two.

4 Extended GL

Even though Pustejovsky's four qualia express inherent properties of referents, I propose supplementing lexical semantics with information about the referents. Besides type, argument, event, and qualia structures in GL (cf. Johnston and Busa 1996, 79), the referential module (REF) has subcategories of TIME, LOC, and MANNER roles.

(8) Original GL Template

$$\begin{bmatrix} \alpha \\ \text{TYPESTR} = \begin{bmatrix}\text{ARG1 = THE TYPE OF } \alpha\end{bmatrix} \\ \text{ARGSTR} = \begin{bmatrix}\text{D-ARG1 = OTHER ARGUMENTS IN THE QUALIA}\end{bmatrix} \\ \text{EVENTSTR} = \begin{bmatrix}\text{E1 = EVENTS IN THE QUALIA}\end{bmatrix} \\ \text{QUALIA} = \begin{bmatrix}\text{FORMAL = ISA-RELATION} \\ \text{CONST = PARTS OF } \alpha \\ \text{TELIC = PURPOSE OF } \alpha \\ \text{AGENT = HOW } \alpha \text{ IS BROUGHT ABOUT}\end{bmatrix} \end{bmatrix}$$

(Johnston and Busa 1996, 79)

(9) Template for Extended GL

$$\begin{bmatrix} \alpha \\ \text{TYPESTR} = \begin{bmatrix}\text{ARG1 = THE TYPE OF } \alpha\end{bmatrix} \\ \text{ARGSTR} = \begin{bmatrix}\text{D-ARG1 = OTHER ARGUMENTS IN THE QUALIA}\end{bmatrix} \\ \text{EVENTSTR} = \begin{bmatrix}\text{E1 = EVENTS IN THE QUALIA}\end{bmatrix} \\ \text{QUALIA} = \begin{bmatrix}\text{FORMAL = ISA-RELATION} \\ \text{CONST = PARTS OF } \alpha \\ \text{TELIC = PURPOSE OF } \alpha \\ \text{AGENT = HOW } \alpha \text{ IS BROUGHT ABOUT}\end{bmatrix} \\ \textbf{REF} = \begin{bmatrix}\textbf{LOC} = \text{IN}\left(\boxed{e2}, \boxed{x}, \boxed{l}\right) \\ \textbf{TIME} = \text{AT}\left(\boxed{e2}, \boxed{x}, \boxed{t}\right) \\ \textbf{MANNER} = \text{WITH}\left(\boxed{e2}, \boxed{x}, \boxed{y}\right)\end{bmatrix} \end{bmatrix}$$

For example, *Operaza-no* "of the Opera" in *operaza-no kaijin* "the Phantom of the Opera" in (10a) and *mayonaka-no* "midnight" in *mayonaka-no kaigan* "the midnight beach/the beach in midnight" in (11a) modify referential modules of the Phantom and the beach. In *baiku-no karera* "those on scooters" in (12a), scooter-riding is one of the temporary properties of the referents, so that it is MANNER role modification.

As a result, selective binding not only applies to qualia structure but also to a referential module, which enables the computation of the meaning of the NP_1-*no* NP_2 construction. For example, *Operaza-no* "of the Opera" specifies the location of the Phantom as the Opera, *mayonaka-no* "midnight" modifies time and *baiku-no* "on scooters" fills the manner role as shown in (10b), (11b) and (12b).

(10) a. Operaza-no kaijin
The Opera-GEN phantom
"The Phantom of the Opera

b. $[\![The\_Phantom\_of\_the\_Opera]\!]$ = λx[phantom(x) ∧ [REF = ∃e[be-phantom(e) & theme(e) = x ∧ location(e) = The Opera]]]

(11) a. Mayonaka-no kaigan-e it-te
midnight-GEN beach-GOAL go-and
sakende-kudasai.
shout-IMP.HON
"Go to beach during midnight and shout there."

(BCCWJ 2011, oc 104343)

b. $[\![midnight\_beach]\!]$ = λx[beach(x) & [REF = ∃e[be-beach(e) ∧ theme(e) = x ∧ time(e) = midnight]]]

(12) a. Baiku-no karera-mo
scooter-GEN they-also
kekkona ritsu-de te-o
high freuency-by hand-ACC
agete-kure-ta
raise-BENEF-PAST
"Those on scooters also raised their hands often."

(BCCWJ 2011, oc 56711)

b. $[\![those\_on\_scooters]\!]^g$ =λx[g(1) = x & [REF = ∃e[born(e) & manner(e) = with-scooter]]]

(13) a. kinjo-no
neighborhood-GEN
seikeigeka-ni-wa iki-mashi-ta
orthopidics-DAT-TOP go-HON-PAST
"I visited the orthopedics in neighborhood."

(BCCWJ 2011, oc 97196)

b. $[\![neighborhood - \text{GEN}\_orthopedics]\!]$ = λx[orthopedics(x) ∧ [REF = ∃e[location(e) = neighborhood ∧ theme(e) = x]]]

Kinjo-no "in the neighborhood" in (13a) and *mayonaka-no* "midnight" in (11a) represent the temporary location and time of the referents of *seikeigeka* "orthopedic clinic" and *kaigan* "beach."

Therefore, I propose the addition of a referential module to the lexical meaning in GL, for incorporating temporary location, time, manner and others of referents, in addition to the qualia structure. The possessive or genitive phrases NP_1-*no* in these examples modify the referential modules of NP_2 which cannot be captured within the framework of the already existing GL.

5 EGL Database

I have made a small database of fifty lexical items taken from BCCWJ (2009) in the format of the Extended GL.

6 Conclusion

A quantitative survey of the meaning of the NP_1-*no* NP_2 construction in Japanese revealed the need for the expansion of the GL for the computation of the meaning, although many examples were of the qualia structure modification in GL.

References

Barker, C. (1995). *Possessive Descriptions.* Stanford: CSLI Publications.

BCCWJ (2009). *Balanced Corpus of Contemporary Written Japanese, BCCWJ2009 edition.* The National Institute of Japanese Language.

BCCWJ (2011). *Balanced Corpus of Contemporary Written Japanese.* The National Institute of Japanese Language.

Johnston, M. and F. Busa (1996). Qualia structure and the compositional interpretation of compounds. In *Proceedings of the ACL SIGLEX Workshop on Breadth and Depth of Semantic Lexicons*, pp. 77–88. Kluwer.

$$
\begin{bmatrix}
\textbf{ASA-NO KOEN} \text{ ``PARK''} & \\
\text{TYPESTR} = & \begin{bmatrix} \text{ARG1} = \boxed{y}\ \text{OUTDOOR'S\_LOCATION} \end{bmatrix} \\
\text{ARGSTR} = & \begin{bmatrix} \text{D-ARG1} = \boxed{w}\text{HUMAN} \\ \text{D-ARG2} = \boxed{z}\text{HUMAN} \\ \text{D-ARG3} = \boxed{l}\text{LOCATION} \\ \text{D-ARG4} = \boxed{t}\text{TIME} \\ \text{D-E1} = \boxed{e1}\text{TRANSITION} \\ \text{D-E2} = \boxed{e2}\text{STATE} \\ \text{D-E3} = \boxed{e3}\text{PROCESS} \end{bmatrix} \\
\text{QUALIA} = & \begin{bmatrix} \text{FORMAL} = \boxed{x} \\ \text{CONST} = \left\{\text{LAWN, BENCH, FOUNTAIN,...}\right\} \\ \text{TELIC} = \text{RECREATIONAL\_ACTIVITY}\left(\boxed{e3}, \boxed{w}, \boxed{y}\right) \\ \text{AGENTIVE} = \text{MAKE\_ACT}\left(\boxed{e1}, \boxed{z}, \boxed{y}\right) \end{bmatrix} \\
\text{EXT} = & \begin{bmatrix} \text{LOCATION} = \text{IN}\left(\boxed{e2}, \boxed{y}, \boxed{l}\right) \\ \text{TIME} = \text{AT}\left(\boxed{e2}, \boxed{x}, \begin{bmatrix} \textbf{ASA} \text{ ``MORNING''} & \\ \text{TYPESTR} = & \begin{bmatrix} \text{ARG1} = \boxed{x}\ \text{TIME} \end{bmatrix} \\ \text{ARGSTR} = & \begin{bmatrix} \text{D-ARG1} = \boxed{t}\text{DATE} \\ \text{D-ARG2} = \boxed{t1}\text{TIME} \end{bmatrix} \\ \text{QUALIA} = & \begin{bmatrix} \text{FORMAL} = \boxed{x} \\ \text{CONST} = \text{PART-OF}\left(\boxed{t}, \boxed{x}\right) \wedge \text{PART-OF}\left(\boxed{t1}, \boxed{x}\right) \end{bmatrix} \end{bmatrix}\right) \end{bmatrix}
\end{bmatrix}
$$

Langacker, R. W. (1993). Reference-point constructions. *Cognitive Linguistics 4:1*, 1–38.

Montague, R. (1973). The proper treatment of quantification in ordinary english. In K. J. J. Hintikka, J. M. E. Moravcsik, and P. Suppes (Eds.), *Approaches to Natural Language : Proceedings of the 1970 Stanford Workshop on Grammar and Semantics*, pp. 221–242. Dordrecht: Reidel.

Moravcsik, J. M. (1975). Aitia as generative factor in aristotle's philosophy. *Dialogue 14*, 622–636.

Nishiguchi, S. (2012). *Disambiguation of Possessives: The Extended Generative Lexicon*. Saarbrücken: Lambert Academic Publishing.

Partee, B. H. (1983, 1997). Genitives: A case study. In J. van Benthem and A. ter Meulen (Eds.), *Handbook of Logic and Language*, pp. 464–470. Amsterdam: Elsevier.

Pustejovsky, J. (1995). *The Generative Lexicon*. Cambridge: MIT Press.

Vikner, C. and P. A. Jensen (2002). A semantic analysis of the english genitive. interaction of lexical and formal semantics. *Studia Linguistica 56*, 191–226.

Features of Verb Complements in Co-composition: A case study of Chinese baking verb using Weibo corpus

Yu-Yun Chang
Graduate Institute of Linguistics,
National Taiwan University
No. 1, Sec. 4, Roosevelt Rd.,
Taipei, Taiwan (R.O.C.) 10617
yuyun.unita@gmail.com

Shu-Kai Hsieh
Graduate Institute of Linguistics,
National Taiwan University
No. 1, Sec. 4, Roosevelt Rd.,
Taipei, Taiwan (R.O.C.) 10617
shukaihsieh@ntu.edu.tw

Abstract

In the Generative Lexicon Theory (GLT), co-composition is one of the generative devices proposed to explain the cases of verbal polysemous behavior where more than one function application is allowed. The English baking verbs were used as one of the examples to illustrate how their complements co-specify the verb with *qualia unification*. In this paper, we begin by exploring the polysemy of Chinese baking verb, where the first two senses in Chinese Wordnet (CWN) are assumed. Features including linguistic cues and common sense knowledge are involved in the experiment with Weibo corpus and computed with SVM for closer investigation. From the analysis, it is found that though there are various cases found in senses of *change of state* and *creation*, a coarse but systematic approach combined with certain features in disambiguating CWN senses could be arranged. In addition, we further observe that the usage of various instruments cases and classifiers would be harnessed by underlying background knowledge to help select an appropriate sense based on the context.

Keywords: The generative lexicon, co-composition, baking verbs

1 Introduction

In Generative Lexicon Theory (GLT), the co-composition theory in discussing the logical polysemy of verbs illustrates that in some verbal meaning alternations, arguments of verbs would shift the meaning of verb in the compositional interpretation. This poses difficulties for word sense disambiguation (WSD) task in contextualizing the underlying sense, i.e., putting semantic weights on the non-functor elements, to give rise to a derivative sense.

Firstly, we start with exploring the representative example of baking verb "bake" used in GLT regarding co-composition, to see whether two assumed senses, *change of state* and *creation*, can be derived through the proposed generative mechanisms in composition with its argument in the case of Chinese baking verb *kao* 烤 'bake' with the Chinese examples *kao malingshu* 烤馬鈴薯 'bake a potato' and *kao dangao* 烤蛋糕 'bake a cake'.

We choose WordNet to depict the contrast. In regard to the differences in senses *change of state* and *creation* of the English verb "bake", the definition of the verb in WordNet [1], carry diverse glosses as well in the examples "bake a potato" and "bake a cake"; however, considering the verb *kao* 烤 'bake' in Chinese WordNet (CWN) [2], both the Chinese examples *kao malingshu* 'bake a potato' and *kao dangao* 'bake a cake' could be included into the first CWN gloss "use heat to cook and make the food edible" (CWN_sense_1). Whereas, it is discovered that the example *kao malingshu* 'bake a potato' could also be applied to the secondary CWN gloss "use heat to heat the object" (CWN_sense_2). That is to say, in Chinese, although *change of state* sense would be assigned to *kao malingshu* 'bake a potato' and *creation* sense would be attached to *kao dangao* 'bake a cake' as in English, both examples would be primary grouped into CWN_sense_1; but there are situations that *kao malingshu* 'bake a potato' also occur with CWN_sense_2, based on the context. Therefore, in the above Chinese cases, it seems to be clear that examples with *creation* sense would only be assigned to CWN_sense_1; while the con-

[1] http://wordnetweb.princeton.edu/perl/webwn

[2] http://lope.linguistics.ntu.edu.tw/cwn/

ditions for examples with *change of state* sense, to distinguish interpretation differences between CWN_sense_1 and CWN_sense_2, need to be further investigated.

Nonetheless, there are situations that examples with *creation* sense would be assigned to CWN_sense_2 as well. For instance, *kao tusi* 烤土司 'toast a loaf of bread / toast a slice of toasted bread' would not only be assigned to CWN_sense_1, but also CWN_sense_2, based on some occasions. Additionally, a sense shifting would be prompted as well, from *creation* sense to *change of state* sense. Moreover, it is investigated that cases such as *kao dofu* 烤豆腐 'grill tofu' though along with *change of state* sense, yet possesses some features from *creation* sense, and could merely be specified with CWN_sense_2.

Therefore, this paper aims to search out a coarse but systematic approach with linguistic cues, with the help of applying the Support Vector Machine (SVM) computational technique by taking Leidon Weibo Corpus (van Esch, 2012) [3], to help identify and analyze what the sets of conditions for *change of state* and *creation* senses are that would lead to different mappings between CWN_sense_1 and CWN_sense_2, by investigating the Chinese baking verb *kao* 'bake'.

2 Co-composition in GLT

Qualia structure (Pustejovsky, 1995), adapted from the modes of explanation by Aristotle, depicts that there are four main essential factors (*constitutive*, *formal*, *telic*, and *agentive*) to drive and capture the interpretation of an object as well as a relation (Moravcsik, 1975). Although many models of semantics agree that words have simple denotations, but there are various perspectives in the methods of lexical composition. Some formal models argue that the composition approaches are truth-value denotation and computation within logical inferences; while in the perspective of GLT, it is the semantic transformations (including type coercion, selective binding, and co-composition) of words' denotations that shift from one to another to form new meanings. Therefore, in GLT, the use of qualia structure could be applied to better specifying a word's meaning.

[3]Leidon Weibo Corpus collects messages from China's most popular micro-blogging platform, Sina Weibo. The corpus is open-access and can be found here: `http://lwc.daanvanesch.nl/`

As mentioned in Pustejovsky (1995), among the four interpretive levels of qualia structure, the *agentive* quale of the lexical item is encoded with the knowledge of what an object may identify or refer to and be able to explain an artifact comes into being. Therefore, it would be an important manner if something is created in order to distinguish natural kinds (e.g. potatoes, carrots and so on) from artifacts (e.g. cookies, cakes, bread).

In addition, the *agentive* role of a lexical item would be represented as an event predicate while the lexical item is a noun. For example, "potato" and "cake" could all be event predicates in "bake a potato" and "bake a cake"; however, the verb "bake" is polysemous with two meanings: a sense of *change of state* and a sense of *creation*, as stated in Atkins et al. (1988). Since this kind of logical polysemy occurs in many cases, a relation of co-composition is introduced by Pustejovsky (1995) (originally named as co-specification (Pustejovsky, 1991)) to capture the words' meanings.

Under the notion of co-composition, the verb "bake" itself is not polysemous but the complement that follows derives other meanings can be re-examined, not only through the *agentive* quale, but also *constitutive* role. From the example (51) provided by Pustejovsky (1995), it is further discovered that though a complement makes reference to an *agentive* quale, the *constitutive* quale plays an important role to the baking act. That is, if the material in a *constitutive* quale of a complement is an individual as a default argument, the derived sense from *agentive* role would be *change of state*. On the other hand, when the material in a *constitutive* quale of a complement is a mass of individual components, the selected sense from *agentive* role would turn out to be *creation*.

Therefore, the verb "bake" originally has one event type but with two argument types in the lexical structure, it is the complement that chooses one of the two arguments to govern. When in the case of "bake a potato", the *agentive* role of "potato" is simply a natural kind and an individual material, the process only involves state changes with event type makes no shifting, and thus the sense *change of state* is assigned; whereas in "bake a cake", "cake" is an artifact created from a mass of components, its event type would shift from one to the other, thus obtain the sense of *creation*. The kind of event type shifting in a complement, is what that makes the verb "bake" to be polysemous, not the verb itself.

The co-composition operation on VP proposed by Pustejovsky (1995) includes the following process:

1. The governing verb would apply to its complement;

2. The complement would then co-specify the verb;

3. A new sense of the verb would be derived resulting from an operation called *qualia unification*, where the agentive roles of both the verb and its complement match with each other; and the *formal* quale of the complement is also the *formal* role of the entire VP.

Since the process of co-composition will arouse new senses to the governing verb based on its complement, it is also worth noting that the thematic roles played by the complement of a verb needs to be taken into consideration. As mentioned by many researchers (Tanenhaus et al., 1989; Jackendoff, 1987; Gentner, 1981), thematic role knowledge is part of a verb's meaning and can be construed as a claim that the concept of a verb is its relation to the entities participated in the event. Though numerous thematic taxonomies have been proposed by linguists, six thematic roles are typically involved: agent, patient, theme, goal, instrument and location (Cook, 1979; Fillmore, 1968).

In this paper, we are interested in investigating the verb *kao* 'bake' with its complements in Chinese examples under co-composition theory, and focus on exploring one of the thematic roles "instrument" within context. This study thus aims to further seek empirically for what the linguistic features are in deciding or shifting the CWN senses of *kao* 'bake' under the notion of *change of state* and *creation* senses. A corpus-based machine learning approach is taken for the analysis, which is introduced in the following section.

3 Data Analysis using Weibo Corpus

3.1 Data Collection

Since Weibo is the most prevalent Chinese social communication and microblogging platform, recent studies in corpus data analysis have taken Weibo data as corpus, in order to further and better investigate the up-to-date language usage. By taking the Weibo corpus into study, we can not only freely accessed large amount of timely data without expensive computing, but also discover the linguistic cues that best display current language usage. Therefore, in this paper, with the open-sourced weibo corpus, Leiden Weibo Corpus (van Esch, 2012), freely accessed online, the posts containing *kao* 'bake' could all be easily retrieved using R programming language. At present, due to the efficiency in data processing, convenience in applying statistical models and powerfulness in plotting, an amount of 9688 parsed posts involving the verb *kao* 'bake' have been successfully extracted for the preparation of following data analysis.

3.2 Complements, Linguistic Features and Common Sense Knowledge

By observing the extracted *kao* 'bake' posts, 53 nouns that could be taken as complements of the verb are randomly chosen, and manually tagged with one of the two senses based on its complement role to the verb *kao* 'bake'(e.g. 41 nouns are tagged as *change of state* sense and the other 12 are tagged as *creation* sense), as target data for running SVM approach. Since complements may trigger VPs to select a *change of state* or *creation* sense, there might be some certain embedded and underlying information (including linguistic cues and common sense knowledge) beneath a complement, which causes the complement to select one of the two senses for an VP. Therefore, by applying SVM approach with related implicit information of complements, we may roughly further investigate what the information are influencing the decision of senses between *change of state* and *creation*. In addition, via the analysis of SVM results, a more detailed exploration can be carried out from the observed essential implicit information, in determining CWN_sense_1 and CWN_sense_2 under *change of state* and *creation* senses.

Hence, a data frame targeted on the complements with features such as relevant linguistic cues and common sense knowledge, to learn whether these features would help deciding *change of state* and *creation* senses, is shown in Figure 1. We tend to add in as many relative linguistic cues and shared knowledge as possible, and by using the characteristics of SVM to help quickly derive a set of effective features from a pool of various infor-

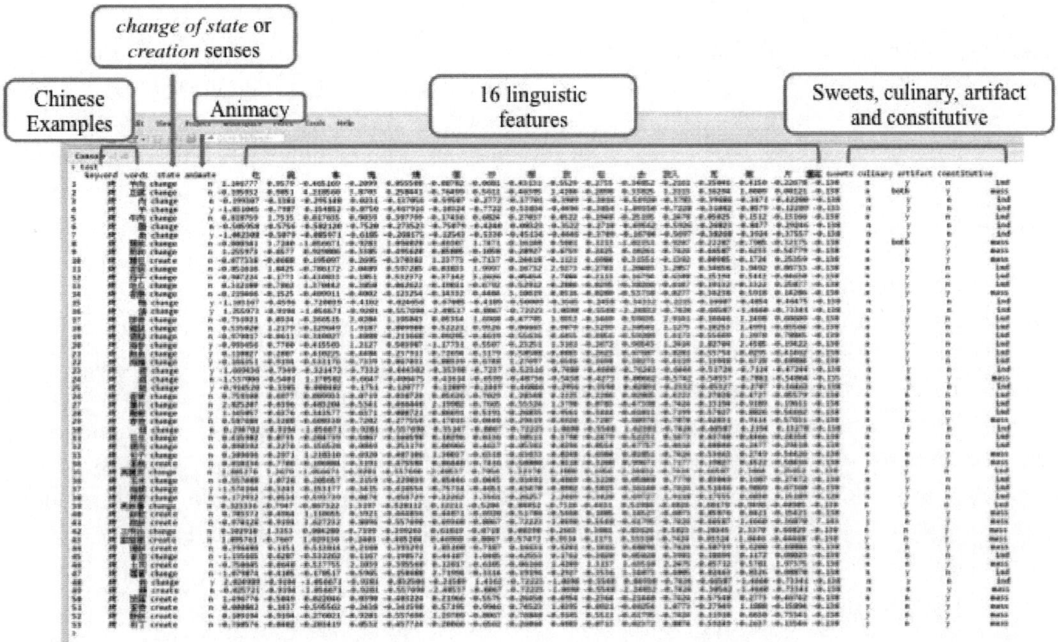

Figure 1: A data frame with complements and features prepared for applying SVM approach

mation for further observation.

In the data frame, since the collocation of a word has been taken as an approach in computational linguistics for presenting its relationships with a word, the collocations are also involved for SVM. The span of the collocation is set to three before the position of the nouns for automatically extracting and computing, and the first collocation method in Gries (2009) is applied. Since it is observed in GLT that the sense of a verb would be influenced by the followed noun, despite the verb *kao* 'bake', it would be interesting to see whether there are shared or common interactions between the complements and other verbs that follows. In addition, studies of classifiers have shown to be an important feature in representing a noun and have been applied to various classifiers to help make divisions. Therefore, in regard to linguistic features adapted in this paper, only the collocations of each noun with the highest frequency counts in verbs and classifiers, will be selected. The 16 selected linguistic features (including 9 verbs and 7 classifiers) are computed and each given a scaled[4] Point-wise Mutual Information (PMI) value to each noun. Equation is shown in (1).

[4]The numbers shown in Figure 1, are all scaled by applying collocation frequencies to Z-score, in order to get the data weighted for a better investigation. Therefore, the scaled numbers would have positive and negative values.

$$PMI = \frac{P(X,Y)}{P(X) * P(Y)} \qquad (1)$$

Unlike the 16 linguistic cues that could be retrieved easily from the data, the underlying common sense knowledge is hard to be revealed. Accordingly, 5 common sense features are manually analyzed and tagged, which include animacy (animate or inanimate), artifact (an artifact or natural objects), culinary (needed to be cooked before eating or not), sweets (could be generally categorized as sweets or not), and constitutive (whether its default argument is an individual or a mass).

3.3 Data Training and Testing

In order to see the interactions between the 21 features and the 53 nouns, the SVM approach is introduced to investigate whether the features mentioned above could possibly provide sufficient information of a complement to select *change of state* or *creation* sense for the verb, and furthermore, make a further research on finding essential features from the potential information in helping disambiguate CWN_sense_1 and CWN_sense_2. Therefore, the data in the data frame is randomly divided into two groups, which 70% of the data is used for training a model and the rest of the 30% is for testing. Furthermore, the results of SVM is presented by involving F-score, see equation (2), to present a weighted average of the precision and recall, and the score ranges from 0 (the worst) to 1 (the best).

$$F = 2 * \frac{precision * recall}{precision + recall} \quad (2)$$

4 Analysis

From SVM approach, the F-score presents 0.67 value for the model. Although the F-score only shows 67% chance to correctly make the complement choose the right *change of state* and *creation* senses for the verb *kao* 'bake', some inconsistency could be found within the 5 manually tagged common sense knowledge features and could be considered for the further discussion in dividing CWN_sense_1 and CWN_sense_2.

- Animacy - For complements that are inanimate are all tagged with *creation* sense; however, there are some that would be grouped as *change of state* sense.
- Sweets - For complements that are not sweets are all tagged with *change of state* sense; however, some would be assigned with *creation* sense.
- Culinary - For complements that do not needed to be cooked before eating, are tagged with *creation* sense; however, some would be fixed with the *change of state* sense.
- Artifact and Constitutive - It is found that the tags between artifact and constitutive are consistent. This might lead to the reason that if an item is an artifact instead of natural objects, a lot of materials would included for an artificial process. Therefore, for complements that are assigned as artifacts, are also tagged as mass; and vice versa. In addition, for complements that are tagged as artifact and mass, are all tagged with *creation* sense; however, some would be categorized as carrying *change of state* sense.

As observed from the above features, there are some complements containing the characteristics of being a *creation* sense, but are assigned with the sense of *change of state*. Though features change along with the senses, a typical combination of deriving a *creation* sense based on the complement could still be found, which including features such as inanimate, a kind of sweets, not culinary, an artifact and coming from a mass of materials.

As mentioned in GLT, the *constitutive* quale of whether a material is individual or a mass within a noun, would help identify a sense for a VP. Thus, as the examples described in Pustejovsky (1995), when the *constitutive* role is an individual, the sense of *change of state* is chosen; and when the *constitutive* role is a mass, the sense of *creation* would be assigned. However, in Chinese, it is found that there are examples that would be specified as *change of state* sense when the *constitutive* role is a mass. More examples and illustrations will be presented in the following section, and a brief process in identifying CWN_sense_1 and CWN_sense_2 under *change of state* and *creation* senses, are presented in Figure 2.

4.1 *Change of state* sense

4.1.1 *Constitutive* role: individual

By applying the *constitutive* quale, Chinese examples with constitutive quale identified as an individual, would be mapped to CWN_sense_1. These examples observed from the corpus, with the state changing from raw to cooked, could be roughly categorized as three groups: meat (e.g. *kao niurou* 烤牛肉 'roast beef' and *kao yangrou* 烤羊肉 'grill mutton'), seafood (e.g. *kao yu* 烤魚 'grill fish' and *kao longxia* 烤龍蝦 'grill lobsters'), and vegetables (e.g. *kao malingshu* 烤馬鈴薯 'bake a potato' and *kao xianggu* 烤香菇 'grill mushrooms').

4.1.2 *Constitutive* role: mass

For those examples with *change of state* sense but possess the *constitutive* role as a mass, which is one of the features to be specified as *creation* sense, observed from the corpus are *kao daofu* 烤豆腐 'grill tofu', *kao xiangchang* 烤香腸 'grill sausages', *kao mianjin* 烤麵筋 'grill gluten', *kao regou* 烤熱狗 'grill hotdogs', *kao jiu* 烤酒 'heat liquor', *kao chunjuan* 烤春捲 'grill spring rolls', *kao boazi* 烤包子 'grill steamed buns', and *kao sanmingzhi* 烤三明治 'grill sandwiches'.

Mostly these examples would only be led to CWN_sense_2, with the state changing from cold/cool to heated; however, this is not the case when considering *kao xiangchang* 'grill sausages' and *kao regou* 'grill hotdogs', which could be assigned to CWN_sense_1 as well.

Taking *kao xiangchang* 'grill sausages' for instance, as presented in example (3):

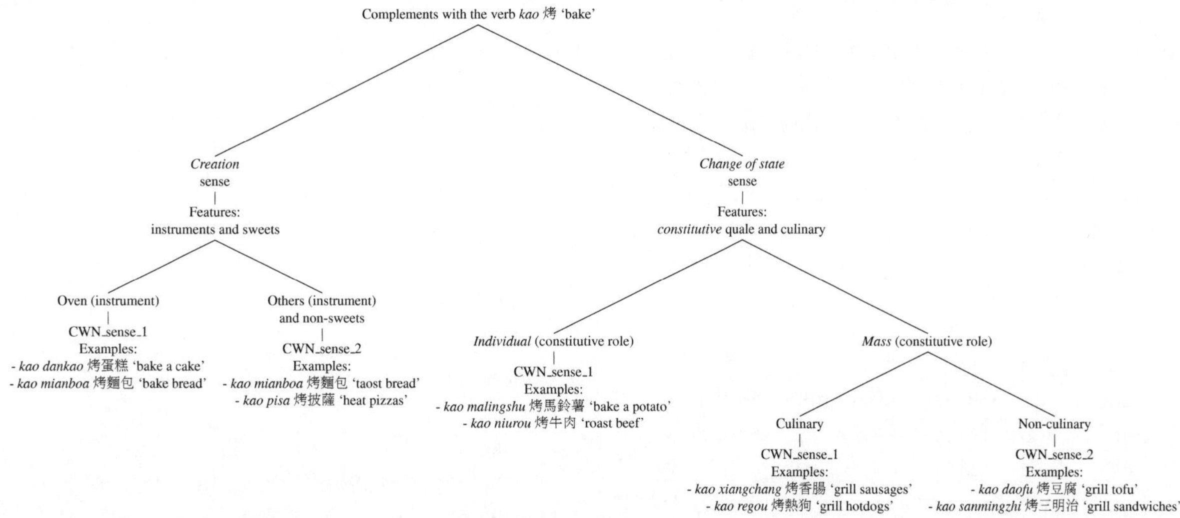

Figure 2: The process of identifying CWN_sense_1 and CWN_sense_2 under *change of state* and *creation* senses

(3)

回家	高速路	上	的	
huijia	gaosulu	shang	de	
on the way home	freeway	SHANG	DE	
休息站	開始	賣	烤	香腸
xiuxizhan	kaishi	mai	kao	xiangchang
rest area	start	sell	grill	sausage
和	烤	肉丸	了	
he	kao	rouwan	le	
and	grill	meat ball	LE	

'On the way home, the rest area beside the freeway, starts to sell grilled sausages and meat balls.'

As presented in example (3), though the *constitutive* role of sausages would be specified as a mass by containing a lot of ingredients, it is CWN_sense_1 that would be assigned to rather than CWN_sense_2. Such cases could be re-analyzed and distinguished by the manually tagged feature: culinary. For cases that are tagged as culinary, which illustrates "need to be cooked before eating", would then be grouped as CWN_sense_1; whereas, those that are tagged as non-culinary, expressing "edible without being cooked", would be specified as CWN_sense_2. Therefore, since *kao xiangchang* 'grill sausages' in example (3) is identified as culinary, it would be directed to CWN_sense_1.

4.2 *Creation* sense

4.2.1 Using instrument: oven

Considering the examples carrying *creation* sense: *kao dangao* 烤蛋糕 'bake a cake', *kao binggan* 烤餅乾 'bake cookies', *kao gaobing* 烤糕餅 'bake pastries', *kao tiantianquan* 烤甜甜圈 'bake donuts', *kao danjuan* 烤蛋捲 'bake egg rolls', *kao subing* 烤酥餅 'bake shortcakes', *kao buding* 烤布丁 'bake puddings', *kao mianboa* 烤麵包 'bake bread', *kao shaobing* 烤燒餅 'bake sesame seed cakes', *kao tusi* 烤土司 'bake a loaf of bread', *kao xiang* 烤饟 'bake a kind of traditional bread from north China', and *kao pisa* 烤披薩 'pizzas', it is investigated that these cases specified as CWN_sense_1 all share the same feature, using oven as instrument.

One of the example *kao dangao* 'bake a cake' is used for the following illustration.

(4)

沒	注意	看	烤箱,	蛋糕
mei	zhuyi	kan	kaoxiang	dangao
not	notice	watching	oven	cake
烤	過了頭			
kao	guoletou			
bake	overtime			

'Not noticing the oven, the cake is over-baked.'

Therefore, as presented in example (4), it is the use of instrument *kaoxiang* 烤箱 'oven' that frequently follows when cases that are tagged as *creation* sense.

In addition, the use of oven in a *creation* sense among the examples with the verb *kao* 'bake' becomes a common sense in shared knowledge. For example in *kao dangao* 'bake a cake', it may be the bakery bakers, not anyone else, that would frequently use 'oven' to bake a cake. Hence, the stereotype of using an oven for baking a cake is then implanted into the mind as background knowledge. That is to say, even without the instrument 'oven' occurred in the context, the act of baking a cake already possesses the default information of instrument 'oven', and thus would still be assumed as carrying the meaning CWN_sense_1, as shown in example (5).

(5)

我們	的	家庭	生活!	周末
women	de	jiating	shenghuo	zhoumo
our	DE	family	life	weekend

烤	蛋糕	嘍!
kao	dangao	lou
bake	cake	LOU

'Our family life! Bake a cake during weekend!'

However, there are still some examples that take not only the oven as the only instrument, but others such as toasters, grills and so on, would be assigned to CWN_sense_2 with *change of state* sense in some occasions. The discussion about these would leave to section 4.2.2 for more details.

For those that only use oven as instrument are typical examples with *creation* sense, which would not also possess the *change of state* sense depending on the context. Examples that meet with the requirements are: *kao dangao* 'bake a cake', *kao binggan* 'bake cookies', *kao gaobing* 'bake pastries', *kao tiantianquan* 'bake donuts', *kao danjuan* 'egg rolls', *kao subing* 'bake shortcakes', and *kao buding* 'bake puddings'. Furthermore, it could be inspected that these cases not only share the feature of merely using oven as instrument, but also are all consistently manually tagged as sweets, which is one of the 5 manually tagged common sense features. Therefore, if an example with *creation* sense is investigated to be a kind of sweets and only uses oven as instrument for baking, it could then be directly grouped to CWN_sense_1.

4.2.2 Using instrument: others

For examples that are tagged with *creation* sense and are not sweets, might also possess *change of state* sense with CWN_sense_2 depending on the context, such words are *kao mianboa* 'toast bread', *kao shaobing* 'heat sesame seed cake', *kao tusi* 'toast a slice of toasted bread', *kao xiang* 'heat a kind of traditional bread from north China', and *kao pisa* 'heat pizzas'.

The following takes the example *kao mianboa* 'toast bread' for illustration.

(6)

眼看	烤箱	裡	的
yankan	kaoxiang	li	de
see	oven	inside	DE

羊角麵包
yangjiaomianbao
croissant

'See the croissant inside the oven'

(7)

轉載	我	用	東菱	麵包機
zhuanzai	wo	yong	dongling	mianbaoji
forward	I	use	Donlim	toaster

烤	麵包	的	配方	與
kao	mianbao	de	peifang	yu
toast	bread	DE	cooking recipe	and

步驟
buzou
step

'Forward the cooking recipe and steps that I use for toasting bread on the Donlim toaster.'

As presented in example (6) and (7), the instrument for bread could either be an oven or a toaster. The sense in example (6) stays as what it is originally tagged, the *creation* sense with the usage of instrument 'oven'; whereas in example (7), when the instrument is other than an oven, such as a toaster, *change of state* sense would then be selected. This could lead to the reason that the instrument, toaster, is mainly used for heating the bread, rather than baking or creating the bread. Thus, the process of applying the instrument toaster to perform the act *kao mianboa* 'toast bread', would simply be *change of state* sense, along with state changes from cool/cold to heated.

Besides, by considering whether examples are using an oven as instrument or not, classifiers may provide some contributions in helping identifying the occasions that cases with *creation* sense would become *change of state* sense.

(8)

早餐	吃	了	兩	片	烤
zaocan	chi	le	liang	pian	kao
breakfast	eat	LE	two	piece	toast

土司
tusi
bread

'(Someone) eats two pieces of toasted bread for breakfast.'

(9) 他 烤 了 一 條 牛奶土司
ta kao le yi tiao niunaitusi
he bake LE one loaf milk bread
'He bakes a loaf of milk bread.'

As shown in example (8) and (9), different classifiers also implicate the using of certain instruments that may implicitly select a *change of state* sense for example (8) and a *creation* sense for example (9). Though the instruments are not revealed in the two examples, the classifier *pian* 片 'piece' in example (8), indicated the implicit instrument 'toaster' which would usually be used for toasting slices of bread or toast. Hence, due to the underlying usage of a toaster instead of an oven, the *change of state* sense could be affirmed. Considering the example (9), using the classifier *tiao* 條 'loaf' suggests that it is often the instrument oven that would bake a loaf of bread. On that account, the*creation* sense could be verified.

5 Conclusion

Under the point of co-composition, in order to observe an approach with linguistic cues that influence a complement to select a *change of state* or *create* sense for the Chinese baking verb *kao* 'bake', the investigation and analysis are carried out by using Leiden Weibo Corpus along with the application of SVM technique.

From the analysis, it is figured out that the sense of a complement with the verb *kao* 'bake' might be influenced by two of the five manually tagged features: sweets and culinary, usage of instruments and *constitutive* quale.

In Chinese examples, when a complement follows the verb *kao* 'bake', conditions for assigning *change of state* or *creation* sense to a CWN_sense_1 or CWN_sense_2 are as below: [1] *change of state* sense: if the *constitutive* role of a complement is an individual, or a mass but tagged as culinary, a CWN_sense_1 would be assigned; while if its *constitutive* role is a mass and tagged as not culinary, a CWN_sense_2 would be chosen. [2] *creation* sense: if the instrument oven for performing the act of *kao* 'bake', then a CWN_sense_1 would be selected; however, if using the instrument other than oven and not being tagged as sweets, a CWN_sense_2 would be specified.

Therefore, in *change of state* sense, by combing the *constitutive* role and culinary feature, the CWN_sense_1 and CWN_sense_2 could be identified; whereas, in *creation* sense, with the help of instrument usage and sweets feature, the situations by assigning CWN_sense_1 or CWN_sense_2 could be affirmed. Moreover, if the instrument is omitted, the classifiers could further help decide which sense to be assigned to under the situation.

As could be observed from the results, it seems that most of the CWN_sense_1 could be shifted to CWN_sense_2 according to the context. This is due to the reason that the *change of state* sense in Chinese examples would have two meanings: [1] state changes from raw to cooked, which is CWN_sense_1; [2] state changes from cool/cold to heated, which is CWN_sense_2. Thus, since most state changes in Chinese need to be firstly altered through the process in CWN_sense_1, the situations that cooked food get cool/cold and would like to get heated, have been discovered in context.

Consequently, in this paper, inspired by the analysis of discussing English baking verb "bake" under co-composition theory, we take this as a starting point for a preliminary study in a specific sub-task of Chinese Word Sense Disambiguation (WSD). Future works include extending the model to handle other underspecified phenomena, e.g. creation verbs and performance verbs, where information from complements and other non-functor elements co-compose to give rise to derived sense.

References

B. T. Atkins, J. Kegl, and B. Levin. 1988. Anatomy of a verb entry: From Linguistic Theory to Lexicographic Practice. *International Journal of Lexicography*, 1:84–126.

W. A. Cook. 1979. *Case grammar: The development of the matrix model (1970V1978)*. Washington: Georgetown University Press.

C. Fillmore. 1968. *The case for case*. New York: Holt, Rinehart and Winston.

D. Gentner. 1981. Some interesting differences between nouns and verbs. *Cognition and Brain Theory,*, 4:161–178.

Stefan Th. Gries. 2009. *Quantitative Corpus Linguistic with R: A Practical Introduction*. London & Newyourk: Routledge, Taylor & Francis Group.

R. Jackendoff. 1987. The status of thematic relations in linguistic theory. *Linguistic Inquiry*, 18:369–411.

J. Michael Moravcsik. 1975. Aitia as generative factor in aristotle's philosophy. *Dialogue*, 14:622–636.

James Pustejovsky. 1991. The generative lexicon. *Computational Linguistics*, 17(4):409–441.

James Pustejovsky. 1995. *The Generative Lexicon*. The MIT Press.

M. K. Tanenhaus, G. N. Carlson, and J. T. Trueswell. 1989. The role of thematic structures in interpretation and parsing. *Language and Cognitive Processes*, 4:211–234.

Daan van Esch. 2012. Leidon weibo corpus. http://lwc.daanvanesch.nl/index.php.

A Lexico-Semantic Analysis of Chinese Locality Phrases

- A Topic Clustering Approach

August F.Y. Chao
Department of M.I.S, National Chengchi University Taipei, Taiwan
fychao.tw@gmail.com

Siaw-Fong Chung
Department of English National Chengchi University Taipei, Taiwan
sfchung@nccu.edu.tw

Abstract

In this paper, we present a novel approach using LDA (Latent Dirichlet Analysis, Blei, David, Andrew, Michael, and Jordan, 2003) to analyze synonym groups appearing in fixed frames containing Chinese locative phrases, such as [*zái* noun phrase (*yǐ*/*zhī*) *shàng*/*xià*/etc. *biān*/*miàn*/etc.], and to understand noun meanings related to the syntactic forms of locative phrases. We mapped the different noun phrases to their collocating synonym groups before we generated similarity comparison among different combinations. We collected locative phrases using 11 monosyllabic locative words and 5 locative compound-formation patterns from Sketch Engine, and we aligned these compounds with Chinese Synonym Forest (Mei, Zhu, & Gao 1983) before clustering. A Hive Plot (Krzywinski, Birol, Jones, and Marra, 2012) visualizer was constructed in order to help understand the relationship of locative nouns and their synonym groups. The results showed not only the semantic meaning within a locative phrase, but also the corresponding semantic meanings among locative phrases.

1 Introduction

Locative phrases express the locative and directional information in relation to a certain object or entity. In Chinese, locative phrases have the following structure (Li and Thompson, 1989, pp 390):

zái noun phrase ~ (*locative particle*)
'at'

Within this structure, the locative particles can be monosyllabic or disyllabic compounding with prefixes, like *yǐ* and *zhī*, as well as suffixes, like biān, miàn, and tóu. (See Table 1).

Many scholars have done research on locative phrases to understand the language context through frame reference (Hsu and Tai, 2001; Liang and Wang, 2010) and image schema (Liang and Wang, 2010; Wang and Hsieh, 2011), but not on cross-comparing the different locative words with their suffix/prefix combinations.

Table 1 Combinations of Chinese Locative Nouns

	Suffix			Prefix	
	~邊 *biān*	~面 *miàn*	~頭 *tóu*	以 *yǐ* ~	之 *zhī* ~
上 *shàng*	上邊	上面	上頭	以上	之上
下 *xià*	下邊	下面	下頭	以下	之下
前 *qián*	前邊	前面	前頭	以前	之前
後 *hòu*	後邊	後面	後頭	以後	之後
左 *zuǒ*	左邊	左面	N/A	N/A	N/A
右 *yòu*	右邊	右面	N/A	N/A	N/A
裡 *lǐ*	裡邊	裡面	裡頭	N/A	N/A
外 *wài*	外邊	外面	外頭	以外	之外
東 *dōng*	東邊	東面	東頭	以東	之東
西 *xī*	西邊	西面	西頭	以西	之西
南 *nán*	南邊	南面	南頭	以南	之南
北 *běi*	北邊	北面	北頭	以北	之北
內 *nèi*	N/A	N/A	N/A	以內	之內
中 *zhōng*	N/A	N/A	N/A	N/A	之中

In this study, we collected data from the Chinese Giga-word corpus[1] (Ma, and Huang, 2006) in Sketch Engine to retrieve the combinations of

[1] Giga-word corpus contains 2466840 news articles in Taiwan's CNA and Mainland China's XIN.

Chinese locative nouns in Table 1, and we categorized each compound into synonym groups according to the categories provided by the Chinese Synonym Forest (Mei, et. al. 1983) disregarding the part-of-speech information [2]. Then we adapted the LDA (Latent Dirichlet Analysis, Blei, et. al. 2003) methods to cluster each synonym group to extract meaningful groups of combinations existing in our data set. Instead of a network view, we used Hive Plot (Krzywinski, et. al. 2012) to visualize the comparison result of each locative noun combination. The graphical decomposition of concept categories in locative phrases, hopefully, would benefit the analysis of Chinese locative nouns.

2 Methodology

2.1 Latent Dirichlet Allocation

The LDA model involves drawing samples from Dirichlet distributions and from multinomial distributions. This method is widely used in biomedical studies and can profile genes (Flaherty, Giaever, Kumm, Jordan, and Arkin, 2005) by considering DNA sequences are simple 4-letter combination (A, T, G, and C). The formally probabilistic generative process is defined (Blei and Lafferty, 2009) as:

1. For each topic *k*, draw a distribution over words $\phi_d \sim Dir(\alpha)$.
2. For each document *d*,
   a) Draw a vector of topic proportions $\theta_d \sim Dir(\beta)$.
   b) For each word *i*,
      i. Draw a topic assignment $z_{d,i} \sim Mult(\phi_d), z_{d,i} \in \{1,\dots, K\}$
      ii. Draw a word $w_{d,i} \sim Mult(\phi_{z_{d,i}}), w_{d,i} \in \{1,\dots, V\}$

where *K* is a specified number of topics, *V* is the number of words in vocabulary; *Dir(α)* is a *K*-dimensional Dirichlet; *Dir(β)* is a *V*-dimensional Dirichlet; and $z_{d,i}$ is the *i*-th word in the *d*-th document.

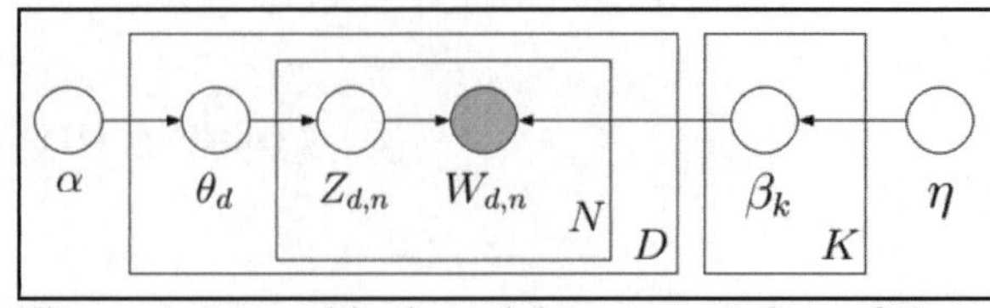

Figure 1 A graphical model representation of the latent Dirichlet allocation (LDA). (Nodes denote random variables; edges denote dependence between random variables. Shaded nodes denote observed random variables; unshaded nodes denote hidden random variables. The rectangular boxes are "plate notation," which denote replication.)

In large corpus experiments, LDA topic model can explain why some parts of the data are similar by observing different sets of various words' probabilities in topics, such as arts, budgets, children and education word groups (Blei, et. al., 2003).

2.2 Chinese Synonym Forest

The Chinese Synonym Forest (or Chilin 同義詞詞林, Mei *et al.,* 1983) is a collection of 5300 Chinese synonyms. In this synonym forest, synonyms were categorized into 3 levels hierarchical groups. The top level of this hierarchy is the upper concept labeled from "A" to "L" including *human*, *object*, *time/ space*, *abstract entities*, *characteristic*, *movements*, *psychological*, *phenomenon-condition*, *activities, relationship*, *auxiliaries*, and *honorifics*, (see Appendix I). Within each top level, there are several middle and specific synonym groups, and each one has its own group code representing the hierarchical information and synonym relationship symbols: "=" means a semantic equal group, "#" means semantic unequal but in the same group, and "@" is a self-enclosed and independent group. The extended version of the Chinese Synonym Forest by the HIT IR Lab expended the original 3 level hierarchies to 5, deleted rarely usage words, and included modern words from news corpus. Table 2 (next page) shows several examples from the extended version (hereafter Chilin).
In Table 2, we can see that each synonym group has a unique code: the initial capital letter represents the top level concept, the last symbol represents the semantic relationship within a synonym group, and the other letters or numbers in between represent the position of a word in a synonym hierarchy.

[2] The locative suffixes and prefixes are also interfered by the concept combination in locative phrases. Because lack of part-of-speech information in Chinese synonym forest, we can't not create explicit formation for locative phrases.

Table 2 Samples of Extended Chinese Synonym Forest. (The synonym meanings are translated by the authors.)

Synonym Groups	Synonym Meanings
Aa01B03# 良民 順民	obedient civilians
Aa01C05@ 眾學生	students
Bp20B03= 招子 **幌子** 市招	signboard *
Bg02B07# 超聲波 低聲波 聲波	sonic wave
Bg03A01@ 火	fire
Dd15A09= **幌子** 招牌 牌子 旗號 金字招牌	brand *

This synonym list has two major problems while applying it in computation algorithm: first, because of the lack of clearly definition of each synonym group, we can only conjectured the meaning; second, because Chinese compounds have many senses, a word can be found in many synonym groups, such that *幌子 huǎngzi* (asterisked in Table 2) originally means 'signboard of hotel' and it also commonly means 'brand' (a metaphor when referring to performing an activity under the guise of the name). Despise the problems presenting above, Chilin is the state-of-art collection of synonym wordlist.

2.3 Statistics of Collected Data

We used 11 directional words: *上 shàng*, *下 xià*, *前 qián*, *後 hòu*, *裡/裏 lǐ* *外 wài*, *東 dōng*, *西 xī*, *南 nán*, *北 běi*, and 5 prefixes/suffixes: *～邊 biān*, *～面 miàn*, *～頭 tóu*, *以 yǐ～*, *之 zhī～* to collect data from the Chinese Giga-word corpus, and the results of locative nouns, disregarding the presents of *zái*, can be found in Table 3 below. The reason of excluding *左 zuǒ*,*右 yòu*, *內 nèi*, *中 zhōng* is because these words cannot be found in all 5 prefixes/suffixes.

Because the Chinese Giga-word corpus is a news corpus, we found that not all the combinations can be found. The usage of *~tóu* is significantly lower than other formations in every locative word and statistics shows that the usages of *shàng*, *xià*, *qián*, *hòu*, *lǐ*, *wài* as prefixes of *biān*, as well as *dōng*, *xī*, *nán*, *běi* as suffixes of *yǐ* cannot be found in news corpus. Even *dōng*, *xī*, *nán*, *běi* as media addressing directional information are barely found using *biān* as suffix.

Table 3 Statistics of Collected Data

	~邊 *biān*	~面 *miàn*	~頭 *tóu*	以 *yǐ* ~	之 *zh*~
上 *shàng*	11	788	51	1557	15559
下 *xià*	6	169	3	8273	7547
前 *qián*	3	1085	154	31618	12596
後 *hòu*	9	1028	215	22051	3751
裡 *lǐ*	9	1086	97	0	0
外 *wài*	28	1254	154	4370	1918
東 *dōng*	139	33	0	0	424
西 *xī*	147	66	3	0	874
南 *nán*	118	20	0	0	390
北 *běi*	199	78	0	0	731

2.4 Clustering using LDA and Hive Plot

Pustejovsky (1991:437) points out that "much of the lexical ambiguity of verbs and prepositions is eliminated because the semantic load is spread more evenly throughout the lexicon to the other lexical categories." Here, we differentiate different uses of locative phrases through observing their groups of nouns in a fixed frame. In order to find the meanings corresponding to the locative nouns appearing in the fixed frame [*zái* noun phrase (*yǐ/zhī*) *shàng/xià*/etc. *biān/miàn*/etc.] in all combinations in Table 3 above, we used LDA to cluster in the nouns appearing in each combination by first mapping each noun to its synonym group in Chilin. Before we used Chilin, we needed to translate the original synonym list which is in simplified Chinese into traditional encoding. In order to avoid any translation problems, we uses Simplified/Traditional Chinese conversion table[3] with maximum matching phrases for the conversion. In our study, in order to retrieve the patterns in Table 3, we used *zái* as a keyword to locate any fixed locative phrases. Thus, the pattern we are looking for is [*zái* noun phrase (*yǐ/zhī*) *shàng/xià*/etc. *biān/miàn*/etc.]. To locate this pattern, we searched for occurrences of *zái* within the left window size of 3 from all locative compounds. When mapping each compound onto the synonym group codes, some compounds may be located in more than one synonym group. We enlisted all synonym group codes before doing LDA process, because LDA topic model considering each vocabulary entry (here is

[3] Simplified / Traditional Chinese conversion tables can be retrieved on Wikipedia source code web site: http://svn.wikimedia.org/svnroot/mediawiki/trunk/phase3/includes/ZhConversion.php

synonym code) to be multinomial distribution to each specific topic (see in 2.1). While clustering each mapped locative phrase containing several translated synonym group codes into topics, each topic (or cluster) also presents a multinomial distribution. While clustering, we set the minimum data set to 5 to filter out *xià tóu* and *xī tóu*, and commanded LDA to cluster each locative phrase in to 5 topics with parameters chunk-size at 10% of dataset during 20 passes. The selected results as follows:

Table 4 Selected Results of LDA model at 5 clusters

Cluster for :北邊
#1 0.166*3-Ka + 0.122*1-Kc + 0.120*2-Kc + 0.082*1-Bn + …
#2 0.250*1-Cb + 0.144*1-/Nca + 0.139*1-Kd + 0.073*2-Cb + …
#3 0.150*2-Kb + 0.141*1-Kb + 0.097*3-Kb + 0.089*3-Di + …
#4 0.152*1-/Nb + 0.102*2-Ka + 0.069*2-Gb + 0.064*1-/Nab + …
#5 0.321*1-Di + 0.134*1-/Nc + 0.130*2-Di + 0.098*2-Jd + …
Cluster for :下面
#1 0.167*3-Ka + 0.116*2-Ka + 0.082*1-Di + 0.079*1-Hi + …
#2 0.176*1-Kd + 0.141*1-Bo + 0.141*2-Dn + 0.060*2-Kd + …
#3 0.175*1-Kc + 0.114*3-Kd + 0.107*1-Bp + 0.078*2-Kb + …
#4 0.149*2-Kc + 0.146*1-Kb + 0.089*1-/Na + 0.057*2-Ka + …
#5 0.155*3-Jb + 0.138*2-Bn + 0.105*1-Bn + 0.089*3-Kc + …

LDA creates 5 clusters according to the percentage of the existing synonym groups. Because all information, including parts of speech, were inputted into LDA, if a part of speech is considered more prominent by LDA (as in 0.152*1-**/Nb** above where the initial is marked with a "/"), the part of speech will be listed as one of the most important features of a particular cluster. The elements without the "/" represent the Chilin synonym group codes.

However, the results in Table 4 are hard to us to recognize the patterns of correlation between synonym groups and parts of speech in locative nouns. Therefore we adapted the Hive Plot (Krzywinski, *et al*, 2012) method to construct a network viewer for comparison by using each coefficient weight larger than 0.05 (Figure 2). Furthermore, we also incorporated the synonym-group-occurring frequency into the Hive Plot diagram if this occurring frequency ratio is higher than 0.005 within each pattern. As the occurring frequency represents the most prominent pattern in each locative phrase, the LDA topic coefficients are able to show the significant differences among topics with each locative prefix/suffix formation.

In our study, we used GENSIM (Řehůřek and Sojka, 2010) library to perform the LDA clustering of the essential synonym groups appearing in different formations of locative nouns, and we analyzed the coefficient within each generating groups.

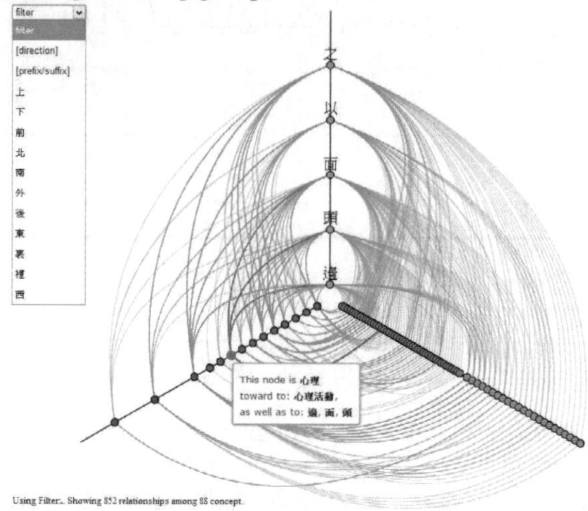

Figure 2 The Hive Plot viewer for Locative Clusters. Red Single links from *psychological activities* to *biān, tóu*, and *miàn.*

In Figure 2, we used the Hive Plot to integrate information of LDA clusters and Chilin hierarchy within an interactive diagram for 5 patterns of locative noun formations. The upper left drop-down bar shows the select function, and the bottom text provides the basic statistics of the current diagram. There are 3 axes in each diagram: the upward axis is the pattern we used in LDA (the top two nodes are prefixes and the last three are suffixes); the right-downward axis is the mapped (sub)synonym groups (green nodes)[4] or P.O.S tag (pink nodes) in the LDA topics or high occurring frequency nodes; and the left-downward axis is the upper-level synonym groups (red nodes) and the initial letter of P.O.S tags (the coarse categories of 'N', 'V', etc.) (brown nodes) corresponding to the nodes locating in right-downward axis.

Each node in the upward axis represents a single LDA clustering processing, which processes all locative nouns matching the node label (e.g., all patterns containing *biān*) , and the links (grey) represent the aggregated coefficient (weighting) of each clustered topic. While users put the mouse on any node, the over-layer will show the information about the mouse-over node including the meaning of the node and the target nodes it links to. In Figure 2, currently it shows the *psychology 心理* has three links toward to *頭 tóu*, *邊 biān*, and *面 miàn,* as well as one link toward

[4] Sub-synonym groups refer to the lower subordinate synonym groups under each synonym group in Chilin.

psychological activities 心理活動. The linkage represents a general idea of common usage (occurring frequency) which LDA clusters regard as significant difference among topics for this 3 patterns of locative noun formations.

3 Results

3.1 Prefixes/Suffixes of Locative Nouns

In order to understand the locative phrases, it is necessary to provide some of the meanings of the prefixes/suffixes in this section. Noun phrases are appearing in the fixed frame [*zái*~ (*yǐ*/*zhī*) *shàng*/*xià*/etc. *biān*/*miàn*/etc.] may occur with 5 prefixes/suffixes: *～邊 biān*, *～面 miàn*, *～頭 tóu*, *以 yǐ～*, *之 zhī～*. Each prefix/suffix word has its specific meaning, according to http://www.zdic.net/. *Biān* means "edge, margin, side, border", *miàn* means "face; surface; plane; side, dimension", *tóu* means "head; top; chief, first; boss", *yǐ* means "by means of; thereby, therefore; consider as; in order to", and *zhī* means "marks preceding phrase as modifier of following phrase; it, him/her, them; go to". When these prefixes/suffixes form compounds with locative words such as *zái*, they can be used to describe the locative information of *time/space* and *abstract entity* (Figure 3), as well as *object*, and *characteristics* (Figure 4), for example.

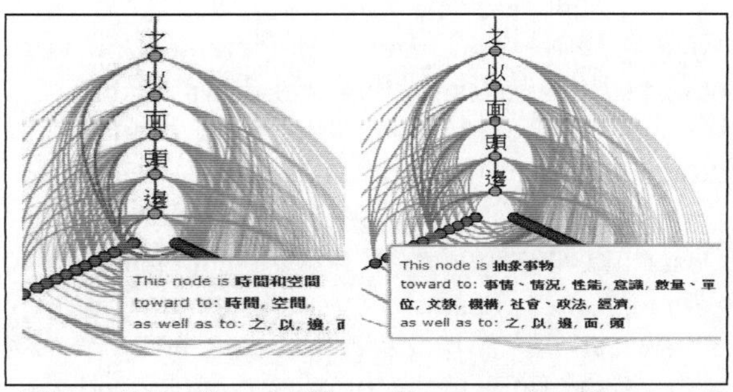

Figure 3 Prefixes/suffixes Connected to the Synonym Groups of *time/space* and *abstract entity*.

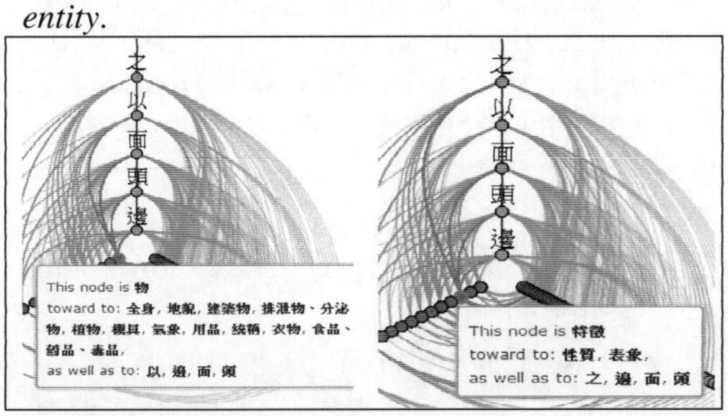

Figure 4 Connections of *object* and *characteristics* toward to prefix/suffix axis.

In Figure 3, we can see *time/space* and *abstract entity* are all connect to every prefixes and suffixes, and "toward to" illustrate the links from the node which your mouse pointing on to sub-categories, and the top-ward dimension is the nodes of prefixes and suffixes which can be compounded with locative nouns (*上 shàng*, *下 xià*, *前 qián*, *後 hòu*, *裡/裏 lǐ 外 wài*, *東 dōng*, *西 xī*, *南 nán*, *北 běi*), such as "*上面*"(*shàng miàn*), and "*以下*"(*yǐ xià*).

When expressing location information of the synonym group *object* (in Figure 4), the data showed that nouns compounding with all prefix patterns (*biān*, *miàn*, *tóu*) and the suffix pattern of *yǐ* are significant, because these physical features like "edge", "surface", and "top" can only be found in the physical existence of objects. And the connection of *zhī* is not presenting in Figure 4, because of less frequent and not significant in LDA clusters. Similar to *object* the synonym group called *characteristics* is an upper group of *shape*, *appearance*, *color/taste* for physical objects, and *nature*, *moral*, *circumstances*, and others for abstract events. Therefore, all prefix patterns (*biān*, *miàn*, *tóu*) can be used while expressing the locative information related to physical objects. As to the prefix formation of *zhī*, it usually modifies the features of abstract events. More examples like *human* and *movement* are presenting in Figure 5.

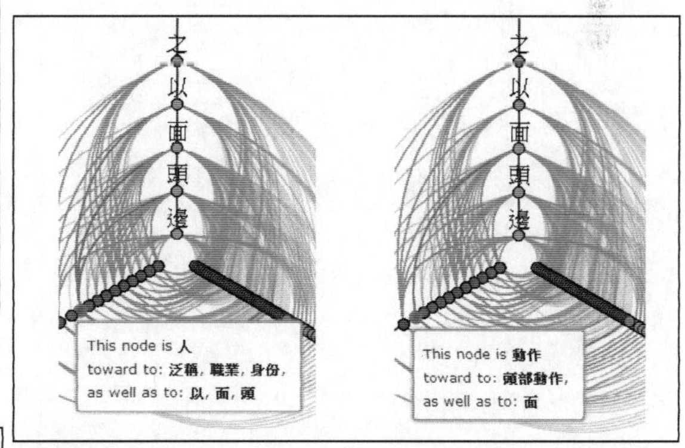

Figure 5 Connections of *human* and *movements*

When referring to directional information about *human*, linkage to sub-synonym (green nodes) groups such as *occupation* or *social positions* (*labors*, *land lord*, *loyal families*, and etc.) were seen. Data also show that only *yǐ*, *tóu*, and *miàn* are found in corpora. Considering the meaning of *tóu* and *miàn*, it is clear to find "face" and "head" senses of *human*. Another interesting finding is the linkage of *activities* to *head movements* (*kissing, blinking, listening, biting* … and etc.) and to *miàn*.

3.2 Directional Words

In this section, we analyzed 11 directional words (excluding *zuǒ*, *yòu*, *nèi*, *zhōng* but including two forms of *裡/裏 lǐ*; cf. Table 1), and we also used the same setting in 3.1 (using LDA model to create 5-topic clusters and combining most frequent synonym groups to plot Hive diagram). After mapping all noun phrases onto Chilin synonym groups, we used Hive Plot for interactive investigation and we enlisted the selected results in Figure 6.

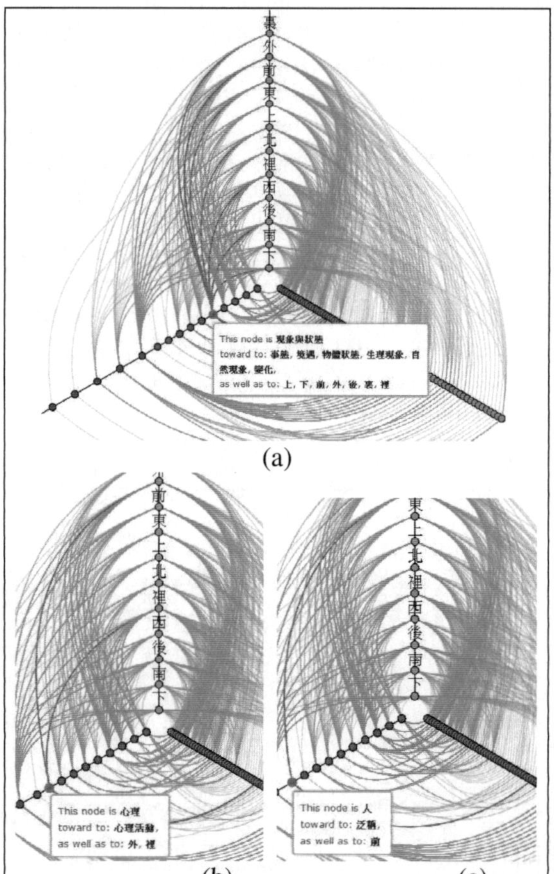

(a) (b) (c)

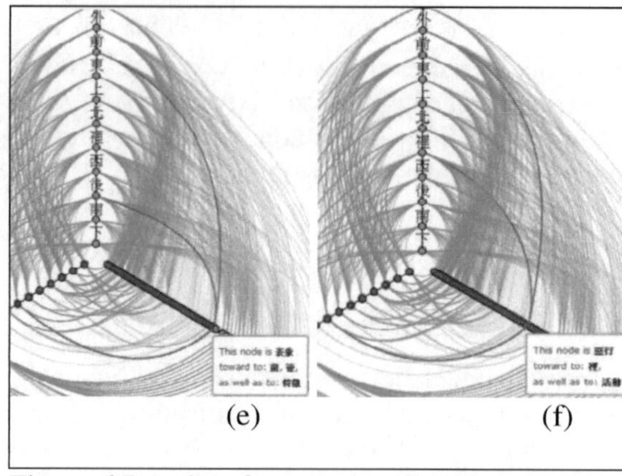

(e) (f)

Figure 6 Results of comparing directional words. (a) focuses on *phenomenon-condition*; (b) focuses on *psychology*; (c) focuses on *human*; (e) focuses on *appearance*; (f) focuses on *sin activities*

In Figure 6, we show differences when comparing directional words in the LDA results,. We selected some interesting patterns for discussion, as follows: in Figure 6(a), *phenomenon-condition* (including sub-synonym groups) is not connected to *dōng*, *xi*, *nán*, *běi*, because it is awkward to address any direction of a *phenomenon* or *conditio*; in (b), *psychology* nouns exclusively use *裡/裏 lǐ* and *外 wài*, such as "*在 發現 裡面*" (discover something inside..) and "*在 支持 之外*" (besides supporting); in (c), *human* nouns only show the usage of *前 qián* "*在 民眾 之前*"(before citizens). In Figure 6(e), if we observed the nodes on the right-downward axis, we can find even more interesting usages of directional nouns. For example, only *前 qián* and *後 hòu*, such as "*在 明朗 之前*" (before event clear) and "*在 明朗 之後*"(after event clear), can be addressing *appearance* (sub-synonym groups are *less*, *fertile*, *bare*, *dense*, *sparse*, and etc.), as well as the only usage of *sin activities* and *lǐ*, such as "*在 治罪 條例 裡面*" (in offences ordinance), can be found in news corpora. Unfortunately, we cannot enlist all 1,509 relationships among 104 concepts in Hive Plot of all directional words. The above are just some interesting observations.

3.3 Combination of Directional Words and Patterns

It is possible to dig in each formation of directional words and prefixes/suffixes combination. We used the same method to create

Hive Plot for each directional word and prefix/suffix formation pattern. We combined all statistical results of LDA and the occurring frequency of synonym groups using the same directional words. Similarly, in this paper, we just selected some findings for discussion.

(A) *Time/space*

In Chilin synonym groups, *time/space* is the upper-level groups of *time* (its sub-synonym groups including: *A.D.*, *B.C.*, *end of year, four seasons*...and etc.) and *space* (its sub-synonym groups including: *position, direction, neighborhood, surrounding,* etc.). Our data showed very interesting results while comparing each opposite direction in pairs (Figure 8).

In Figure 7(a), we can see *shàng* is used in the suffix patterns (*zhī* and *yǐ)*, and *xià* is used with the prefix *biān* and suffix *yǐ*. If we consider the semantic senses of *biān* – "edge, margin, side, border", example like "*在 朝/往 下邊*" (To the following), it seems that *xià biān* shows a distance closer to an observed point. On the contrary, when addressing *shàng*, data showed that most uses ignored the distance with regarding to the observation point. In addition, in (b), we can see *lǐ* and *wài* are totally different. When expressing *time/space* in *wài,* just like all other directional nouns (*qián*, *hòu*, *dōng*, *xī*, *nán*, *běi*), they are connected to every prefix/suffix pattern. As to *lǐ*, no matter its sub-synonym groups are *time* or *space*, we can find only one linkage to *miàn* which means "face; surface; plane; side, dimension", such as "*在 時間 裡面*" (during that time).

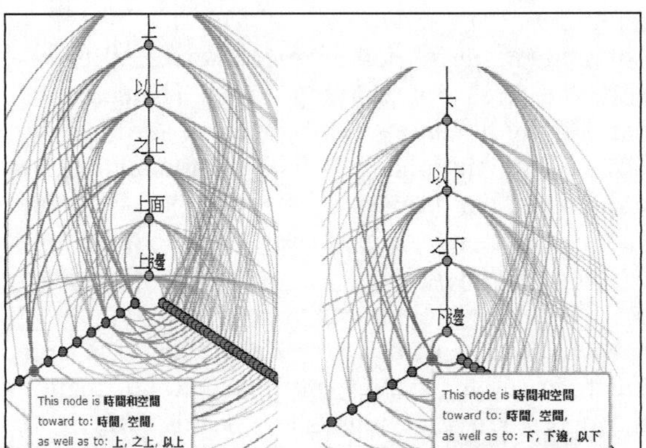

(a) focuses on *time/space* and comparing *shàng*, *xià*

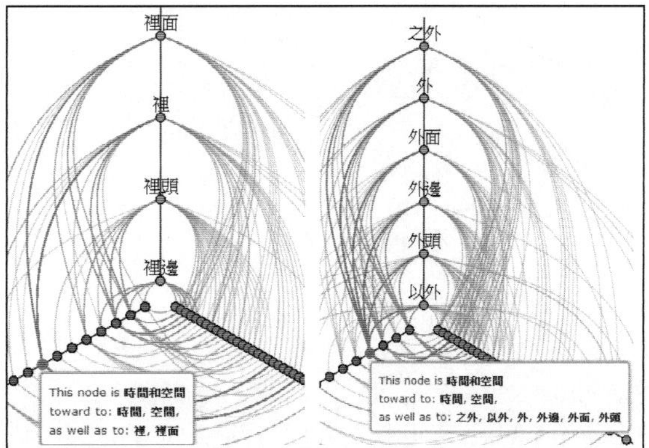

(b) focuses on *time/space* and comparing *lǐ* and *wài*

Figure 7 comparing *time/space* in pairs of directional words with opposite meanings

(B) *Psychology*

In Chilin, *psychology* has only two sub-synonym groups, *psychological activities and psychological status.* However, we can only found *psychological activities* is connected in collected corpora. In Figure 2, we found that nouns in *psychology* synonym groups are usually used with *biān, tóu*, and *miàn*, and we could only find 5 linked graphs in every locative noun and pattern combination (Figure 8).

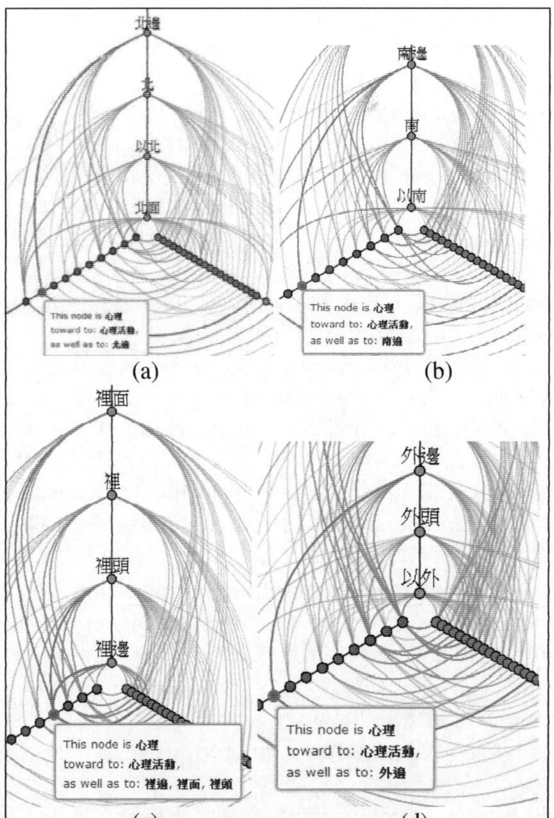

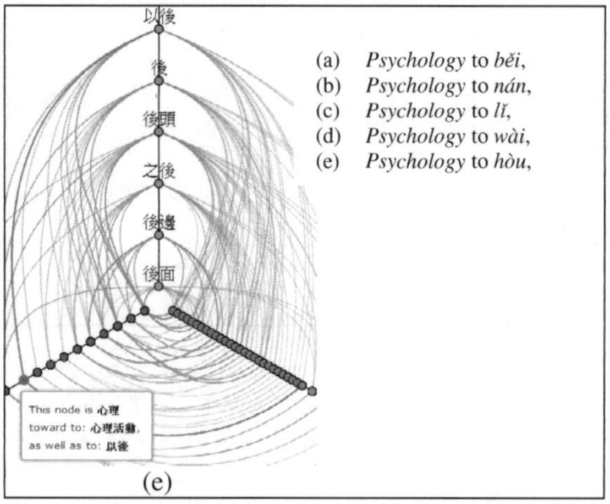

Figure 8 Connections of synonym group *psychology* in different locative nouns

First, the synonym group *psychology* is linked to *běi* (a) and *nán* (b), and the linkages are relatively lower than other linkage weighting in the same graph, such as "*在 支持 中國 北邊*" (supporting northern China) and "*在 規劃 濁水溪 以南*" (planning south of Zhuoshui River). When expressing locative information, *psychology* nouns use only suffix *biān* in our corpora. More significant results can be found in locative nouns *lǐ*, *wài*, and *hòu*. In Figure 8(c), when using locative noun *lǐ* to address directional information of synonym group *psychology*, we can only find evidences support using suffixes of *biān, tóu,* and *miàn*, but not with prefixes. The LDA result of no linkage to pattern node *lǐ* is different from all other graphs. In Figure 8(d), *psychology* nouns are relatively close to the observation of *object* because both use *wài biān* instead of using suffixes *tóu* and *miàn*. In Figure 8(e), locative information of *psychology* appears as *abstract entities* by using *yǐ hòu*.

(C) *Example of Generating Locative Structure*
Although the complexity of analyzing Chinese locative nouns which accompany with 5 different suffixes and prefixes, it is possible to generate locative structure for a locative nouns. We take *裡 lǐ* as an example. In Figure 7(b), while addressing concept regarding to *time/space*, the frequency of using suffix combination, *miàn*, is significant in diagram, and the usage of *miàn* only can be found in compounds in *space* category, if we look into right-downward axis (sub-synonym groups).(Figure 9)

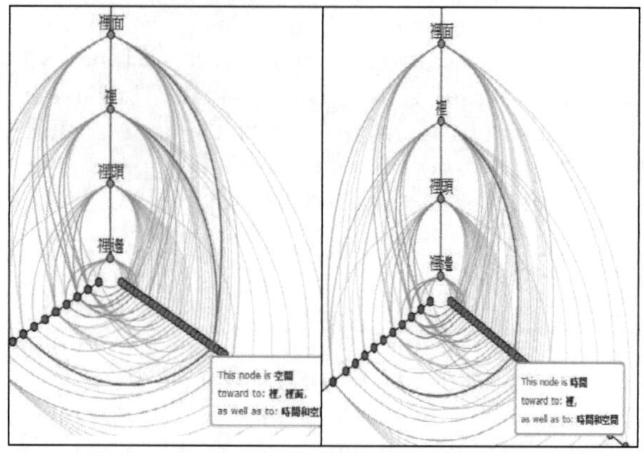

Figure 9 Connections of sub-synonym groups, *time* and *space,* to different locative nouns

The translations of using *lǐ miàn* and *lǐ* are different, because the translated senses depend on the concept before locative nouns (here, one is *time* period, and the other is *space*). For example, "*夏日*" is compounds addressing summer days and be collected in *times* category, therefore "*在 夏日 裡*" is translated into "in/during summer days". As to *space*, locative nouns like "*在 城市 裡面*" can be translated into "in/inside city", other suffixes and prefixes, such as *～邊 biān,～頭 tóu, 以 yǐ～, 之 zhī～*, are rarely found in corpus.

4 Conclusions

Locative phrases are formatted compounds which contain directional nouns and referring scope at the same time. The combinations of locative phrases are difficult for us to analyzing the formation and to establish formal rules for representation and composition for locative nouns. Our study tries to re-categorize all nouns appearing in a certain fixed frame. The semantic meaning of the nouns can be seen in our study by observing their concepts. Instead of using human judgments, we propose a novel method by using LDA model and its clustered topics parameters, as well as integrating the statistical frequency and Chinese Synonym Forest hierarchical information to inspect the differences between locative nouns and prefix/suffix formation through Hive Plot interface. In this study, we discover several findings regarding locative nouns and syntactic locative phrases using synonyms nouns. Our study is limited by the news genre of Giga-word corpus in Sketch Engine. It is possible to use different machine learning mechanisms, and to adapt interactive visual investigating method to help us understand more relationships beyond statistical data. As Pustesjovsky (1995:26) points out that "the ways in which words carry multiple meanings can vary", by observing the nouns in a fixed frame, we can see how different, and some closely-related, locative phrases vary in their concepts.

Acknowledgements

This research is supported by National Science Council grant 101-2410-H-004-176-MY2 directed by Siaw-Fong Chung.

References

J. J. Mei, Y. M. Zhu, Y. Q. Gao, and H. X. Yin. 1983. Tongyici Cilin (Chinese Synonym Forest).

J. Pustejovsky, 1991. The generative lexicon. Computational linguistics, 17.4 (1991):409-441.

J. Pustejovsky, 1995. The Generative Lexicon: A Theory of Computational Lexical Semantics. Cambridge, MA: The MIT Press.

D. M. Blei,A. Y. Ng, and M. I. Jordan. 2003. Latent dirichlet allocation. The Journal of Machine Learning research, 3:993-1022.

C. N. Li and S. A. Thompson. 1989. Mandarin Chinese: A functional reference grammar. Univ of California Press.

Yuqi Sheng. Modern Chinese online course (現代漢語網絡課程), http://www.yyxx.sdu.edu.cn/chinese/, visited on 2013/06/01.

Ya-chen Hsu and James H.I. Tai. 2001. An analysis of the Chinese spatial term shang in three reference frames. Unpublished dissertation.

Kan-Yuan Liang and Song-Mu Wang. 2010. Study on the Image Schemata of Modern Chinese Cian: Based on Frames of Reference. Unpublished dissertation.

Chao-Mei Wang and Ching-Yu Hsieh. 2011. The Cognitive Analysis of Mandarin Locative Expressions from the Perspective of Emotion: With Reference to Shang and Xia. Unpublished dissertation.

W. Y. Ma and C. R. Huang. 2006. Uniform and effective tagging of a heterogeneous giga-word corpus. In 5th International Conference on Language Resources and Evaluation (LREC2006):24-28.

M. Krzywinski, I. Birol, S. J. Jones, and M. A. Marra. 2012. Hive plots—rational approach to visualizing networks. Briefings in Bioinformatics, 13(5):627-644.

D. Blei and J. Lafferty. 2009. Topic Models. In A. Srivastava and M. Sahami, editors, Text Mining: Classification, Clustering, and Applications. Chapman & Hall/CRC Data Mining and Knowledge Discovery Series.

R. Řehůřek and P. Sojka. 2010. Software framework for topic modelling with large corpora. In Proceedings of LREC 2010 workshop New Challenges for NLP Frameworks:46-50.

Flaherty, P., Giaever, G., Kumm, J., Jordan, M. I., and Arkin, A. P. 2005. A latent variable model for chemogenomic profiling. Bioinformatics, 21(15):3286-3293.

Gao, Z.M., Extraction and Integration of Chinese Lexical Semantic Information, Proceedings of the 19th Conference on Computational Linguistics and Speech Processing, ROCLING 2007, Taipei.

Appendix I: Chinese Synonym Forest (Chilin 同義詞林)

Chinese synonym group code and translated senses by the authors.

Codes	Group Name	Translated sense	Codes	Group Name	Translated sense	Codes	Group Name	Translated sense
A	人	*People*	C	時間和空間	*Time/Space*	H	活動	*Activities*
Aa	泛稱	*General term*	Ca	時間	*Time*	Ha	政治活動	*Political activities*
Ab	男女老少	*Men and Women*	Cb	空間	*Space*	Hb	軍事活動	*Military activies*
Ac	體態	*Posture*	D	抽象事物	*Abstract*	Hc	行政管理	*Administration activities*
Ad	籍屬	*Nationality*	Da	事情、情況	*Things/situation*	Hd	生產	*Production activities*
Ae	職業	*Profession*	Db	事理	*Affair*	He	經濟活動	*Economic activities*
Af	身份	*Identity*	Dc	外貌	*Appearance*	Hf	交通運輸	*Transportation*
Ag	狀況	*Status*	Dd	性能	*Performance*	Hg	教衛科研	*Education/Research activities*
Ah	親人、眷屬	*Relatives/dependents*	De	性格、才能	*Character/Talent*	Hh	文體活動	*Sports*
Ai	輩次	*Seniority*	Df	意識	*Awareness*	Hi	社交	*Social activities*
Aj	關係	*Relationship*	Dg	比喻物	*Metaphor*	Hj	生活	*Life*
Ak	品性	*Moral*	Dh	臆想物	*Imaginary*	Hk	宗教生活	*Religious*
Al	才識	*Ability*	Di	社會、政法	*Social, political and legal*	Hl	迷信活動	*Superstitious*
Am	信仰	*Faith*	Dj	經濟	*Economy*	Hm	公安、司法	*Public security, justice*
An	丑類	*Bad title*	Dk	文教	*Culture*	Hn	惡行	*Sin activities*
B	物	*Object*	Dl	疾病	*Disease*	I	現象與狀態	*Phenomenon-condition*
Ba	統稱	*General term*	Dm	機構	*Agency*	Ia	自然現象	*Natural phenomenon*
Bb	擬狀物	*Proposed substance*	Dn	數量、單位	*Quantity/Unit*	Ib	生理現象	*Physiological condition*
Bc	物體的部分	*Part-of*	E	特徵	*Feature*	Ic	表情	*Expression*
Bd	天體	*Astronomical*	Ea	外形	*Shape*	Id	物體狀態	*Object condition*
Be	地貌	*Landforms*	Eb	表像	*Table*	Ie	事態	*Situation*
Bf	氣象	*Meteorological*	Ec	顏色、味道	*Color/Taste*	If	境遇	*Circumstance*
Bg	自然物	*Natural*	Ed	性質	*Nature*	Ig	始末	*Begin and end*
Bh	植物	*Plant*	Ee	德才	*Moral*	Ih	變化	*Changes*
Bi	動物	*Animal*	Ef	境況	*Situation*	J	關聯	*Relevance*
Bj	微生物	*Microorganism*	F	動作	*Movement*	Ja	聯繫	*Contact*
Bk	全身	*Whole*	Fa	上肢動作	*Upperr limb movements*	Jb	異同	*Differences*
Bl	排泄物、分泌物	*Excretions/secretions*	Fb	下肢動作	*Lower limb movements*	Jc	配合	*Coordinate*
Bm	材料	*Material*	Fc	頭部動作	*Head movements*	Jd	存在	*Exist*
Bn	建築物	*Building*	Fd	全身動作	*Full body movements*	Je	影響	*Affect*
Bo	機具	*Machines*	G	心理活動	*Psychology*	K	助語	*auxiliaries*
Bp	用品	*Articles*	Ga	心理狀態	*Psychology status*	Ka	疏狀	*Sparse*
Bq	衣物	*Clothing*	Gb	心理活動	*Psychology activities*	Kb	仲介	*Agency*
Br	食品、藥品、毒品	*Food/medicines/drugs*	Gc	能願	*Wishes*	Kc	聯接	*Link*
						Kd	輔助	*Aid*
						Ke	呼歎	*Call*
						Kf	擬聲	*Onomatopoeia*
						L	敬語	*Honorifics*

Author Index

Keyword Index

Association for Computational Linguistics
209 N. Eighth Street
Stroudsburg, Pennsylvania 18360

CURRAN ASSOCIATES INC
proceedings.com